3rd Edition

Making It Legal

A Guide to Same-Sex Marriage, Domestic Partnerships & Civil Unions

Attorney Frederick C. Hertz
with Attorney Emily Doskow

THIRD EDITION	JANUARY 2014
Editor	LINA GUILLEN
Cover and Book Design	SUSAN PUTNEY
Proofreading	SUSAN CARLSON GREENE
Index	SONGBIRD INDEXING SERVICES
Printing	BANG PRINTING

Hertz, Frederick, author.

  Making it legal : a guide to same-sex marriage, domestic partnerships & civil unions / Frederick Hertz, Emily Doskow. -- 3rd Edition [reprinted].

    pages cm

  Summary: "With the only comprehensive guide to same-sex relationship laws in the U.S., Making It Legal discusses the important factors involved in the personal decision to marry, along with the issues that every married couple may face: What are the special needs of same-sex couples with kids? What happens when you want to file your taxes? When is a will or a living trust needed? "-- Provided by publisher.

  ISBN 978-1-4133-1983-5 (pbk.) -- ISBN 978-1-4133-1984-2 (epub ebook)

1. Same-sex marriage--Law and legislation--United States. 2. Civil unions--Law and legislation--United States. 3. Gay couples--Legal status, laws, etc.--United States. 4. Gay rights--United States. 5. Divorce--Law and legislation--United States. 6. Estate planning--United States. I. Doskow, Emily, author. II. Title.

  KF539.H475 2014

  346.7301'68--dc23

                              2013036343

Please note

We believe accurate, plain-English legal information should help you solve many of your own legal problems. But this text is not a substitute for personalized advice from a knowledgeable lawyer. If you want the help of a trained professional—and we'll always point out situations in which we think that's a good idea—consult an attorney licensed to practice in your state.

Acknowledgments

My deepest gratitude goes to my many law and mediation clients, who have brought so many of their questions and problems to me over the past 25 years. They have turned to me with their troubles, uncertainties, and fears, and while I hope that I have guided and advocated for them, in turn, I have learned a great deal. This book reflects the lessons I have learned from working with so many of them, often in the most painful situations. I hope that the lessons that have emerged from their difficulties can be useful to others facing similar challenges.

It has been my honor to work with an abundance of smart, dedicated, and collegial professionals working to clarify and resolve the complex challenges that same-sex couples face as marriage and marriage equivalent relationships become available—both in my home state of California and across the country. I've been able to share stories and ideas with a great many lawyers, mediators, therapists, and accountants, and the concepts and approaches discussed in this book have benefited greatly from these discussions.

I have been extraordinarily fortunate to have Emily Doskow as my coauthor, both on this book and our *A Legal Guide for Lesbian & Gay Couples*. Emily doesn't just fix up my sentences, paragraphs, and pages. She inspires me, reins me in when necessary, and asks the probing questions I need to consider. She also comes to the table as my friend and counselor when that is what I need, and I am grateful for her help and guidance.

Finally, I could not imagine doing this kind of work without the loyalty, affection, and support of Ran, my (unmarried) partner of more than 30 years. He distracts me when that is what I need, shows me the best ways to nurture our love, and provides me with the encouragement and friendship that enables me to stay afloat. Truly, I could not have survived the dramas of being a gay divorce lawyer without his steady presence in my life.

—Frederick Hertz

Foreword

By Kate Kendell, Executive Director, National Center for Lesbian Rights

On June 16, 2008, I witnessed the marriage of two of the most extraordinary women in my life, when I watched Del Martin and Phyllis Lyon exchange vows in San Francisco, the first to do so under the California Supreme Court's landmark decision granting same-sex partners the right to marry. I was so proud to pay witness to that moment in history and pay tribute to two of the founding mothers of our movement.

Sadly, we lost Del only six short weeks later. And on November 4, 2008 we all lost the right to marry in California when the voters passed Proposition 8, a constitutional amendment banning same-sex marriage. In May of 2009, the California Supreme Court rejected our legal challenge to Prop. 8 and upheld this unprecedented measure eliminating the right to marry for same-sex couples. On the heels of that loss, Ted Olson and David Boies filed their federal challenge to Prop. 8. It took more than four years of litigation in the federal courts to finally rid our state constitution of the stain of Prop. 8, but eventually justice prevailed and marriages of same-sex couples resumed in California on June 28, 2013.

In June 2013, we also saw the U.S. Supreme Court strike down Section 3 of the Defense of Marriage Act (DOMA), which had barred the federal government from recognizing the marriages of same-sex couples.

All of these events demonstrate the speed at which things change in the human rights movement for the freedom to marry. Amid the confusion of legal rules and court actions it can be complicated, from a legal standpoint, to be in a committed same-sex relationship these days. Even though it's legal to marry in fourteen jurisdictions and seven other states recognize some form of legal commitment, the majority of states still do not honor or allow marriages between same-sex couples, resulting in a patchwork of benefits, taxation, and parentage rules.

Given all this, it can be hard to figure out what marriage or another legal partnership will mean to your family. Will it benefit you financially to make a legal commitment, or cause more problems than positives? What does it mean to your plans to have children?

Making It Legal addresses all these confusing issues, bringing some measure of order to the chaos that remains same-sex family law in 2013 and beyond and helping you to make the all-important decisions about how you want to structure your life together. Living happily ever after is more likely if the happy couple shares not only love and adoration, but also clear-eyed expectations and a mutual understanding of the answers to the hard issues. This book brings to life the realities that same-sex partners face when considering making it legal and it illuminates the nuances of the decision-making process.

The freedom to marry is a fundamental human right and make no mistake: we are very close to our goal of achieving full marriage equality. With that equality, comes the right to choose. Make your decisions wisely, and may you live happily ever after.

San Francisco, 2013

About the Authors

Frederick Hertz is an attorney and mediator working in Oakland, California, specializing in the property aspects of the formation and dissolution of marital, nonmarital, and other forms of family relationships.

Emily Doskow is an attorney in Berkeley, California, specializing in LGBT family law, and an author and editor for Nolo. She is the author of *Nolo's Essential Guide to Divorce*, and coauthor of numerous Nolo books, including *A Legal Guide for Lesbian & Gay Couples* and *The Sharing Solution: How to Save Money, Simplify Your Life & Build Community*.

Table of Contents

Appendixes

"*Gays and lesbians getting married—haven't they suffered enough?*"

Your Same-Sex Marriage Companion

Following the California Supreme Court's historic ruling legalizing same-sex marriage in May 2008, June was christened "gay bride month" by comedienne Kate Clinton. Over the course of that summer, like many others, I attended a bounty of same-sex weddings. Each wedding featured unique moments that exquisitely captured the power of the social transformation that was happening, but two of them stood out as especially illustrative of the changes precipitated by the court's decision.

Alan and Bill had been living together for more than five years; Alan is in his mid-60s and had been single for decades, while Bill is in his 40s and was briefly in a straight marriage. This was the first serious same-sex relationship for both of them. Near the conclusion of their joyous reception Bill's straight boss took the microphone and offered a toast, and his was a tender expression of support for the couple as he spoke openly about his feelings to the assembled guests—many of them straight and married as well. He recalled his own wedding and talked about his journey toward full acceptance of Bill and Alan as a married couple, and I knew that hearts and minds were being changed throughout the room.

Later that summer I walked into San Francisco City Hall, the very place where then-Mayor Dianne Feinstein vetoed the city's domestic partnership ordinance in 1982 and where the flurry of unauthorized marriages had been celebrated in 2004, to attend another wedding. I had attended Terry and Carol's first, nonlegal, wedding more than a decade ago. Terry is the deputy San Francisco city attorney who argued the marriage case before the California courts, arguing so powerfully that "words matter." No one better deserved the accolades of celebration that she and her partner received that afternoon, and when the judge officiating referred to "the power vested in me by the State of California," whoops of joy rose from the crowd. These were words that could not have been uttered at their earlier commitment ceremony, and indeed, the event was the perfect manifestation of the Court's decision, as quoted in the ceremonial program:

The substantive right of two adults who share a loving relationship to join together to establish an officially recognized family of their own—and, if the couple chooses, to raise children within that family—constitutes a vitally important attribute of the fundamental interest in liberty and personal autonomy that the California Constitution secures to all persons for the benefit of both the individual and society.

Meanwhile, I found myself consulting with prospective spouses almost daily, fielding questions raised by the new option of marriage—about divorce, remarriage, adoption, property purchases, and financial arrangements. Even those already registered as domestic partners had questions, often wanting to renew their vows as fully legal married partners. I was drafting an average of one premarital agreement per week, nearly four times my usual workload.

I was also meeting nearly as often with couples seeking to end their relationships and resolve their legal and financial entanglements so that they could avoid the agony of court litigation. While some people can manage it, others find themselves mired in conflict. Dissolutions can be excruciating to be around and at times it seems impossible to resolve even the tiniest of disputes. Yet I'm convinced that the end of even a long-term relationship does not have to be so awful, and I am continually pondering whether and how these couples could have avoided their ugly endings.

And then a few month later on November 4, California voters passed a constitutional initiative to reinstate the ban on same-sex marriage. The vote was close, painfully so, and suddenly we all had to confront the extent of the hostility that exists toward our relationships. The validity of the summer's marriages was in question for some time, and a whole new batch of messy legal quandaries began to surface. My own emotions included a sense of fatigue in the face of the continuing legal complexities—couldn't we just have ordinary marriage and be done with all these complications? In May 2009, the California Supreme Court upheld Prop. 8, answering "No" to my question. Federal litigation followed and in August 2010, Judge Vaughn Walker of the Northern District federal court held Prop. 8 unconstitutional and finally in June 2013, the Prop. 8 appeals were dismissed for lack of standing by the appellants. Full marriage equality for Californians was reinstated a few weeks later.

In the midst of the chaos of 2008, it became clear that it was the perfect time for this book. Every client meeting reminded me of another topic to add to my list, and every negotiation or mediation session was a window into how couples attempt to address these difficult issues. The long-awaited demise of the federal Defense of Marriage Act has simplified the lives of lesbian and gay couples to some degree, but many questions and challenges remain.

Locally, I'm often branded as the antimarriage lawyer, because I tend to focus on the risks and downsides of this powerfully attractive institution. This reputation surprises me, as I'm a sincere fan of long-term relationships—last year my partner and I celebrated our 30th anniversary, and I hope we will be together forever. But it's true that I am cautious. I sometimes envision myself standing in the middle of a wildly busy freeway, watching couples speed by me either toward or away from their marriages, with me holding up a puny sign that says to the marrying partners, "Be careful," and to the fleeing spouses, "Be nicer." I implore everyone to slow down, please.

My caution derives from two sources. First, the legal structures of conventional marriage and the patchwork of nonrecognition by other jurisdictions create fairly serious legal problems for many couples, and it is just plain unwise for anyone to get married without fully understanding the potential risks and benefits. And second, marriage creates a social partnership that is tighter and potentially more restrictive than most of us comprehend, and for many couples it simply is not the best way to organize their affairs. I want every one of our relationships to be happy and long lasting, so I don't want couples to grab the marital ring out of a sense of political exuberance if it is not the best arrangement for them. It is my hope that this book will help each of you make your marriage or partnership decision fully informed of the benefits and the risks.

I also hope that everyone who has some connection to same-sex marriages or legal partnerships will take the time to read these chapters—this book is also intended to inform and advise therapists, lawyers, spiritual advisers, accountants, and of course, the friends and relatives of lesbians and gay men.

Finally, a word about the many stories I relate in this book. I have both a professional duty and an ethical commitment to protect the privacy of each of my clients, and so I have created case studies that are just that, my creations. While they are inspired by the situations my clients find themselves in, I have changed names, residences, and even genders, and I have reconstituted and combined the underlying facts in many respects in order to shield my clients from any kind of public exposure. If any of you recognize yourselves in any of these stories, it is simply because the situations and the conflicts they describe recur so frequently in our community.

—Frederick Hertz

Get Updates and More Online

When there are important changes to the information in this book, we'll post updates online, on a page dedicated to this book:

www.nolo.com/back-of-book/LGM.html

You'll find other useful information there, too, including author blogs, podcasts, and videos.

A Brief History of the Same-Sex Marriage Movement

Why read about the history of the gay marriage movement? For one thing, you don't have to worry that it will take up a lot of your time. We have come so far, so fast, in so many ways, that the time period you'll be reading about is fairly compressed (and this summary is a compressed version of it). For another, it's a fascinating story of a diverse community evolving in the face of political and social forces that no one could have anticipated even 50 years ago. The current confusion of rules for same-sex couples has emerged from a complex political and legal history, and the recent legal and political victories did not occur in a vacuum. Knowing the history will help you in trying to make sense of your legal options.

Just over fifteen years ago, in the introduction to my previous book, *Legal Affairs*, I offered readers the following caution: "If same-sex marriage is ever allowed, you will need to think about whether marriage is right for the two of you, not just whether it's politically correct." Little did I imagine in 1998 that we would all be facing this question so soon.

The Not-So-Good Old Days

While there certainly were same-sex relationships back through the ages, and even cultures where such relationships were socially acceptable, the modern movement for relationship recognition in the United States only began around 1969. In those years, getting married was of little interest to most lesbians or gay men—either legally or personally. If the topic of marriage ever arose, it usually related to getting out of a straight marriage—not getting into a gay one. Even long-term same-sex couples lived in a world of personal bonds, social networks, and private commitments—not a world of formal marriage or legal recognition. (And by the way, we were all simply "gay" back then, not LGBT, Q, or I.)

Both personal and political struggles in those early years focused on obtaining recognition and validation as gay individuals, not as couples, and on winning the basic right to be safe from harassment, discrimination, violence, and social exclusion. Couples knew that their relationships were not likely to be acknowledged, and most of us accepted, sometimes almost happily, the lack of any public recognition of our relationships. (The quintessential novel of gay coupledom in that period was Christopher Isherwood's *A Single Man*, which tells the story of a recently widowed gay man whose long-term partnership was invisible even to those closest to him, and who must therefore endure the pain of mourning his recently deceased lover alone.)

This was a time when most homosexuals lived deep in the closet, and coming out at all could jeopardize one's physical safety, never mind one's social standing or economic security. Among the small minority of gay folks who were open about their lives, many appreciated the experience of living outside of the social framework of marriage and divorce, creating their own living arrangements in isolation from most of mainstream society.

The legal battles of those years reflected this reality. For gay men, the relevant law was criminal law. Men were frequently arrested if they attempted to pick up a sexual partner in a public place, subscribed even to a non-pornographic gay magazine, or frequented a local gay watering hole. Given this oppressive atmosphere, legal and political organizing was directed at lifting the criminal prosecutions. Legalizing a love relationship in any way, let alone by marriage, would have seemed an impossible and, for most of us, an irrelevant quest.

For lesbians, the battlefields were typically located on quite different legal terrain. There were fights to keep women's social institutions free from harassment, to publish lesbian magazines, or to form social organizations, but for the most part, lesbians were in court most often when they tried to retain custody of their children after leaving a heterosexual marriage. Newly out lesbian moms often faced legal fights with ex-husbands over the right to continue coparenting their children, and for the most part, courts were not sympathetic. Homosexuality alone was often seen as sufficient grounds for denying a lesbian parent all access to her children or for justifying limitations on custody or visitation.

Given these realities, legal marriage was the last thing that most lesbians and gay men worried about. Also, many newly liberated lesbians and gay men had already served their time in heterosexual marriages and were not eager to re-create the same arrangements in their new lives. For women, negative experiences as the subordinate partner in a heterosexual marriage, coupled with an emerging feminism, led to a view of marriage as a restrictive, confining, sexist institution that had little appeal. And for gay men, marriage meant gender roles, conventionality, and monogamy, none of which matched the real lives of most sexually active gay men. Even those who were living in long-term relationships did not view them as marriages, but rather, as long-term partnerships that thrived outside of any legal framework.

This self-image as outsiders was reinforced by the living arrangements and political values of those who were the most vocal in the gay community—for the most part a younger, more activist crowd. Gay liberation itself was framed as a "movement" that existed in opposition to mainstream society—a struggle for liberation, not assimilation. Marriage, to the extent it was even discussed at all, was viewed as an institution that resided deep in the heart of the mainstream, and that was not where many of us wanted to live.

In that political context, lesbians and gay men who had the audacity to advance a campaign for legal marriage were seen as retrograde—to the extent they were even noticed at all. Marriage simply was not a high legal or political priority, despite the fact that the lack of marriage equality was broadly understood to have discriminatory consequences for many lesbians and gay men.

The Marriage Pioneers

In 1969, the historic Stonewall riots took place in New York City—the first time in the United States that the LGBT community fought back visibly and powerfully against oppression and homophobia. It was a time of enormous social change and agitation, with liberation movements breaking out in the women's community and other marginalized communities everywhere. The sexual "revolution" of the 1960s was spreading wildly—for gays and straights alike. And then in Minneapolis, Minnesota, of all places, Jack Baker and Mike McConnell walked out on that highly charged political stage. In contrast to Stonewall and other political events, and even against the backdrop of a fairly active gay community in Minnesota, Baker and McConnell were about as mainstream as a gay couple could be. Baker was a law student and later student body president at the University of Minnesota, and his lover McConnell was a university librarian. Together they went to Minneapolis City Hall and applied for a marriage license.

I well remember their story, as I was living in Minnesota at the time—not as a gay activist or lawyer, but rather, as a high school senior trying to figure out my own sexuality and my place in the larger society. I had sat in the back row of a meeting of Minnesota's vibrant gay liberation organization, named "F.R.E.E.," which stood for "Fight Repression of Erotic Expression"—not the sort of organization that would ever be fighting for the right to get married. I'd even been taken by my older sister and her gay best friend to the local gay bar, where I got to see men kissing and enjoyed watching the drag queens having a great old time. But marriage?

As news of Baker and McConnell's rejection at City Hall and subsequent lawsuit spread, the reaction from the gay community was intensely and universally negative. Baker and McConnell were not expressing the rejection of straight society that was the gay norm, but rather, a desire to enter the most conventional core of the heterosexual mainstream. Their agenda appeared to defy everyone's sense of how the world worked. Homosexuals wanting to get married was as strange a concept for gay people to absorb as it was for straight folks—and for the latter, it was virtually unthinkable.

Not surprisingly, Baker and McConnell's efforts were not successful, either legally or politically. Their application for a marriage license was denied, and in a series of rulings over the next few years the Minnesota courts upheld that denial—resulting in the world's first published appellate court case on the issue of gay marriage.[1] Applying reasoning that presaged the recurring basis for rejecting such appeals over the next three decades, the Minnesota justices concluded that because marriage was "by definition" the union of a man and a woman, homosexual couples could not assert a right to marry. The court rejected any application of *Loving v. Virginia*, the U.S. Supreme Court case that lifted the ban on interracial marriage.[2] In other words, the definition of the word "marriage" set the rules for the reality of marriage—end of story. It took more than 40 years before the Minnesota legislature reversed this ruling —in 2013, it legalized same-sex marriage in my home state.

A few couples launched similar efforts to marry legally in other states over the ensuing years, but each attempt was isolated and none garnered much support. Each of these efforts simply failed. Gay people remained outside of mainstream society, and while we would fight vigorously to improve the

[1] *Baker v. Nelson* (1972) 291 Minn. 310, 191 N.W.2d 185.
[2] *Loving v. Virginia* (1967) 388 U.S. 1, 87 S.Ct. 1817.

quality of our marginalized lives, we didn't really expect—and some of us didn't desire—to be invited back in from the margins.

The Emergence of Gay Families

It seems ironic now, but looking back through the prism of subsequent legal developments, the dramatic successes of a gay liberation movement that disdained marriage may actually have sowed the seeds for the later marriage campaign. Throughout the 1970s and 1980s, lesbians and gay men emerged from the closet, embraced their sexual identities and formed new and lasting relationships, gathered the courage to come out at work, and (primarily in the women's community in the early decades) found ways to raise children proudly and openly—all in the absence of legal marriage. We weren't getting married, but we were sexually active, socially alive, and creating loving relationships and solid communities across the United States.

Although no one was trying to do it, the movement's establishment of greater freedom and visibility for lesbian and gay couples created underlying societal conditions that made the creation of legal relationships both desirable and, in the end, achievable. As the number and visibility of long-term same-sex couples grew, and especially as so many couples formed lasting bonds that ended up looking very similar to traditional heterosexual families, it was only a matter of time before the injustices wrought by the denial of legal marriage would become increasingly unacceptable. In this way, a path of liberation that was not directed toward the legalization of gay marriage ended up taking us there.

Not that it happened in any straightforward or direct way. Instead, in an odd congruence of political realism with legal practicalities and the community's underlying discomfort with the institution of marriage, domestic partnership was born.

Domestic Partnership: In the Beginning

By the early 1980s I was a young lawyer living in the San Francisco Bay Area, and it was there that the gay community launched a series of campaigns designed to obtain limited benefits for couples at the local level—with health insurance coverage for city employees as the highest priority—under the newly minted term for nonmarital relationships: "domestic partnership."

Domestic partnership appeared to be an ideal alternative to marriage. It covered the immediate practical needs of socially conventional cohabiting partners, like health insurance, without trying to barge into any established social norms such as marriage, and thus it was unlikely to offend the heterosexual community. The fact that the campaign wouldn't be seen as a quest for conventional marriage was also a plus within the gay activist community. In some settings, it even offered an option for opposite-sex couples who wanted to escape the confines of traditional marriage.

In practical political terms that were key to its success, domestic partnership was a legal status that could be granted by local governments and private employers without getting into political fights on a national or even a statewide level. Progressive cities like Berkeley or innovative companies like New York City's *Village Voice* newspaper could extend spousal benefits to their own residents or employees, with no need to ask permission from any less enlightened entities.

Even so, these early efforts were not always an easy sell. It took five years of lobbying by a stalwart city employee before the city of Berkeley enacted the nation's first domestic partnership ordinance in 1984. At the outset only city employees could register, and the program offered only dental insurance coverage and leave benefits to city employees, but within a year Berkeley began including medical insurance benefits as well. In 1985, West Hollywood took a major step forward by creating a domestic partnership registry open to all residents, not just city employees. Private employers now could extend similar benefits to those who signed up on the city's registry.

Access to health insurance and having a say in the treatment of one's seriously ill partner were the central concerns in the debate about the domestic partnership ordinance that was submitted to the San Francisco Board of Supervisors in 1982. The legislation was approved, but vetoed by then-Mayor Dianne Feinstein, who felt it was too radical for the time. (This was only two decades before San Francisco issued the nation's first marriage licenses to same-sex partners. Change indeed has occurred quickly.)

It took the city several more years before the "gay capital" was ready to embrace a domestic partnership ordinance, but eventually, in 1989, San Francisco followed Berkeley and West Hollywood and enacted a citywide domestic partnership law (which exists to this day).

Domestic partnership in the 1980s meant different things to different people, but one thing it was not was marriage. It did not require a solemnization ceremony; the state system of marital property law did not apply; it had no hint of religious sanctification; and it did not fundamentally change the legal or financial relationship between the partners. The local rights and employment benefits that it provided were only marginally beneficial to the gay community at large, though they were of real value to the affected employees. Nevertheless these new laws were meaningful to the extent they established the first legal framework for governmental recognition of same-sex relationships.

Early domestic partnership ordinances also set up a system of registration that other cities and private employers could use as a model. Recognizing that domestic partnership was an alternative to marriage, many jurisdictions and companies allowed opposite-sex unmarried couples to register as domestic partners as well—but overall it was the LGBT community that carried the domestic partnership campaign forward.

The Impact of AIDS

Shortly after the first domestic partnership registration systems were set up in 1984, AIDS began to spread through the gay community. What had begun as a thin trickle of sad stories about how the absence of marriage affected lesbian or gay couples turned into a torrent. The realities of illness and death transformed a theoretical injustice into a daily tragedy for thousands of people. At the same time, the heartrending story of Karen Thompson, a lesbian who was barred from caring for her partner, Sharon Kowalski, after a car accident left the latter incapacitated, became the poster story for the lack of rights, standing in for the stories of many others.

All across the country, gay men were being kept out of their sick lovers' hospital rooms, denied the right to make medical decisions for their partners, and deprived of their rightful share of financial assets, all because they were not legally "related" to their dying partners. The refusal by families and social institutions to recognize these caregiving partners as family brought home in a powerful way the truth about the legal discrimination that had existed for so many decades. Domestic partnership registration became all the more valuable, as it offered a set of basic rights, like hospital visitation and health insurance, that could make a critical difference in the lives of those with AIDS (and other medical conditions) and their same-sex partners.

AIDS didn't just bring to the surface the discriminatory treatment of our relationships. It also changed, sometimes for the better, the way in which others viewed those relationships. As a San Francisco lawyer doing legal work for men with AIDS in the mid-1980s, I witnessed many families arrive in San Francisco and meet the partners of their dying sons and brothers for the first time. Parents were forced to acknowledge their son's chosen community, and often helped to care for their dying relative under the welcoming umbrella of their host, the surviving "domestic partner." At the same time, same-sex relationships were gaining new respect and recognition in films, plays, and personal stories about the epidemic.

The Expansion of Domestic Partnership

In the 1980s and early 1990s, a growing number of cities began offering local tax benefits to registered domestic partners, and others extended employment benefits, such as bereavement and parental leave. By 1992, even some publicly traded companies were offering such benefits, as were many of the larger university systems. Eventually, a majority of Fortune 500 companies began extending benefits to domestic partners—some only to same-sex partners, and others to opposite-sex unmarried partners as well. However limited the benefits were, they bestowed an increasingly meaningful symbolic benefit to the entire community, and they raised the expectations of same-sex couples.

In 1987, just when life in our gay community seemed as bad as it could be amid the widening scourge of AIDS, it got worse. The United States Supreme Court ruled that it was not unconstitutional for the state of Georgia to criminalize homosexual acts simply because, in effect, the Bible said so.

If sentencing two adult men to jail for enjoying a consensual sexual relationship in the privacy of their own home was legally acceptable in the eyes of the highest court in the land, then it was evident that extending the rights of legal marriage to our families was utterly beyond hope. Activist attorneys weren't just discouraged, we were preoccupied with other tasks. The growing needs of gay men who were dying from—and then, as medical progress was made, learning to live with—AIDS, and increasingly, the needs of lesbians raising their own children, were much higher legal priorities for most of us.

The Question of Marriage

During this same period of the 1980s and 1990s, the number of same-sex couples in long-term committed partnerships and the number of lesbian families raising children continued to grow. Nonetheless, marriage was still not a front-burner issue for our community.

The marriage issue was framed very differently in the early 1990s than it is now. Gay civil rights groups openly debated whether to devote resources to a fight to legalize same-sex marriage. The pro-marriage-equality camp argued that marital relationships are the basis of significant material benefits and social legitimacy. For that reason alone, advocates argued, lesbians and gay men should have equal access to marriage and the right to make the same choices as opposite-sex couples. Many shared the view that marriage was not the ideal way to organize society, but still felt that justice required allowing lesbians and gay men equal access to the institution.

On the other side of the debate, skeptics took the position that marriage was fundamentally a sexist institution based upon a social model that presumes a dominant and higher-paid husband, a deferential and lower-earning wife, a presumption of monogamy and permanence in the relationship ("till death do us part"), and a societal favoritism of couples over single people—all of which fostered values directly contrary to those espoused by the gay liberation movement. The marriage skeptics argued that it was better to work toward building a society that would provide housing, health insurance, and social dignity for every individual, single or coupled, instead of trying to squeeze everyone into a marriage "box" that was constricting and narrow.

This debate still exists, but it continues under the surface, as the marriage equality movement has emerged as the primary battleground for equality.

Gay Soldiers and Lesbian Moms

In the mid-1990s, two seemingly unrelated developments occurred: The opposition to the military's policy of discharging gay soldiers became more vocal and visible, and there was a noticeable "gayby" boom in the lesbian community. While on the surface these developments had little to do with the marriage movement, they had a profound impact on how society saw our relationships, and in turn, how we envisioned our own place in society. Gay soldiers? Lesbian moms? Clearly, this was not the 1970s picture of homosexual activists rioting in the streets, and certainly it was not the world of radical lesbian feminist separatists and sexually adventurous gay men. Over time, and quite unpredictably, these two trends didn't just change the way the straight world saw us; they also fostered and then highlighted a noticeable trend toward the mainstream in our own communities. Call it conservative or call it assimilationist—or call it equality. Whatever you call it, what it meant to be gay was changing dramatically. Lesbians and gay men were moving out of gay ghettos, raising kids of their own, demanding to join the military, and at the same time coming out in the corporate workplace all over the country.

These changes could be felt and seen everywhere. I certainly saw them in my legal practice. Couples throughout the San Francisco Bay Area were buying houses, raising kids, taking on corporate leadership positions, and entering politics. Over time, some of them were, inevitably, breaking up. All of them needed advice about how to structure their family lives in the face of a still-homophobic world where marriage remained unavailable.

In light of these social changes, it should have been no surprise to see a blossoming of the desire to legalize same-sex marriage. Couples were already living lives that resembled marriage in many ways, and yet they were continually confronting the discriminatory reality of the lack of marriage equality. It was frustrating, not to mention expensive, for partners in marriage-like relationships to try to craft protections without the support of the legal framework of marriage. The gap between social reality and legal exclusion was growing intolerable.

Aloha: Marriage Equality Comes and Goes in Hawaii

Despite the growing awareness of marriage inequality on the part of couples and the lawyers working with them on structuring (and dissolving) their relationships, the first marriage cases did not originate with any of the legal advocacy groups. On the local level, lawyers were too focused on meeting the practical needs of clients, and on the national level the advocacy groups were too discouraged by negative court decisions. The early lawsuits were grassroots efforts—brought by idealistic couples who were tired of being mistreated and disenfranchised, with the help of lawyers who were not always part of the gay legal mainstream.

This new chapter of the marriage story began to unfold in 1993, when a few gutsy couples in Hawaii linked up with a straight civil liberties attorney and sued to lift the state's ban on same-sex marriage. Around the same time, a couple in New York State launched a parallel battle, also on their own, without the support of any national gay rights legal group.

Gay People Can Save Themselves for Marriage, Too

While the New York case was never able to achieve any legal success, the plaintiffs in that case exemplified just the sort of maverick independence that was fueling the marriage effort. To them, their case was a simple matter of justice, not political strategy. They were in love, and they were so traditional that they didn't even want to live together until they were married! All they wanted was what their straight friends and relatives had: a traditional marriage, public legal recognition, and the identity of spouses to each other. They didn't care if the courts seemed unsympathetic or if the timing of their case didn't seem "prudent" to the gay legal strategists. They were outraged by the injustice of their situation and they wanted to right that wrong, right away. Even though they went on to lose their case in the courts, this couple and others like them deserve much of the credit for helping to bring us to where we are today.

The Hawaii marriage campaign was a telling illustration—and a precursor —of how unpredictable the struggle for legal marriage would be. Initially, the courts were not persuaded by the arguments for legalizing gay marriage, but eventually the Hawaii Supreme Court sided with the gay plaintiffs and ordered the parties to return to court for a trial on the question of whether there was any legal justification to ban gay marriage.

This ruling was itself a tremendous victory, as it set a new standard of questioning the government's position and distinguished between civil and religious marriage, rather than simply deferring to a dictionary definition of marriage. It opened the possibility of actually winning such a battle. No longer was a mere citation to Webster's dictionary or the Bible the end of the legal analysis.

After the trial, the lower court found that the government was not justified in prohibiting same-sex marriage, and legal marriage suddenly seemed possible. But then, as would happen later in so many other states, antimarriage activists switched tactics, bolted out of the courtroom, and launched a statewide ballot campaign to ban same-sex marriage. If they couldn't win in court, they would take the issue to the voters—and in a terrible blow for the marriage movement, the people of Hawaii voted to enact a constitutional amendment banning same-sex marriage. A few more years of political wrangling ensued, but Hawaii's great marriage victory was left in tatters. In the end, the state only managed to offer a "reciprocal beneficiary" registration scheme that provides very few substantive rights. (In 2010, the Hawaii legislature passed a marriage equivalent civil union bill, but governor Linda Lingle vetoed it.)

The Political Game

The Hawaii victory invigorated antigay activists, who ramped up efforts to prevent same-sex marriage at both the state and federal levels. The anti-equality forces won their biggest victories in the legislatures. In 1996, the United States Congress enacted the "Defense of Marriage Act" (DOMA), which (until 2013) precluded federal recognition of any same-sex marriage— even one that is lawful in the state where it occurred and recognized in the couple's home state. Over the next five years, more than 40 states passed "mini-DOMA" statutes, prohibiting same-sex marriage. Some passed so-called "super-DOMA" laws, which provide not only that a state itself doesn't sanction same-sex relationships of any kind, but also that same-sex relationships that are legal in other states won't be recognized there.

Whether marriage as an institution was good for people and whether marriage was the right choice for any particular couple were no longer the pressing political issues for the LGBT community, which had no choice but to respond to the homophobic activism. And so, very quickly, and quite surprisingly to some of us older gay rights advocates, marriage equality became the frontline gay civil rights battle.

The Marriage Equivalent Movement

Even as the marriage equality campaigns progressed, domestic partnership continued to play an important role. For politicians, domestic partnership offered a safe harbor—it provided an expandable package of practical rights without stepping into the political danger zone of marriage, instead keeping the focus on the practical and legal dimensions of the relationship.

In an odd juxtaposition of political agendas, antimarriage and promarriage forces could join in support of domestic partnership, with one faction (ours, that is) viewing it as a stepping-stone to marriage, and the other side hoping that it would be the only status ever granted to same-sex couples. More and more companies, universities, and municipalities enacted domestic partnership programs.

For a while it appeared as though the "domestic partnership but no marriage" stalemate would rule the day. Starting in the late 1990s, however, the line between domestic partnership and legal marriage began to blur. The roots of the U.S. breakthrough came from Europe: A comprehensive civil partnership system called PACS was enacted in 1999 in France, granting some marriage rights to registered couples of any gender configuration, without calling it marriage. Again, the idea was to avoid the highly charged language and the symbolic dimensions of marriage, while providing marital rights as practical benefits.

Inspired by this blended approach, a new kind of in-between arrangement emerged in the United States as well. In 1999, the Vermont Supreme Court ruled that denying marital benefits to same-sex couples was unconstitutional. The court didn't say there had to be marriage, but rather, that it was wrong to deny marital rights to lesbian and gay couples. After a great deal of statewide political haggling, the Vermont legislature opted not to legalize same-sex marriage, but instead to establish a civil union status that came with all of the same rights and duties of marriage.

The resulting political compromise made sense historically and was probably unavoidable, but the adoption of the model in other U.S. states has created a messy patchwork of laws that can make life extraordinarily complex for many same-sex couples. Several states have established some form of domestic partnership or civil union—some nearly identical to marriage except by name, and others offering only a limited selection of marital benefits. Meanwhile, as this book goes to press, 16 states and the District of Columbia allow same-sex marriage, and every state is following its own course with regard to the recognition of partnerships or marriages originating elsewhere. (See Chapters 2 and 4 and Appendix A for the specifics of the state rules.) It's a crazy and, in the end, an unworkable system, but it is our current legal reality.

The Marriage Equality Movement

To an extent that would have been unforeseeable even five years ago, the "just don't call it marriage" compromise was itself not destined to last very long. In 2003, the Massachusetts Supreme Court rejected the compromise approach and issued a landmark ruling declaring that nothing short of marriage would remedy the discriminatory impact of the state's opposite-sex-only marriage rules. The court's written opinion was deeply touching, as it spoke of the need to impart dignity and respect to all couples. This wasn't just a matter of extending practical benefits that could be conferred by state registration, but rather, an insistence by the court on full marriage equality, including the name.

After the ruling, the Massachusetts legislature resisted the clamoring demands of antigay activists to rescind the court's ruling, and in May 2004, the nation's first legal gay weddings were celebrated in the Bay State. Since then, more than 15,000 same-sex couples have married in Massachusetts.

Gay activists weren't the only ones demanding change. Also in 2004, San Francisco's new mayor, Gavin Newsom, was so deeply offended by antigay comments made by then-President Bush in his State of the Union address that he came back to San Francisco and ordered city officials to start issuing marriage licenses to same-sex couples.

The result was an episode of political theater that was extraordinary even by San Francisco standards. Lesbians and gay men lined up in the pouring rain to receive official blessings on their relationships, and San Francisco City Hall was awash in wedding gowns and tuxedos, buoyantly happy couples, and beaming relatives celebrating the weddings of their children, parents, and friends. The California courts shut down the unauthorized weddings within a few weeks (and soon after that invalidated all of the marriages), but the genie was out of the bottle. Within a day of the California Supreme Court's issuance of an order to stop the San Francisco marriages, four separate lawsuits challenging the ban on gay marriage were filed in California courts.

The California legal train had left the station, and four years later, on May 15, 2008, it arrived at the ultimate destination when the California Supreme Court threw out the ban on same-sex marriage. The court's ruling was eloquent in its defense of the rights of all people in loving relationships to enjoy the rights and privileges of marriage. While the justices recognized that couples already had access to the technical rights of marriage under California's domestic partnership laws, they ruled that the creation of a second-class status was constitutionally unacceptable and—for the first time—included lesbians and gay men in the category of suspect classes entitled to the highest level of constitutional protection in the courts.

But just six months after the court ruled, and after nearly five months' worth of weddings had taken place, California voters approved Proposition 8, which provided that only marriage between a man and a woman was valid and recognized in California. Once again, the marriage door had slammed shut. Supporters of marriage equality protested the proposition in a lawsuit to the California Supreme Court, which ruled in May 2009 that Prop 8. was valid and allowed the constitutional amendment to stand. Same-sex couples thus continued to be barred from legal marriage in California—but the Supreme Court also ruled that those who married between June and November 2008 were still married. The California legislature also passed a law clarifying that California would recognize same-sex marriages, as well as civil unions and domestic partnerships, from other states. In 2009, two same-sex couples filed a federal lawsuit challenging Proposition 8, and a trial was held, ending in a ruling by Judge Vaughn Walker that Proposition 8 was unconstitutional. The case was immediately appealed to the Ninth Circuit Court of Appeals and eventually, in June 2013, the United States Supreme Court tossed out the Prop. 8 appeals, and the same-sex marriage door reopened in California. All of these important developments do nothing to mitigate the fact that continuing inconsistencies in the laws create confusion for families as well as the institutions, like employers and insurers, for whom family relationships are relevant.

In another landmark decision in 2008, the Connecticut Supreme Court ruled in October that the state's ban on same-sex marriage was unconstitutional, and that the civil union option already in effect there was separate and, thus, not equal. Following the same reasoning as the California Supreme Court, the Connecticut justices ruled that segregating same-sex couples into a lesser form of partnership—even one offering the same rights and duties of marriage—was unacceptable. That decision stood firm through the November 2008 elections, and that month same-sex couples began marrying in Connecticut. Then, within a few short months, the Iowa Supreme Court and the Vermont and New Hampshire legislatures opened the door to legal marriage for same-sex couples. In 2010, Washington D.C. also began issuing marriage licenses to same-sex couples. Within the next three years, voters, legislators or courts in Maine, New York, Maryland, Washington State, Rhode Island, Delaware, Minnesota, New Jersey, Illinois, and Hawaii granted same-sex couples the right to marry.

And so, as of this writing, same-sex marriage is legal in 16 states and the District of Columbia. Massachusetts originally prohibited out-of-state couples from marrying there if they lived in a state that barred same-sex marriage, but that ban has been lifted, and currently couples from anywhere in the world can travel to Canada, or any of the marriage equality states and be legally married. In addition, Oregon now recognizes valid, out-of-state same-sex marriages, even though same-sex marriage is not legal in the state.

In other words, it took just 40 years for the marriage equality movement to evolve from the lonely fantasy of two Minnesota men to a reality for every same-sex couple in the country.

Timeline	
1578	–Several male couples married in a Catholic church in Rome, 11 of whom were later burned to death as heretics
1969	–Stonewall Riots in New York City
	–Jack Baker and Michael McConnell apply for a marriage license in Minnesota
1972	–Minnesota Supreme Court rejects marriage claim
	–Washington State court rejects marriage claim
1977	–Anita Bryant forms a group called "Save Our Children" to repeal antidiscrimination laws in Florida
1978	–Antigay teachers campaign in California (Briggs Initiative)
	–Assassination of Harvey Milk
1981	–First reported case of AIDS (originally known as GRID)
1982	–Lawsuit seeking domestic partnership rights defeated in San Francisco
	–San Francisco's domestic partnership ordinance vetoed
	–*Village Voice* newspaper gives domestic partner benefits
	–Liberace sued for palimony by ex-lover
	–Wisconsin passes first statewide antidiscrimination law
1984	–Berkeley city employees win domestic partnership protection
1985	–West Hollywood establishes public domestic partnership registry
	–Rock Hudson dies of AIDS
	–First lesbian second-parent adoption approved in Oregon
1987	–U.S. Supreme Court upholds antisodomy criminal laws
1989	–San Francisco establishes domestic partnership registry
	–Denmark legalizes same-sex domestic partnerships
1991	–Berkeley enacts public domestic partnership registration
1993	–Hawaii couples file a lawsuit to legalize same-sex marriage
	–"Don't Ask, Don't Tell" gays in the military rules enacted
1996	–U.S. Congress enacts the Defense of Marriage Act
1997	–Hawaii voters pass constitutional amendment banning same-sex marriage

Timeline, continued	
1999	–Vermont court rules marriage ban unconstitutional
	–France establishes PACS (domestic partnership registration)
	–California enacts first statewide domestic partnership registration
2000	–Vermont legislature creates civil union (marriage equivalent) registration
2001	–Same-sex marriage legalized in the Netherlands
2003	–Massachusetts court invalidates ban on same-sex marriage
	–Belgium legalizes same-sex marriage
	–U.S. Supreme Court invalidates antisodomy statutes
2004	–San Francisco allows same-sex marriages; court says no
	–Massachusetts allows first legal same-sex marriages
2005	–Same-sex marriage legalized in Spain and Canada
2006	–South Africa legalizes same-sex marriage
	–New Jersey civil unions (marriage equivalent) commence
	–Civil partnership (marriage equivalent) authorized in Great Britain
	–Mexico City legalizes same-sex domestic partnership
	–Uruguay legalizes same-sex civil unions
2008	–California Supreme Court lifts ban on same-sex marriage
	–California voters enact Proposition 8, reinstating ban on same-sex marriage
	–Connecticut court invalidates ban on same-sex marriage
	–New Hampshire authorizes marriage equivalent civil unions
	–New York State recognizes legal marriages from other states
2009	–Norway legalizes same-sex marriage
	–California Supreme Court upholds Proposition 8, limiting marriage to a man and a woman; court also upholds validity of existing same-sex marriages
	–Iowa Supreme Court invalidates ban on same-sex marriage
	–Vermont, Maine, and New Hampshire gain marriage equality through legislative action, but equality in Maine is lost after a public vote
	–Nevada legislature creates domestic partnership law

Timeline, continued	
2010	–Maryland recognizes legal marriages from other states
	–District of Columbia legalizes same-sex marriage
	–Argentina legalizes same-sex marriage
	–Mexico's Supreme Court upholds marriage equality law for Mexico City
	–Iceland's lesbian prime minister marries her partner
	–Illinois passes civil union bill, goes into effect June 2011
2011	–New York State approves same-sex marriage legislation
2012	–Washington State, Maine, Maryland, and Denmark legalize same-sex marriage
2013	–Delaware, Rhode Island, and Minnesota enact same-sex marriage legislation
	–Brazil, France, New Zealand, Uruguay, England, and Wales legalize same-sex marriage
	–Proposition 8 is overturned and same-sex marriages resume in California
	–Section 3 of the Defense of Marriage Act is invalidated by U.S. Supreme Court
	–The U.S. Treasury Department rules that same-sex married couples will be recognized as legally married for all federal tax purposes, regardless of where they live, so long as they were married in a jurisdiction that recognizes same-sex marriage
	–A State Superior Court Judge in New Jersey overturns the state's ban on same-sex marriage. The New Jersey Supreme Court indicates it will not reverse the decision and the Governor decides not to appeal. New Jersey becomes the 14th state to legalize same-sex marriage
	–The Oregon Department of Justice rules that the state must recognize valid, same-sex marriages from other jurisdictions, even though same-sex marriage is not yet legal in Oregon
	–Illinois passes a same-sex marriage bill, which the Governor has promised to sign. Same-sex marriage will begin taking place on June 1, 2014
	–Hawaii passes a same-sex marriage bill which will allow same-sex marriages to take place on December 2, 2013

As later chapters will explain, there is still significant uncertainty about relationship recognition between states, and it may be years before the federal government honors every same-sex partnership. There are maddening inconsistencies regarding parentage and custody rights, lingering problems resulting from disparate tax treatment of same-sex couples, and terrible dilemmas for couples who move across state lines, or who break up in nonrecognition states. But the right to enter into a legal marriage—or at least some reasonable facsimile of it—is now available to each of us.

Marriage is no longer just a theoretical question. It's now a personal one for each of us. That's why you are free to ask—and obligated to ask—whether you and your partner should walk down the proverbial aisle. Wholly apart from what activists and lawyers have been fighting over for the past four decades, when we meet Mr. or Ms. Right and want to settle down, each of us is now free to ask whether we should simply cohabit as we used to do, without any formal legal relationship between us, or whether we should "make it legal."

It's taken the heroic legal and political efforts of thousands of your gay brothers and sisters to bring us to this transformative point in our history. It's now up to you to answer this all important personal question for yourselves—and we hope this book will help.

RESOURCE

To stay up to date on the progress of marriage equality, check the legal updates at www.nolo.com and the blogs at www.makingitlegal.net and www.queerjustice.com.

Same-Sex Marriage Around the World and at Home

'm convinced that having a solid grasp on today's changing legal environment will help you make the best possible decisions about your relationships. The last thing you want to do is to get married or partnered just because your state allows it, without finding out whether marriage is a good option for you personally. And, if you fail to comprehend where you stand under the current law or to account for possible future developments, there is a chance you will make mistakes; couples who downplay the problem of obtaining legal dissolutions in the states they live in, for example, could experience some mighty powerful regrets should their relationships go awry.

Just 12 years ago, this chapter would have been extremely short—no matter where you were in the world there was little in the way of recognition for same-sex relationships. Now, things are very different. Our survey of the legal landscape starts overseas, where the first same-sex marriages in the world were performed in 2001.

The International Landscape

In my view, Europeans seem less concerned about the "morality" of same-sex marriage than Americans generally. There's a greater acceptance of informal cohabitation, and many Europeans view marriage as a legal relationship rather than a religious one. This phenomenon manifests in various ways: (1) In nearly every European country, only a civil authority can conduct a marriage—couples are not allowed to be married by a priest or another religious leader; (2) while statistics are notoriously difficult to pin down, marriage rates in northern Europe tend to be about half of those of the United States; recent figures put the annual marriage rate at approximately ten for every 1,000 residents in the United States and somewhere around four or five per 1,000 in Europe; and (3) legalization of gay relationships has happened rapidly in Europe, even in countries such as Spain that have traditionally been dominated by religious conventions.

Same-Sex Marriage in Europe

The Netherlands, ever enlightened, was the first country in the world to legalize same-sex marriage, in 2001. The country already had a system of registered partnership law on the books, providing limited benefits and a degree of official recognition of gay relationships. Expanding the laws to include more of the elements of marriage was thus an easy step. The Dutch marriage law started with some discrepancies between same-sex and opposite-sex marriage, mostly involving adoption of children, but at this point none of these discrepancies remain.

Belgium was the second European country to legalize same-sex marriages, in 2003. And to the surprise of many observers, Spain was next. Spain's history as a conservative society with a strong Catholic Church presence and ultra right-wing politics made it an unlikely seat of gay liberation. In the past several decades, however, socialist and secularist political parties have come to dominate the social conversation, resulting in a widespread tolerance for "alternative" lifestyles.

Norway was the next European country to come into the light—not really a surprise, given that civil unions with nearly all of the rights and duties of marriage have been available there since as far back as 1993. Full-scale marriage went into effect in Norway as of January 2009. Portugal and Iceland followed in 2010.

Same-sex marriage continues to make its way through Europe, with Sweden granting the full legalization of same-sex marriage in 2009. France, England, and Wales joined the club in 2013.

In case you're starting to imagine a European vacation with a wedding thrown in, take note that each of the European countries that allow same-sex marriage require that at least one partner be a citizen or resident of that country.

Same-Sex Marriage Elsewhere

South Africa is the only African country that permits same-sex marriage. Legal marriage for same-sex couples arrived in South Africa in December 2006, a product of the new constitution formed when apartheid was abandoned—and a powerful statement of the new government's support of full equality for all of its citizens. Couples may call their legal relationship either a marriage or a civil partnership, but in either case all the rights and duties of marriage apply. There is no residency requirement to marry in South Africa, so any same-sex couple in the world can travel there and get married.

Mexico City allows same-sex couples to marry (and to adopt children), and other Mexican districts must recognize the legal relationships. And in July 2010, Argentina became the first Latin American country to allow same-sex couples to wed. Brazil and most of Mexico followed in its footsteps soon thereafter.

Governmental Structures Matter

In most foreign countries, the legal battles—as well as the decisive political or judicial actions that legalize same-sex marriage—are played out on a national stage, not in a local or regional locale. With the exception of Australia, Canada, and the United States, every major country in the world treats marriage as a national issue, not a local or state matter. Many of the world's larger countries have regional provinces that are equivalent to our states, and there are some legal differences between provinces on other topics. But marital laws are national, and so the entire country tilts in one direction or the other.

Our each-state-for-itself set of marriage rules is the source of many of the inconsistencies that cause legal problems for same-sex couples in the United States. At the same time, the lack of a national system of marriage in this country also allows for more incremental change, enabling the more progressive states to move forward to allow gay marriage at a time when Congress and less progressive state legislatures have been unwilling to make such moves.

The Canadian Story

Like the United States, Canada has provincial (the equivalent of the U.S. state) as well as federal marital rules. Some basic rules and rights are set out in the national laws, while provincial legislatures and their courts have a certain degree of autonomy, including setting some of the rules of marriage and divorce. Because of this political system, change in Canada happened both regionally and nationally at the same time.

Starting in 2003, a series of local lawsuits achieved court victories in the more liberal provinces. By 2005, eight of the ten provincial courts or legislatures had ruled in favor of same-sex marriage. There is no local residency requirement preventing anyone from traveling from one province to another to get married and each province recognizes the others' marriages, so national acceptance of local marriages was pretty much a foregone conclusion at that point. Canada legalized same-sex marriage nationally as of July 2005, and soon thereafter that new order was imposed on all of the provinces.

Canada does not require that either of the spouses be a Canadian citizen or even reside in Canada in order to marry there. Any same-sex couple can travel to Canada and get married there legally after complying with local rules to get a marriage license—some of which require a few weeks of public notice before the marriage can be solemnized.

CAUTION

We don't know whether a Canadian marriage between two partners of the same sex (whether Canadians who have moved south or U.S. residents who came to Canada for their wedding) will be recognized in the states here that currently do not allow same-sex marriage. It's equally unclear whether all branches of the federal government will recognize Canadian marriages. This means there's no guarantee that you would receive the benefits of marriage or, for that matter, be able to get divorced, in Kansas after marrying in Canada. Similar problems will be encountered by couples marrying abroad and then returning home to the United States. There's more about the issue of recognition in "When Is a Spouse Not a Spouse?" below, and in Chapter 4.

Recap: Countries Offering Same-Sex Marriage		
Argentina	France	Portugal
Belgium	Iceland	South Africa
Brazil	Mexico	Spain
Canada	The Netherlands	Sweden
Denmark	New Zealand	Uruguay
England and Wales	Norway	

Separate but Equal: Marriage Equivalent Countries

While only 11 foreign countries offer full legal marriage, the list of those with some form of relationship recognition is growing. Civil union or domestic partnership status is available to same-sex couples in nearly 20 European countries, including the United Kingdom (England, Scotland, Wales, and Northern Ireland). A few years ago, Hungary granted all marital rights to same-sex couples—the first formerly "Eastern Bloc" country to do so. However, their own constitutional court threw out the new law (as violating the constitutional status of heterosexual marriage because opposite-sex couples were included). Subsequently, a reduced-scale partnership law was enacted extending most marital rights to same-sex couples.

Most of these countries provide just about every right of marriage to registered couples, though the laws differ on a variety of lesser matters, such as whether or not the couple has to use the courts to dissolve the relationship. England comes the closest to legal marriage—registered partners have all the rights and obligations of marriage, and must dissolve their relationships in court if they separate. In other countries, such as France, registered couples have limited inheritance and tax protections, but are considered married with respect to all property rights and support obligations.

In Australia, same-sex marriage per se is banned, but a majority of the regional provinces offer civil-union-type registration, with some but not all of the rights and duties of marriage.

The Future of Marriage Worldwide

A frustrating limitation in Europe is that the European Union doesn't require member countries to recognize same-sex marriages or partnerships from elsewhere on the continent—similar to the United States' problem of lack of interstate recognition. But in my opinion, the tide has turned, and I believe that in the coming decade, legal marriage for same-sex couples will become the new norm, with full recognition by most European countries of marriages entered into elsewhere—and eventually, as a mandate binding on all members of the European Union.

Other than in Australia, where marriage is a real possibility in the coming decade, legal marriage—or any marriage equivalent relationship—is probably a long way off for same-sex couples on the other continents, especially in Africa and Asia.

Recap: Countries Offering Relationship Recognition		
Andorra	Finland	Portugal
Austria	Germany	Slovenia
Colombia	Hungary	Sweden
Croatia	Luxembourg	Switzerland
Czech Republic	Mexico (locally only)	Scotland, Northern
Ecuador	New Zealand	Ireland

The Domestic Landscape

As exciting as the international developments may be, changes closer to home are the ones that will have the greatest impact on your decisions about what is the best legal arrangement for the two of you.

A Brief History of Marital Law in the United States

The United States is a federal system of government, based upon the notion of a federation of independent states. As is true of many of our laws, from colonial days, the rules of marriage and divorce in our country have generally been left up to each individual state.

Over time, the federal government has increased its control over things like business dealings and interstate commerce, but for the most part stayed out of the laws of birth, marriage, divorce, and death, which remain state-based. That is why each state can maintain its own rules about who is and isn't allowed to marry, and its own rules and procedures related to divorce. It is also why the federal government has never been in the business of creating marriage or divorce laws, and why federal agencies (such as the IRS) traditionally have recognized marriages from every state. In short, until the Defense of Marriage Act (DOMA) was passed in 1996, there was no such thing as a federal definition of marriage.

Heterosexual couples may marry in any state, whether they live there or not, as long as they meet that state's requirements for marriage (such as age and degree of relation). Then every other state treats them as legally married, even a state that wouldn't allow the couple to marry there. So too, if a couple divorces, it doesn't matter where they got married; their marriage will be recognized as valid and the laws of the state where they have been living will apply to the divorce. Residency requirements prevent spouses from moving to another state just before a divorce in order to avoid financial obligations imposed by the actual home state. Child custody disputes are handled by the courts in the state where the kids actually live.

These rules make for almost total marital mobility and provide a rational system for managing the marital lives of a mobile population—at least for opposite-sex couples.

Religious and Civil Marriage

Marriage laws are entirely civil in nature, meaning they are governed by laws made by an elected legislature. A couple obtains a license to marry from the county clerk, but has the option to become legally married in a church, synagogue, mosque, or other symbolic location. While not of any real legal significance, this cultural practice has led many to blur the lines between religious and civil marriage—severely hampering efforts to remove the legal prohibition on same-sex couples' enjoying the benefits of civil marriage.

A Brief History of Divorce

The history of divorce in this country is actually quite complicated. Full legal divorce as we know it today was very hard to obtain in colonial America, where English protocols were generally followed and sometimes even a vote of the state legislature was required for a divorce to be granted. In the 19th century, most couples wanting to end their marriages were limited to the option of legal separations that allowed them to live apart but precluded marriage to others. Some states loosened their rules by the end of the 19th century, but divorces granted in one state were not always honored in other states.

By the early 20th century, divorce was available more or less everywhere—but it could take years of legal wrangling to end a marriage. Typically, one partner had to be found at fault before the court would grant a divorce, and the division of money and property rested on the fault finding as well. To prevent spouses from moving around to try to find the most advantageous divorce laws, most states established minimum residency requirements for filing a divorce petition. As a result, you could get legally married wherever you wanted to, even if you didn't live in that state, but you could only file for divorce in your home state (or after establishing residency somewhere else). The federal government recognized all marriages and divorces, and the only federal regulations relating to divorce dealt with child custody, the prevention of parental kidnapping, and tax exemptions for assets transferred upon divorce.

This basic structure has held for many decades. The biggest change in divorce law in the 20th century was the development of no-fault divorce, which allowed couples to divorce by agreement, based on "irreconcilable differences" instead of on one partner's fault.

A Wrench in the Works: Same-Sex Marriage

Until the 1967 United State Supreme Court decision in *Loving v. Virginia*, some states banned interracial marriage. Thus it was conceivable that a mixed-race couple who married in one state and then relocated to another could find their marriage was not recognized by their new home state. Common law marriage was another outlier issue—only a small minority of states recognize common law marriages, which bestow the rights and duties of marriage on couples who cohabit and act as if they were married but don't go through the formal marriage process. Again, partners who would be considered legally married under the rules of one state might be treated as single by a nearby state, if the second state didn't honor common law marriages.

But these sorts of discrepancies were rare, and never so widespread as to cause any major social policy problems. Between the time that the bans on interracial marriage were tossed out by the Supreme Court and the point when same-sex marriage became an issue, the institution had effectively become a uniform legal status, recognized in every state and on the federal level.

Enter same-sex marriage, and suddenly the well-integrated system of marriage recognition goes haywire. In the United States now, more than 20 states have some form of relationship recognition, in the form of domestic partnership, civil unions, or marriage for same-sex couples. Some of the states that don't offer such relationships have agreed to recognize those entered into in other states. But some states both refuse to allow same-sex marriage and won't recognize lawful marriages and domestic partnerships from other states.

As a result, same-sex couples can't rely on their relationships being honored across state lines.

What follows here is a summary of the current state-by-state rules, as of November 2013.

State by State: Marriage and Relationship Recognition in America

The chart below lists the states that have some form of relationship recognition for same-sex couples, and for the nonmarriage relationships, indicates whether they are marriage equivalents or not. There's a more detailed chart in Appendix A providing the specifics of each state's laws, and there's a longer discussion about each of the states below.

The Marriage States

As this third edition goes to press, 17 jurisdictions have court rulings or laws providing for full marriage equality: California, Connecticut, Delaware, District of Columbia, Hawaii, Illinois, Iowa, Maine, Maryland, Massachusetts, Minnesota, New Hampshire, New Jersey, New York, Rhode Island, Vermont, and Washington. (On November 6, 2013, Illinois passed a same-sex marriage bill which is awaiting Governor Pat Quinn's signature.) In each of these states, same-sex spouses have all of the same rights and responsibilities as opposite-sex spouses—at the state level, that is. As of June 2013, marriage equality was finally extended to the federal level. The lingering problems of federal nonrecognition are discussed in "When Is a Spouse Not a Spouse?" below and in Chapter 4.

State	Relationship	Marriage Equivalent?
California	Domestic partnership/Marriage	
Colorado	Domestic partnership	Yes
Connecticut	Marriage	
Delaware	Marriage	
District of Columbia	Marriage	
Hawaii	Marriage	
Illinois	Marriage (June 2014)	
Iowa	Marriage	
Maine	Marriage	
Maryland	Marriage	
Massachusetts	Marriage	
Minnesota	Marriage	
Nevada	Domestic partnership	Yes
New Hampshire	Marriage	
New Jersey	Marriage	
New York	Marriage	
Oregon	Domestic partnership/Recognition of out-of-state same-sex marriages	Yes
Rhode Island	Marriage	
Vermont	Marriage	
Washington	Marriage	
Wisconsin	Domestic partnership	Nearly

Massachusetts

Massachusetts was the first state to allow same-sex couples to marry, starting in 2004. At the outset, only Massachusetts residents were eligible to marry there. A 1913 law, originally enacted to prevent interracial couples from coming north to get married, stated that if your marriage was illegal in your own state you couldn't get married in Massachusetts. Therefore, from 2004 to mid-2008, the only out-of-state same-sex couples who could marry in Massachusetts were those from the few states that did not prohibit same-sex marriage and those who proclaimed their intention to relocate to the Bay State. A few local clerks didn't enforce the rule strictly, so there were exceptions (and it's unclear whether those marriages are valid—even where such issues would be resolved). This law was repealed in the summer of 2008.

To marry in Massachusetts, you must be 18 or older, not married to anyone else, not related by blood to your intended spouse, and have taken a blood test showing that you do not have communicable syphilis. To get a divorce in Massachusetts, you must have lived there for at least a year.

Massachusetts recognizes marriages from the other states that allow same-sex couples to enter into them. And so far, the state has recognized marriage equivalent relationships from other states, by granting divorces to civil union partners. All of those partners agreed to have their relationships dissolved in Massachusetts, so no one has challenged the state's authority over same-sex couples in relationships other than marriage. However, it's unlikely that such a challenge would be successful—as long as couples meet the residency requirement, most likely courts will grant divorces for marriage equivalent relationships.

California

Like Massachusetts, California opened the door for full marriage equality following the state Supreme Court ruling on May 15, 2008. The Golden State has no residency requirements for marriage, and so anyone who met the legal standards (i.e., was not married to anyone else and was at least 18 years old) was able to get a marriage license and immediately stand before an authorized clerk, judge, or religious officiant and be married.

The excitement over the 2008 court decision was short-lived, as a ballot initiative reinstating the ban on same-sex marriage narrowly passed later that year. A state court challenge soon followed, asserting that because the California Supreme Court had already concluded that we had a constitutional right to marry, this ruling could not be overturned by a voter-initiated ballot vote. That challenge was rejected and the constitutional amendment stands in California. The existing marriages were also upheld, so the 18,000 couples who married in 2008 are still married. However, two same-sex couples filed a federal lawsuit challenging Proposition 8, and a trial was held, ending in an August 2010 ruling by Judge Vaughn Walker that Proposition 8 was unconstitutional. The appeals in that case were eventually dismissed in June 2013, and marriages resumed soon thereafter.

California still has an intact system of domestic partnership registration that extends all of the rights and duties of marriage to registered partners. More about that in "Marriage Equivalents," below. And the legislature enacted a law that provides that same-sex couples who registered or married in other states (and Canada) are subject to California's community property laws and other marital rules. In addition, the most recent California legislation clarifies that couples who are married or registered in California and also married in another state or Canada can use the California courts to end both relationships if they split up. Anticipating the "wedlocked" problem, couples living in nonrecognition states can get divorced in California without meeting the residency requirements.

What Do You Call Yourself?

One thorny question gay couples face is what to call themselves when they get married. "Spouses for life" seems to be a frequently used term of late, but in my opinion it implies that our marriages are more like prison sentences than loving unions. After the Supreme Court ruling, the California Department of Public Health replaced the traditional form with the terms "Party A" and "Party B," which offended everyone as being far too sterile. The state's fix during the five months that marriages were performed was to allow spouses to go with the Party A–Party B designation, or each pick bride or groom (resulting in bride-bride or groom-groom licenses). That seems a good solution; as new marriage laws go into effect, we'll see what other states do as well.

Connecticut

In late 2008, Connecticut joined the ranks of the marriage-equality states under an opinion issued by its supreme court. Before the ruling, Connecticut was a civil union state with a marriage-equivalent system, but the civil union system has now been ended. Connecticut has no residency requirement for marriage, so along with much of the rest of New England, it's a wedding destination for same-sex couples who live in any state.

You can marry in Connecticut if you are over 18, not married to someone else, and not related in a closer relation than first cousins. To get a divorce in Connecticut, there's a rather complicated residency requirement—you must either have lived in Connecticut for 12 months, have married in Connecticut and returned there with the intent of living there permanently, or have decided to divorce after moving to Connecticut. If you meet either of the last two requirements, you don't have to wait a year to start your divorce.

Connecticut will recognize marriages, civil unions, and domestic partnerships entered into in other states.

In the spring of 2009, there was a veritable stampede of change in the world of same-sex relationships. And it began in what might seem like the unlikeliest of places, the Midwest, and then moved through New England.

Iowa

In April 2009, the Iowa Supreme Court lifted the ban on same-sex marriage, in a lucid and compassionate decision that exemplified the best of its heartland sense of fairness and equality. The decision was unanimous, with all seven justices voting for full marriage equality.

Same-sex couples in Iowa may marry after obtaining a marriage license and waiting three days, just like opposite-sex couples. Couples must not be married to someone else, must not be closely related, and must be of the age of consent. Iowa will recognize marriages and marriage-equivalent relationships from other states.

Vermont

Within a week of the Iowa court decision, Vermont became the first state to establish the right for same-sex couples to marry through legislative action, even overriding a governor's veto to accomplish it.

The new law went into effect in Vermont on September 1, 2009, and as of that date, same-sex couples may no longer enter into civil unions. Our advice is that if you are already in a civil union, you renew your legal commitment by marrying. There's nothing to prevent you from being in both relationships at the same time.

You can marry in Vermont immediately after your license is issued, as long as you are both adults, not married to anyone else, and are not closely related to your intended spouse. There's no residency requirement, and Vermont will recognize marriages and marriage-equivalent relationships from other states.

Maine

A few weeks after Vermont's legislature voted for marriage in 2009, the Maine legislature followed suit and Maine's governor, who previously opposed same-sex marriage, signed the bill into law immediately, saying he had changed his mind and now believes that marriage equality is a matter of basic fairness.

The new law was supposed to take effect in September 2009, but Maine voters approved a measure on the November 2009 ballot to ban same-sex marriages, similar to California's Proposition 8. A few years later, Maine's law changed again—this time allowing same-sex marriage.

New Hampshire

In June 2009, the New Hampshire legislature voted to establish the right to same-sex marriage, bringing to four the number of New England states legalizing same-sex nuptials. The law went into effect on January 1, 2010, and New Hampshire residents can no longer enter into civil unions. Couples in existing civil unions were offered the option to convert the civil unions to marriages (with no payment of additional fees or requirement of new licenses). If they didn't do that—or dissolve their relationships—they were deemed married as of January 1, 2011.

Any person otherwise legally authorized to marry in New Hampshire may marry someone of the same sex, with the exception that the state allows marriages by minors as young as 13 if the marriage is between two people of the opposite sex—gay and lesbian youths must wait until they turn 18 to enter into a same-sex marriage.

New York State

After a factious series of legislative hearings, the New York legislature approved same-sex marriage in 2011, and the governor promptly signed the bill into law. For the most part, New York courts recognize both marriages and civil union/domestic partnership registrations entered into in other states and countries.

Washington State

Washington authorized same-sex marriage in 2012. Like many other states with similar histories, the law provides that unless the spouses are over age 62, their domestic partnership registrations will be "upgraded" to marriage in 2014, unless they judicially dissolve their partnerships within a year.

Maryland

The voters of Maryland surprised many observers by approving the legislatively enacted authorization of same-sex marriage in 2012, and the new law went into effect in January 2013.

Delaware

Following the trend of its nearby jurisdictions, Delaware legalized same-sex marriage in 2013.

Rhode Island

Rhode Island enacted a marriage-equivalent civil union registration in 2011, and then in 2013 it authorized same-sex marriage. The existing civil unions will remain valid, but no new civil union registrations will be allowed.

Minnesota

The home state of the first gay marriage litigation (*Baker v. Nelson*) finally came out of the "margins" and enacted a same-sex marriage bill in 2013. This victory was especially sweet, since just a few months earlier, Minnesota had defeated a proposed constitutional amendment to ban gay marriage.

New Jersey

In September 2013, Judge Mary Jacobson of the State Superior Court in Mercer County, New Jersey lifted the state's ban on same-sex marriage. After the New Jersey Supreme Court ruled that same-sex marriages could proceed and that it would likely overturn the ban, Governor Chris Christie dropped his appeal, and same-sex marriage became legal in New Jersey.

Illinois

On November 6, 2013, the Illinois Senate approved a bill to legalize same-sex marriage. The bill must go to Governor Pat Quinn, who has vowed to sign it. Same-sex marriages will begin taking place on June 1, 2014.

Hawaii

On November 12, 2013 the Hawaii Senate passed a bill legalizing same-sex marriage. The bill will allow same-sex couples to marry in the state beginning December 2, 2013.

Marriage Equivalents

There are currently seven states—California, Colorado, Hawaii, Illinois, Nevada, Oregon, and Washington State that extend all of the rights and duties of marriage to same-sex couples without calling it marriage, instead using the terms domestic partnership or civil union. But now that Hawaii and Illinois will allow same-sex marriage, it is unclear whether these two states will continue to grant and recognize civil unions, or convert civil unions into marriages at some future date.

California

California's marriage equivalent domestic partnership law went into effect in 2005, so it existed before marriage became legal there and continues to exist. Domestic partnership remains intact, and there's no rule that says you can't be both registered and married. As long as same-sex marriages aren't recognized in other states, registering as domestic partners in addition to getting married is a smart idea. Couples who are married elsewhere should still register as domestic partners in California so that there will be no question that marital rights and obligations apply.

One of the quirks of domestic partnership law in California is that when marital rights were extended to domestic partners in 2005, couples who were already registered automatically obtained all of those rights and obligations, unless either partner opted out prior to the law's implementation. This means that couples who signed up for registration prior to 2005 when the legal ramifications were relatively insignificant suddenly were in marriage equivalent relationships, whether they knew it or not—and the property rules that come with marriage were retroactive to their dates of registration. Among the many topics that are likely to come up in divorce cases in the next decade will be the question whether this retroactive application of the law was fair.

California has no residency requirement; couples who live anywhere in the world may register as California domestic partners. Moreover, there is no need for a ceremonial solemnization of a domestic partnership—partners can sign and mail in the registration form without even setting foot in California. And domestic partnership no longer requires that the partners be living together at the time they register, which also is not a requirement of a legal marriage. The other requirements for registration are that both people be over 18, not married to or registered with anyone else, and not related by blood. The registration form must be notarized.

California has a unique twist on the residency issue, too: When you register as domestic partners, you agree that the California courts will be able to grant you a divorce even if you live somewhere else. This makes California a prudent choice of venue for an out-of-state couple who wants to enter a legal relationship. Even if they live in a state that won't recognize their relationship by granting a divorce, they won't be stuck in an unwanted marriage. In fact, if they are able to resolve their financial issues amicably, they probably can get their California dissolution by mail, without ever having to travel to California to appear in court.

California recognizes marriages, domestic partnerships, and civil unions entered into in other states. Despite the recognition rule, it may be prudent for California couples who marry elsewhere to protect themselves by registering as California domestic partners as well.

Oregon

As of January 2008, same-sex couples in Oregon can register as domestic partners and enjoy all the rights and obligations of marriage. To register, partners must be of the same sex, be over 18, not be married or in another civil union or domestic partnership with different people, and not be closely related to each other. At least one of the parties must be a resident of Oregon. The domestic partner registry is handled by city clerks, who process a notarized form that both parties sign—no other solemnization is required.

Although Oregon is a DOMA state, the Oregon Department of Justice issued a 2013 ruling that all state agencies must recognize same-sex marriages from other states and countries.

Nevada

To the surprise and delight of many activists, the Nevada legislature overrode the governor's veto and enacted marriage equivalent civil unions in Nevada in October 2009. Partners can be same sex or opposite sex, and must live together. As in other states, to register, couples must file a form with the Secretary of State's office and pay a small fee. Nevada does not recognize domestic partner registration from another state unless the couple is also registered in Nevada. To dissolve the relationship, couples must use a court divorce proceeding unless they meet several very limiting requirements.

Washington State

The state of Washington recently enacted marriage legislation and no longer offers domestic partnership registration.

Colorado

Effective May 2013, same-sex couples in Colorado can register for civil unions and have all the rights (and obligations) of legal marriage.

Marriage Lite

Another group of states has adopted registration schemes that extend some marriage rights and obligations to same-sex couples, without creating a fully equivalent relationship. Colorado, Hawaii, Maine, and Wisconsin all offer limited rights and benefits to same-sex couples. Which benefits a state actually provides is different from state to state, and the chart in Appendix A provides details of each state's rules. If you are considering registering in any of these states, take a close look at the rules there to see how they will affect you and your partner, and then you can use this information to decide whether registration is a good idea for you.

The Marriage Room

Same-sex couples who are registered and living in any of the marriage equivalent states are subject to the same legal rules as married opposite-sex couples, including the sharing of property and debts and access to all state benefits of marriage. The same rules apply to anyone who registered in such a state and now lives in a registration recognition state. In some states, there are some minor distinctions between the partnership rules and the rules of marriage, but these differences don't affect most couples. The chart in Appendix A has the details of the different states' rules.

If you need a visual metaphor to keep all these rules straight, try this one: I frequently explain to my clients that there is a room called "state marriage rights," in which a set of state-based rights and responsibilities are stored. You can enter the room through various doors. For this room, the domestic partnership or civil union door works just as well as the marriage door—but it's still the back door. There's also a room called "federal marriage rights," which is still off-limits for domestic partnerships and civil unions, but has opened to same-sex married couples, for the most part.

Multiple Registrations

Some state LGBT organizations are advising couples who move to marriage equivalent and marriage-lite states and are already registered somewhere else, to register in their new home state as well. While this might seem to make sense—after all, you want to have the recognition of the state where you are living—there are some risks involved. For example, if you took a trip to Vermont to get married while you were living in Kansas, and then you moved to Hawaii, it might seem logical to register in Hawaii when you get there. The problem is that if your relationship ends, you may end up in litigation about which state's laws apply or even which date is your actual date of registration, both of which can affect property rights. There could also be a question about whether your second registration is valid, which could affect not only property rights but, in some circumstances, even parentage. So it's probably best to consult a knowledgeable attorney who can advise you about the current situation at the time you're considering what to do, before you enter into a second legal relationship.

Equality in the Works

The marriage equality map continues to morph on a regular basis.

In addition to the states that now have same-sex marriage or a legal equivalent, a growing number, including Oregon, recognize same-sex marriages from other states. In other places, marriage equality legislation and lawsuits are moving forward quickly.

When Is a Spouse Not a Spouse? Introduction to the Problem of Nonrecognition

If you live in any of the relationship recognition states, you can easily marry or register if you meet the legal requirements. And, if you live in any other American state, you can go to any of the marriage states to marry, or to most of the marriage equivalent or marriage-lite states to register your domestic partnership or civil union. (But make sure you read the fine print; in some states you can't register if you live out of state.)

This means that every same-sex couple in America can be legally married or partnered if they wish, and for many folks that is all they think they need to know. But because of the patchwork of laws covering same-sex relationships, the only place you can be guaranteed that all the rights and responsibilities of the legal relationship will be respected is in the state where you entered into it, and there's no certainty that the relationship will be recognized in other states. There is, on the other hand, complete certainty that your legal marriage will be respected by the federal government, but your civil union or domestic partnership will not.

Thus, in order for you to make decisions about whether a legal marriage or partnership is right for you, you'll have to grasp the basics of at least two, and possibly three, sets of rules. First, you'll need to know the rules that apply to all spouses in the state you live in now. Second, you need to understand the federal laws and how they interact with your state's rules. And if you are considering moving out of state, you will need to learn the basics about any state you might be moving to.

As if this wasn't enough of a burden, each of these three sets of rules is a moving target, subject to frequent changes. It's like you're trying to plan your menu for a dinner party while your guests keep calling every few hours to tell you they've changed their dietary practices, just as you are hearing that the grocery stores in your neighborhood are changing their inventories, and the working condition of your stove is changing hour by hour.

Chapter 4 addresses in detail how the reality of the many homophobic laws and nonrecognition affects you.

CAUTION

If you live in a state that has less than full recognition, state courts and local agencies may act inconsistently. What works in one county may be different for another. As you'll see in Chapter 4, some federal agencies look to the couple's place of residence to determine eligibility for federal benefits, so same-sex married couples living in nonrecognition states won't qualify for all federal benefits. ●

What It Means to Be Married: The Rules of Marriage and Divorce

Approaching marriage as a civil rights struggle can sometimes tempt us to forget that it's also a very intricately developed social institution, with a long history in our culture and many others before ours. Before leaping into the arms of this millennia-old relationship that is so new to you, you need a true understanding of what is involved in being married—for better and for worse. From a political perspective there is no doubt that we all should have the right to marry. But what sort of institution are you actually entering into when you sign up for civil marriage?

The Architecture of Marriage

Marriage imposes social expectations, structures of behavior, and rules of conduct that have been developed over centuries, in a variety of ways across different cultures and communities. The social anthropologists describe marriage as a recurring cluster of human behaviors, social norms, and legal rules that have developed over time, as a way to enable couples to manage their primary interpersonal relationships. There are a few basic elements that developed in patterns distinct to each culture, which typically include a spiritual or religious component and a civil or legal dimension. Over time, these patterns have morphed into formalized rituals and rules in both the civil and religious aspects. Marriage also has typically included prescribed sets of economic expectations, many of which have been codified into a binding legal framework.

The basic components of marriage are fairly universal, though they are carried out differently in different cultures. They typically include:

- the protocols of mate selection
- the formalization of the marriage commitment
- the economics of forming the partnership
- the civil and religious rituals of the wedding
- the financial rules of domestic cohabitation and child rearing, and
- for those wishing to end their marriages, the rules and rituals of divorce.

Within this broad framework, the core ingredients of marriage have remained fairly constant in Western European cultures for more than two thousand years. Yet in many details, marriage has evolved dramatically—including the rules of who can marry and at what age, the role of the extended family in the marital contract, how authority and power is allocated within the marriage, when a divorce is allowed, and how the financial and property assets are transferred upon death or divorce. Despite these changes, marriage itself has been remarkably resilient as a social institution. Every culture on earth has some version of marital or relationship commitment structure, and in most societies, it is the defining framework of family organization. It shapes where people live, whether they are rich or poor, and how they are connected to others.

Status v. Contract

The family law system in the United States treats marriage as a legal status and not as a contractual relationship. This is a very important distinction that underlies many of the rules of marriage. What it means is that when you marry, you and your spouse enter into a relationship that is bound by pre-established legal rules. You adopt those rules by adopting the relationship—the "status." Another status relationship is that of parent and child—the legal obligations of a parent-child relationship are defined in law and not left up to each family to establish. You enter the system voluntarily, but you don't get to design the system. Another way of looking at this is that the marriage contract is already written—you don't get to do it yourself. That is what makes it a "status" relationship.

If marriage were a contractual rather than a status relationship, it would have the characteristic of contracts that allows you to design your own rules to a great extent, so long as both parties are in agreement and your contract meets some minimal legal standards. Cohabiting as an unmarried couple is a contractual relationship, as is going into business with someone.

This legal division is not absolute. The big exception to the status rule of marriage is the right to enter into premarital and postmarital contracts, which you can use to adjust some of the rules of marriage into a contract that is more to your taste. But these options aren't available everywhere and they are subject to significant rules when they are, so you aren't entirely free to design your own contract. There's a good deal more about that in Chapter 7.

Marriage Developments

The status-based rules of marriage control the process of forming and dissolving marital unions—in other words, the way those things happen. They also control the substantive rules related to property and children within a marriage after the process of marrying is complete.

Rules about the marriage process establish who is eligible to marry; the mechanics of the marriage ceremony; whether there is a waiting period between the license and the ceremony; and who may officiate over a wedding. In most states, the process rules even determine which spouse can take the last name of the other spouse. The process rules also control divorce, establishing protocols for resolving disputes and for how long it takes to get a divorce.

The substantive rules of marriage determine parentage; ownership of assets and debts during marriage and in the event of a divorce; and how custody and support are decided at divorce.

Where Do Marriage Laws Come From?

Many of our current marriage practices derive from Roman society, brought to us through European and English laws and culture. The notion of marriage being a civil institution as opposed to being solely a religious rite, for example, derives from Roman law. The Romans were remarkably liberal, not just allowing divorce but even allowing a wife to initiate divorce proceedings against her husband.

The community property model, which applies in states that were formerly part of Mexico, was passed on to us indirectly from Spanish law. In medieval and Renaissance times, marital rules throughout Europe shifted dramatically toward greater religious restrictions (with severe limits placed upon divorce) and the empowerment of the husband. And, to a very great extent in nearly all premodern societies, the marriage formation process was controlled by the extended family. Even in 19th-century France, for example, grooms up to age 30 and brides up to age 25 had to ask their parents for permission to wed.

It is only in the past 50 years that marriage has sprung free of some of its religious overtones and civil marriage has become more popular. But even today, the residue of these histories lingers on.

Three very dramatic changes in marriage rules in the United States occurred in the past 50 years, reflecting major social policy and cultural changes: (1) the emergence of gender-neutral marriage laws, allowing women to be treated as equal in the management of marital assets and property; (2) the loosening of status-based limitations to allow more flexible private contracts between married partners in the form of prenups and postnups; and (3) the near-universal acceptance of no-fault divorce. A short history lesson here will reveal why you probably wouldn't have been very interested in signing up for marriage if these changes had not occurred.

Prior to World War II, men and women in our society were assigned sharply different marriage roles. Husbands had a legal duty to take care of their wives but also had the right to control them as if they were "property." Women did not have the right to manage marital assets and, in some cases, could not even manage their own assets after they married. Private premarital contracts altering the rules of marriage simply were not allowed in most states; if you didn't want to abide by marriage rules, your only option was to remain unmarried. Divorce was only available if one party could prove the other was at fault in ending the marriage, and the assignment of fault affected the allocation of financial support and other rights at divorce.

Starting in the 1950s and accelerating dramatically by the late 1970s, most states rewrote their marriage codes to implement no-fault divorce. (New York State was the last holdout, finally adopting true no-fault divorce in 2010.) This means that spouses can agree to divorce without placing blame on anyone, by stating that the marriage is "irretrievably broken" or that the parties have "irreconcilable differences." This makes a divorce much easier to get, and generally fairer to both spouses.

Next, most states now allow couples to enter into premarital agreements and, in a smaller number of states, postmarital agreements, that significantly deviate from the presumptive rules of marriage. Even in the most liberal of states, however, there are limits on what can be included in a premarital agreement, as well as certain rules (like joint liability for debts) that cannot be waived by contract. In this manner, marriage has morphed closer to being a contractual relationship, but many of the underlying limitations imposed by the older status-based system remain in effect.

Rules of Marriage in the Present

Chapter 2 explained the status of same-sex marriage in the states that offer it or a marriage equivalent relationship. In each of those states, same-sex partners can legally sign up for all of the state rights and responsibilities of marriage, and it is those rights and responsibilities that this chapter discusses. Same-sex couples who enter legal relationships in Colorado, Hawaii, Maine, and Wisconsin have fewer rights, and typically are not subject to marital rules.

Regardless of where you live, if you marry or partner legally through domestic partnership or civil union in any of the marriage or marriage equivalent states, the rules discussed in this chapter apply to you.

You'll notice that although this is a book about marriage, the subject of divorce comes up frequently. That's because many of the rules of marriage, especially those involving property rights, only become important to people if they decide to end their marriage. During marriage, couples generally make whatever choices they want about how they hold their assets and who can use money for what. But if a couple divorces, the government has an opinion about how their property and assets should be treated.

Assets Acquired After Marriage

As a broad generalization, assets acquired by either spouse and debts incurred by either spouse during marriage are shared between the spouses without regard to who earned the money or ran up the debts. This rule applies to:

- earned income
- savings from earned income
- business assets purchased or expanded during marriage
- pension benefits and retirement accounts
- credit card debt
- loans, including mortgages and car loans, and
- stock options (in some instances).

Marital property generally doesn't include property or assets that either spouse inherits from someone else, property or assets that one spouse owned before the marriage and kept separate throughout the marriage, property purchased by one spouse with separate property funds and kept separate throughout the marriage, or gifts that were clearly given to one spouse only. These types of property are called "separate property" and aren't part of the marital property.

These are the very general outlines of marital property rules, but an important distinction is the one between community property states and "marital property" or "equitable property" states.

Ten states are community property states: Alaska, Arizona, California, Idaho, Louisiana, Nevada, New Mexico, Texas, Washington, and Wisconsin. California, Nevada, and Washington are the only marriage equivalent states among these, and in those states, all assets and debts acquired during a marriage (except as an inheritance or gift) are shared equally between the spouses, unless there is a valid written agreement between the parties that says otherwise.

There are some gray areas in community property rules, often arising from the commingling of separate and community property by spouses during marriage. But the rule of equal division of assets and debts is sometimes followed without much regard to the long-term needs of either partner, and without giving much weight to the likely future earnings or inheritance of either spouse. (These issues are considered in the awarding of spousal support, if the marriage was long enough to warrant it.)

In the other 40 or so states, equitable property and asset rules are far less precise. Instead of dividing up marital property equally, the division rests upon general principles of equity that are applied by a judge to the particular facts of each situation at the time of the divorce, based upon broadly defined notions of fairness and economic need and taking into consideration the source of the assets.

During the years a couple is together, spouses have the option of either pooling their assets or keeping them separate; but if they divorce, the court has dominion over all of the assets and debts. The judge is allowed to divide up the financial pie according to a multitude of factors, including the source of funds, the economic needs of each partner, each person's ability to work, and a broad range of equitable factors.

If this sounds a lot like community property, it's because equal division of marital assets is the presumptive rule in most places. But the law is more flexible in equitable division states.

Another important rule involves the legal presumptions about gifts and support between spouses during the relationship. In general, the court will divide only the assets and debts that exist at the time of a divorce. If either of you has been supporting the other, contributing more to the common expenses, or making gifts to your partner, typically you will not get any reimbursement for your generosity. As a result, you can find yourself in a situation where all your past generosity is taken for granted, and yet you still have to share the assets that exist when you divorce. In California, for example, you can reclaim premarital or inherited funds that you invested in the purchase or renovation of a home, but anything that you've contributed to the ongoing household expenses is water under the bridge.

The social policy justifying these rules of marriage is that a married couple is viewed as a single economic unit, and so when either partner heads out to work each day (or to the grocery store or the shopping mall), they are doing so on behalf of their unified economic partnership. That is why it doesn't matter who gets the fatter paycheck, who does the housework, or who indulges in profligate consumer purchases—you are both players on a single financial team. This is also why benefits like health insurance are often provided to both partners: The employer and the government are treating the couple as a single economic unit.

In short, once you elect to get married, you are in business together, no matter how you feel about your spouse's level of ambition or financial habits. This is one of those "status-based" rules that is not easily modified.

Debts and Liabilities Acquired After Marriage

The other dimension of this "joint economic partnership" concept is that you agree to take care of the person you marry, even if you mistakenly married a complete deadbeat. In most states, one partner's income can be tapped to pay the other's debts incurred during marriage; in some states, even debts a spouse incurred before marriage can be collected from either partner's income. In many jurisdictions, spouses are also on the hook for each other's legal claims—again, regardless of who was at fault. And there is an inescapable duty to support each other financially, which means that one spouse can't simply throw the other one out of the house onto the street or onto the ever-diminishing welfare system. And this is why, in many instances, there is a duty to keep supporting one's spouse for some period of time after a divorce, regardless of who was at fault in the breakup or how generous you were during the marriage.

The law in most places also imposes an obligation during marriage to look after the best interests of one's partner, called a fiduciary duty. The exact parameters of this duty are not easily defined, but the fundamental premise is that each partner has a duty to put the interests of the other spouse ahead of—not just equivalent to—the partner's own needs. Because of this rule, if either partner squanders a family resource, invests joint money in a losing business (even funds that the partner wasn't aware were legally joint), or embezzles joint savings, that partner can be held liable financially in the event of a divorce, and can be ordered to repay the injured spouse. Sexual affairs may not be relevant to the economic dimensions of a divorce, but breaches of financial duties certainly are.

Death and Property Transfers

The framework of an economic partnership also imposes constraints on what each spouse can do with assets at death. In community property states, for example, neither partner can bequeath the other spouse's half of the community property to anyone other than the spouse. If either partner tries to leave all the community property to someone else, the bequest can be invalidated and the assets turned over to the surviving spouse.

In other states, there is a "forced share" rule that requires a minimum percentage of the estate, often one-third or one-half, to be bequeathed to the surviving spouse, without exception. Moreover, if either partner fails to give anything at all to a spouse or fails to explain in a will or trust the reasons for that choice, in many states, the widow or widower can claim a hefty percentage of the estate.

EXAMPLES: Marital rules can have some pretty potent consequences. An older woman with adult children gave her second husband nearly a million dollars while they were together and then, when she died, she left all her remaining assets (including her valuable apartment) to her children from a prior marriage. Too bad for the kids: The husband was able to establish that he was entitled under the laws of their state to half of the estate as it existed when she died, without regard to her prior gifts to him.

Similarly, in a California domestic partnership case, a wealthy partner bought a high-value life insurance policy out of his earnings before marital rules were imposed on domestic partners. He designated a nonprofit organization as the beneficiary of his policy. Too bad for the nonprofit: The surviving domestic partner invoked marital rules and established that community property funds had paid the premiums. As a result, he was able to retroactively change the beneficiary to himself.

There's more about estate planning and rules of intestacy and forced shares in Chapter 9.

Tax Consequences of Marriage

Another feature of legal marriage for an opposite-sex couple is that most transfers between spouses are exempt from taxation, and a couple is generally treated as a single economic entity for tax purposes. For state tax laws, these rules only apply to same-sex couples in states that recognize same-sex marriages or marriage equivalent relationships.

With federal tax benefits, it's an entirely different matter. Now that a key section of DOMA has been overturned, if you are legally married, you will file your federal tax returns just like straight married couples do, even if you live in a nonrecognition state. For more on federal tax laws, see Chapter 4.

What's Different About Same-Sex Couples

As you surely have already observed, sharing assets and debts in a marriage-like arrangement is not necessarily the norm for same-sex couples. In fact, I find that this is definitely foreign territory to most of my clients. Moreover, the marriage model is premised on a distinctly old-fashioned family structure: It envisions a couple who married at a relatively young age and lived together from the outset of their career(s), consisting of a working husband supporting a stay-at-home mom or a working wife who is earning less than her husband. This is often not the way that same-sex couples—who are less likely to be raising kids and often partner later in life—choose to organize their financial lives.

Marital property obligations may well make sense when a couple has been together many years or where most of the couple's wealth was acquired while the couple was together. But it is not so clear that this policy makes much sense for many same-sex relationships, where partners often have been self-sufficient for years and where each partner's assets or earning capacity may have been built up long before the marriage took place.

It also may not make much sense in a segment of society where leaving one's assets to charity or to a relative is fairly common, where many couples do not have children, and where the kids are sometimes not the legal children of both partners. More than any other aspect of marriage, this disconnect between the presumptive legal rules of marriage and the daily lives of many same-sex couples is what couples discuss in my office.

But there is no gay exemption from any of these rules—nor would we want one, if our goal is true marriage equality. The bottom line is that the status-based rules of marriage leave you only two options: Accept the rules, or meet the requirements of a premarital agreement, in order to create your own personalized approach to these rules.

Rules of Divorce

The legal implications of marriage take on their real meaning when couples separate. At that point, the state really takes over your relationship by supervising your divorce. That doesn't mean you must split things in a particular way, that you must appear in court, or that you must endure a nasty divorce trial—all those things are in your control. But it does mean that you will have to comply with your state's divorce procedures.

Can You Avoid the Court Divorce?

A few states offer a simplified procedure called a summary dissolution, but that option is available only for couples with short-term marriages, hardly any assets, no children, and no real estate owned by either partner. Even then, most states still require spouses to process their summary dissolution through the courts, though a few (such as California) allow the summary dissolution of a domestic partnership (but not a marriage) to be processed through the Secretary of State's office if you meet some very restrictive conditions.

Divorce procedures usually include the requirements that you:

- establish that you are a resident of the state in which you are seeking a divorce (if you live in a state that doesn't recognize same-sex marriages, you may not be able to process your divorce in that state, as discussed in detail in Chapter 4)
- file numerous forms and disclose the details of your finances, assets, and debts to one another, and sometimes to the judge, and
- reach a settlement or, if that is impossible, submit your disputes to a judge who will resolve them for you.

What a Divorce Looks Like

This choice, between settling (uncontested divorce) or opting for a process that could lead to a court trial (contested divorce), is the one that will determine how much your divorce costs you and how unpleasant the experience will be.

Uncontested Divorce

If you and your partner are able to reach an agreement on how to divide everything up and decide together how you'll share time with your children, then all you have to do is fill out the mandatory forms, prepare a written settlement agreement, and submit your agreement to the local court. After a waiting period of anywhere from six weeks to six months, you can get a divorce judgment. In most instances, the court will approve the agreement unless there is something omitted or drastically unfair about it, and sometimes you don't even have to show up in person.

If you are able to reach agreement and can handle your own paperwork, you have the option of taking care of the divorce yourself without hiring a lawyer. In that case, getting a divorce will only cost you your time and the filing fees, which will range between $200 and $800 depending on where you live. Some places have self-help clinics with lawyers on staff who can help you fill out forms. If you want some help, you may be able to use a paralegal or an online document preparer to help you with your paperwork; you can also hire an attorney to prepare the necessary paperwork. There are many books available to help you through this process; check out the resource list in Appendix B.

Contested Divorce

If you and your spouse can't reach agreement on one or more of the issues at stake in your divorce, then you will have to take the other fork in the road and submit your disputes to a judge for resolution based upon the applicable rules of your state. If your disputes are complicated, each of you will probably need to hire a lawyer. You can represent yourself if you're prepared to spend a great deal of time organizing your documents, researching the law to put together a legal argument that supports your position, and presenting your case to the local family law judge.

Getting your case in front of a judge won't be simple or quick, and trial preparation can cost tens of thousands of dollars. Even though most spouses in contested cases eventually end up hiring lawyers, most cases in the end don't go to trial. Instead, they end up settling after negotiation between the lawyers or meetings with a mediator. If the partners don't reach an agreement, eventually there will be a trial. Divorce trials don't have juries, so a judge will be ruling on your disputes. There's more about contested and uncontested divorce in Chapter 8, "Avoiding the Ugly Gay Divorce."

Unfortunately, for those who really want to take up the sword, a same-sex divorce can involve even more legal disputes than that of an opposite-sex couple. Opportunities for conflict abound in the areas of legal complexity that are discussed throughout this book, including:

- whether the partnership or marriage is technically valid
- what rules apply to premarital assets and debts
- how to deal with tax inequities arising out of federal nonrecognition, and
- whether both spouses are legal parents.

So far, the nastiest same-sex divorce trials have involved parentage conflicts unique to same-sex dissolutions. But as more couples find themselves in divorce court, there are several financial topics that are particularly likely to lead to legal conflicts: spousal support claims, arguments over premarital or preregistration assets, and tax-related disputes.

Spousal Support

My partner once asked me what it means to be married and I said, "It means that if I support you for 20 years and then you leave me, you can demand that I keep supporting you for another ten years!" I wasn't entirely joking—though overly simplistic, my description was accurate, and for that reason the issue of support is a major one in many same-sex dissolutions (as it is in opposite-sex divorces as well).

Marital law in nearly every state provides that when spouses divorce, a lower-earning partner, especially one who is economically dependent on the other partner, can make a claim for alimony, also known as spousal support or maintenance.

Alimony is losing popularity with judges every year, and some states have strict limits on how much can be awarded or how long support can last. Most judges calculate support themselves based on the relevant factors; some courts use guidelines to create an initial figure, and then work up or down from there. In California, for example, support is typically about a third of the difference in incomes—not enough to equalize the incomes, but enough to soften the discrepancies. If both parties are self-supporting and the marriage lasted less than five years, it's unlikely that any support will be awarded at all.

The days of lifetime alimony are long past, and most courts encourage each spouse to become financially self-sufficient. Often, support is awarded for about half as many years as the couple was married or legally partnered. But if a marriage lasted more than ten years or if either partner is unable to work, support can last quite a long time.

Both the duration and the amount of support depend on a number of factors, including:

- how much each spouse earned during the marriage
- the marital standard of living
- each partner's earning capacity
- the age and health of each partner
- the assets each partner is receiving in the divorce
- health- and employment-related factors, and
- the reasonable financial needs of each partner.

For a spouse who needs immediate support following a separation, courts have a procedure for making temporary orders. Spouses then have the opportunity to try to work something out for the long term, without going to court. If they're not able to, they'll go in front of a judge for a hearing (a court proceeding to resolve a single issue) or a full trial (addressing the remaining issues and resulting in a final order that ends the divorce process).

There are two underlying policies behind the concept of alimony. First, there is an assumption that the love and support of the lower earner helped the higher earner get ahead, and so it is only fair that the higher earner share some of the bounty, even after a divorce. And second, it is assumed that over time, the lower earner has come to rely on the higher earner and may have made career decisions over the years that reinforced that reliance, thus justifying postseparation financial support. In addition, spousal support was originally intended to be protective of women, who earned significantly less than men in the marketplace.

I see some problems with applying this hetero-normative framework broadly to the dissolutions of same-sex partnerships (and in fact, it often doesn't work that well for opposite-sex couples in second marriages, either). First, in a same-sex partnership, differences in family roles or earning capacity can't be explained by biological differences or societal differentiation. One partner may indeed have stayed home to raise the kids, but not because of a gender difference. Differences in income between partners is not a result of gender, but of a variety of factors such as education, social class, health, ambition, and choice of career, and often these factors existed long before the couple got married. And, in many cases, the higher-earning partner already had a successful career before the marriage took place—oftentimes before the partners even met.

For partners who have been together a long time and organized their lives according to conventional gender roles (one working spouse and one domestic spouse) before getting married or legally partnered, there is another kind of dilemma. With very few exceptions, divorce courts base the amount and duration of spousal support awards on the length of the marriage—and they don't generally take into account the years that spouses were together before entering into a legal relationship. This rule doesn't make sense when it comes to same-sex divorces, because long-term same-sex partners had no option to register or marry in earlier years. It just doesn't seem fair for a judge to treat a lesbian "wife" of 20 years as though she was only in a two-year marriage—and you can expect to see that issue litigated in upcoming years as well.

Alimony and Same-Sex Couples

There's no evidence on the subject yet, but my personal belief is that same-sex partners claiming long-term spousal support are likely to find less sympathy from courts than heterosexual spouses—especially if the couples don't have children. Many courts believe that most adults without children are fully able to support themselves. And, judges sometimes tend to order support for women where they might not for men—so a gay man without children might have a hard time convincing a judge he's entitled to spousal support, no matter how completely his partner supported him in the past. All this remains to be seen as partner support claims begin making their way into the courts.

Premarital Assets

Most states distinguish between family courts and civil courts. The former handles marital divorces, using special legal and procedural rules that apply only to married couples. The latter handles all other noncriminal disputes, generally about money or property, between parties who aren't related to each other. This leads to a tricky situation when it comes to same-sex couples.

In the past, property disputes between same-sex couples generally ended up in civil court, because marital rules didn't apply. The parties were treated as partners in some kind of business relationship involving money or property. That's still going to be the case for unmarried or unregistered same-sex partners. And for same-sex couples who marry young and acquire all their property together, family court will take care of all aspects of their divorce. But many same-sex couples who are married or legally partnered have two kinds of assets—those acquired before the legal relationship began (which may be subject to civil court division), and those acquired after the start of the legal relationship (resolved in family court).

Each state approaches this division of labor somewhat differently. In Massachusetts, for example, all "family" disputes, whether about premarital or postmarital property, are handled in the same court—but the court applies different rules to each type of property. In California, state-registered partners arguing over a premarital asset that was co-owned after the marriage or registration will find themselves in family court. But the family court may refuse to deal with disputes that involve properties and promises acquired or made before the legal relationship began, or assets that were owned before registration or marriage.

These same rules apply to opposite-sex divorces, but most opposite-sex couples don't acquire all that much before marriage. Even in these modern times, many couples get married before they start acquiring significant property. Because same-sex couples weren't able to register before the year 2000 in any state, and weren't able to marry until 2004 or later, lots of same-sex divorces still involve premarriage or prepartnership assets or contracts. This is likely to continue for the next decade or so, with inevitable complications for those who can't resolve these disputes on their own.

EXAMPLE: Consider the following situation, which is quite typical. Two men live together for ten years, with one investing his inheritance into the purchase of a jointly owned residence. Then, they register as domestic partners and jointly adopt two kids, and one of them switches to part-time work while his partner works overtime and doubles his salary in a few years. Now they are breaking up; the inheritor claims he owns 80% of the house because of his initial investment, and he wants his ex to go back to work full time so that no spousal or child support is owed. The stay-at-home dad says he needs to be available to care for the two young children, and he claims that spousal support should be paid to him based upon a 15-year relationship, not just a five-year legal partnership. This situation illustrates the complexities that only a gay or lesbian divorce would present: uncertainty as to the legal characterization of premarital investments given that the couple couldn't register or marry when the investments were made; uncertainty as to the duration of the "marriage" for spousal support purposes; tax consequences of dividing of the assets; and disputes over the appropriate parenting and work mixture for the same-gendered parents. If either partner wants to ratchet up the conflict, there will certainly be grist for the dissolution mill.

Tax Consequences of Divorce

Married couples have the privilege of passing money and property back and forth between them, both during marriage and at divorce, without any tax consequences at all. No gift taxes, no capital gains taxes, no property tax reassessment, nothing. The transactions are tax neutral, and this eases the flow of property between spouses and keeps the IRS out of divorce court most of the time. These same rules apply to same-sex couples as far as state tax laws in states with same-sex marriage or marriage equivalent laws.

Now that the federal government recognizes same-sex marriages, federal tax exemptions also apply to same-sex couples—both during marriage and at divorce. The IRS will treat transfers at divorce and support payments (if they're ordered by a state court) between same-sex married couples just as they would for straight couples.

There's much more about taxes and nonrecognition in Chapter 4, and about divorce in Chapter 8.

Marriage and Parentage

The question of who a child's legal parents are is one that doesn't come up in most heterosexual relationships, but it is often central to the lives of same-sex partners raising children.

Legal Parentage Generally

A legal parent is a person who has the right to live with a child and make decisions about the child's health, education, and well-being. Legal parents have an obligation to care for and support the child financially.

Marital status used to be much more relevant to the issue of parentage than it is now; in the past a child of unmarried parents was deemed "illegitimate," and financial responsibilities were difficult to pin down. Those days have passed, and now parental status is independent from the parents' marital status. However, advances in reproductive technology have created many new questions, and legal parentage and its relationship to the means of conception has become very tricky.

Each state has its own rules establishing who is and who is not a parent and certain starting presumptions about parentage. Quite a few states have adopted a set of laws called the Uniform Parentage Act (UPA) to govern parentage. The UPA rules say that a child born during a marriage is presumed to be the legal child of both spouses as long as the husband is "fertile and not impotent." The presumption generally applies even if the child isn't biologically related to the husband (for example, if the child was conceived by donor insemination or was the product of the wife's affair with another man). And if a couple is unmarried and the child is biologically related to both parents, they are both legal parents.

This means that when a married heterosexual couple has a child or adopts a child together, both spouses are automatically considered legal parents with equal rights and responsibilities. And when an unmarried heterosexual couple has a child together and the father acknowledges paternity at birth, both partners are legal parents. In either of these situations, if the adults end their relationship, both parents have rights to custody and visitation with their children.

Legal Parentage for Same-Sex Couples

Unfortunately, the same rules don't always apply to same-sex couples. In most of the marriage and marriage equivalent states, the partners are treated like married spouses and both are considered parents of a child born during the marital or registered partner relationship. However, because these rules apply to children "born" into the relationship, they benefit only lesbian couples in which one partner gives birth to a child while she is domestically partnered or married. The nonbiological parent's name can go on the birth certificate immediately, making the parentage presumption one of the most valuable benefits of getting married or legally partnered.

In states that don't have marriage or marriage equivalent relationships, there is no automatic presumption that both partners in a same-sex couple are legal parents. This means that in many cases, only one person has parental rights unless the partners take some legal step, like an adoption, to establish rights for the second parent—the parent without automatic legal rights. In lesbian couples, the legal parent is most commonly the partner who gave birth, and the nonbiological parent is the second parent. When a gay male couple uses a surrogate to carry a child that is biologically related only to one partner, the biological father will use a legal procedure to establish his rights, but unless his partner is included in that proceeding, the partner is the second parent. And for couples of either sex when one partner adopts as a single person, the other partner is a second parent.

The relationships between nonlegal second parents and their children are extremely vulnerable until the parents take steps to establish a legal relationship. Most states, even those that don't allow adoption themselves, do end up honoring adoption decrees from other states—but often it takes an expensive and unpleasant court proceeding to reach that result. If they fail to do an adoption, the second parent may not be able to establish custody or seek visitation if the parents separate.

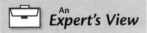 **Expert's View**   **Issues for Couples With Kids**

For lesbian and gay couples with children, the opportunity to marry, register as domestic partners, or enter into a civil union is particularly appealing. Being in a legally recognized relationship with the other parent of one's child is reassuring for all concerned; and it generally has concrete benefits in terms of recognition as a parent. For example, in states like Massachusetts, New Jersey, Vermont, and California, children born into lesbian domestic partnerships, civil unions, or marriages are automatically presumed by the state to be the children of both women, and the child's original birth certificate will include both mothers' names.

That said, it remains extremely important for lesbian and gay couples with children to make sure that each parent's legal relationship to the couple's children doesn't depend on recognition of the legal relationship between the parents. Although states that recognize same-sex relationships may automatically grant parental rights to the legal partner of the biological parent, these rights won't travel with the couple, nor will they necessarily be recognized at the federal level. For this reason, lawyers who work with lesbian and gay couples with children strongly recommend a second parent or coparent adoption, or some other legal proceeding to formalize the relationship between nonbiological parent and child.

The methods available for protecting parent-child relationships within same-sex families vary widely from state to state. It is essential to find an attorney in your state who can help you understand how best to protect your family using your own state's laws. If you don't know how to find an attorney with knowledge in this area, a national organization like the National Center for Lesbian Rights, the ACLU, or Lambda Legal can help.

Deborah Wald has been practicing family law in the San Francisco Bay Area for more than 15 years, with a focus on nontraditional families including lesbian, gay, and transgender families as well as all families created through assisted reproduction and adoption. She is chair of the National Family Law Advisory Council of the National Center for Lesbian Rights.

In fact, most attorneys recommend that even couples who are married or legally partnered should obtain an adoption judgment for the benefit of the nonbiological parent. Why is that? In order to be sure that you don't face problems if you cross state lines or seek any form of federal recognition for your child. Also, if there is another person who has legal rights, such as a sperm donor, the adoption proceeding clarifies who is and isn't a parent. (Whether the donor has legal rights depends on how the sperm was transferred, how the insemination took place, and the laws of the state where the insemination took place.)

There are different ways to establish parentage, including adoptions and actions under the Uniform Parentage Act, and they differ from state to state.

The Benefits of Marriage

Given the complications and legal burdens, why is marriage so popular? Part of it is tradition, and the fervent belief—even among those who have been divorced—that getting married is the best way to solidify and sanctify a love relationship. And, in fact, recent research suggests that long-term married couples tend to be healthier, wealthier, and happier than similarly situated single people, and it appears that it is marital life itself that contributes to their well-being. While these studies have focused on heterosexual couples, it's likely that the outcomes for same-sex couples will be similar. Marriage seems to improve the lives of both spouses by providing a financial safety net, a sense of long-term emotional security, and a place in the broader circle of extended families and the larger society, all of which induces men and women alike to be more responsible to one another, more productive in their own lives, and more at ease about their shared future.

Even if our marriages differ somewhat from those of our straight friends and relatives, there will definitely be benefits coming our way. In fact, there are many reasons to opt for marriage—legal, financial, and emotional. I'm constantly struck by how often couples tell me that getting married has transformed their relationship, giving them a social recognition by their family and the wider community as well as an emotional solidity that they previously lacked. There's a lifting of a mantle of disregard and oppression that may have created an atmosphere of invalidity, in ways that many partners had not even been fully aware of. There is the imprimatur of social approval, the resonance of emotional commitment, and the security of legal interconnectedness, all of which work together to strengthen the relationship. These nonlegal aspects of marriage should never be ignored.

And, by the way, the legal benefits of marriage are indeed very real. If the economic partnership fits with how you intend to live your financial lives, you can agree to pool your assets, share your debts, and take on financial responsibility for each other (both now and in the event of a breakup) in one simple act, by signing up for the marital rules of your state.

Being legally partnered or married guarantees you basic spousal rights and protections on the state level. You will be automatically entitled to act on behalf of your partner in the event of disability, and automatically entitled to a share of your partner's estate even if no will is signed (though no one should rely entirely on intestacy provisions, for reasons explained in Chapter 9). There are literally hundreds of laws in each state's law books that offer benefits to married couples.

As a result of the Supreme Court's DOMA decision, the federal government must now recognize same-sex married couples as married for the purposes of federal benefits. However, federal benefits vary by agency. Not all agencies use the same rules for determining who qualifies for benefits. For example, the Social Security Administration will look at where a married couple lives—not where they were married—to determine if they qualify, so same-sex spouses that live in nonrecognition states aren't eligible for Social Security benefits on their spouses' records.

The IRS on the other hand, will look to the place of celebration (where the couple was married) to determine if a couple qualifies for federal tax benefits.

Let's take a look at some of the marriage benefits you may qualify for:

- You will be entitled to receive a bevy of state and federal benefits, such as federal, state, and local tax exemptions, state retirement protections for your partner, and assistance with many state government programs.

- Many couples will benefit from the presumptions of parentage.

- Depending on where you work, you may be entitled to significant financial benefits, such as health insurance for your partner, survivor's retirement and pension benefits, financial perks or discounts for spouses of employees, bereavement leave, state-based family leave to care for a sick partner or child, and much more.

- If you are legally married *and* live in one of the U.S. jurisdictions that allow or recognize same-sex marriage, you will be eligible for Social Security benefits based on your spouse's work record.

- If you are legally married in any jurisdiction that recognizes same-sex marriage, you will qualify for federal tax benefits, immigration status, Department of Defense benefits, and federal employment benefits (including health and retirement benefits) regardless of where you live.

- You will enjoy immunity from having to testify against your partner in court.

- You will have access to your partner in a hospital, a senior residence, and even in prison.

- If your relationship ends, the family court system will resolve your financial and custody issues. The divorce comes with guaranteed procedural and substantive protections, especially for the benefit of an economically dependent partner.

This is only an illustrative list to show you the many ways that full legal marriage can benefit you and to demonstrate that despite the legal complexities—discussed in detail in the chapter that follows—there are many reasons to marry.

The Real-Life Consequences of Legal Discrimination

Most of my clients here in the San Francisco Bay Area lead day-to-day lives that are blessedly free from any evident anti-gay attitudes or laws. Most of them have good jobs and close ties with their extended families, many are in supportive long-term relationships, and they need not fear social ostracism or physical violence. Many of them are unaware of how precious this happy condition is, especially when compared to what happens to lesbians and gay men in many other countries—as well as in many less-enlightened regions of this country. Some, especially my younger clients, are unaware of how difficult gay life in the United States was just 25 years ago.

We've made enormous progress, especially in the past year, and thus we are, in a sense, fortunate to be burdened with today's remaining legal complications. And even though the absence of full national or global marriage equality is certainly an injustice that causes suffering, it's a far cry from having to live in secret to avoid being gay-bashed or losing your job. I never want to shy away from facing the discriminatory laws that exist, even in the most enlightened regions of this country, but at the same time, I want to keep things in a healthy perspective.

Many of my clients are justifiably angry when they learn the real-life impacts of discriminatory laws, and it remains even more difficult for those living in the nonrecognition states (which still constitute a majority of the states in this country).

Of course, it's my job to warn readers and clients when they may have to pay more in taxes or be prevented from sharing their retirement accounts. Now, with the demise of DOMA, the major burdens are those that are imposed on couples in domestic partnership, civil unions, and those same-sex married couples living in nonrecognition states that are barred from state and certain federal benefits. Since any of us may be faced with the prospect of relocating to such a state, and we should care about every member of our community, nonrecognition is an injustice that affects all of us.

This chapter addresses the remaining problems of federal nonrecognition, and the more serious difficulties arising from the lack of full national recognition for our relationships.

Federal Nonrecognition

Even though there were no lesbian or gay married couples in the United States in 1996, the emerging movement towards allowing same-sex marriage in Hawaii was enough to raise the spectre of such an event happening in the future. In response, the United States Congress passed the Defense of Marriage Act (DOMA). Section 3 of DOMA defined marriage as a legal union between a man and a woman, as husband and wife. This definition allowed the federal government to consider same-sex marriages invalid. DOMA's Section 2 declares that no U.S. state or territory can be required to recognize same-sex marriages performed in other states or territories. To the disappointment of many of his supporters, then-president Bill Clinton signed the bill into law.

It took more than a decade for the federal recognition component of the law to be properly challenged in the federal court system. The cases attacking DOMA began to mount up a few years ago, and just about every federal judge who reviewed the issue declared the federal nonrecognition section of DOMA to be unconstitutional.

Some judges focused on the states rights approach (also known as federalism), saying that marital law had traditionally been left to the states, and so the federal nonrecognition provision of DOMA was an unconstitutional interference with the right of a state to say who is allowed to get married. Others focused on the deeper issues of bias and the fundamental right of liberty, stating that Congress and legislatures should not deny lesbians and gay men their fundamental human right to get married.

Eventually, in June 2013, the United States Supreme Court issued its long-awaited ruling, and it's a wonderful thing to behold—even if it only squeaked through with a 5-4 majority. The case of *United States vs. Windsor,* –U.S.–, 133 S. Ct. 2675, 186 L. Ed. 808 (2013) involved Edith Windsor and Thea Spyer, who married in Canada in 2007 after being in a lesbian relationship for 40 years. When Spyer died in 2009, she left her entire estate to Windsor. Windsor sought to claim the federal estate tax exemption for surviving spouses, but was barred from doing so by Section 3 of DOMA. As a result, Windsor was forced to pay over $363,000 in federal taxes on Spyer's estate, which she would not have had to pay if she'd been Spyer's husband.

Windsor appealed the imposition of the estate tax, and the case went all the way up to the U.S. Supreme Court.

Justice Kennedy, writing for the majority, concluded that because the state of New York recognized the marriage, it was wrong for the United States Congress to ignore the long-standing federal policy of deferring to states when it comes to matters of domestic relations (that is, marriage). Therefore, he ruled that DOMA's Section 3, which limited marriage to a union between a man and a woman, violated basic due process and equal protection guarantees of the U.S. Constitution. Justice Kennedy went on to say that DOMA imposed a disadvantage and stigma on couples in lawful marriages for the sole purpose of harming a group that was disliked and condemned without lawful justification, and thus, the law had no rational basis.

The issue of interstate recognition, that is, whether nonrecognition states must recognize lawful same-sex marriages, wasn't raised in this case, so the Court did not issue a ruling on Section 2 of DOMA.

And so, as of 2013, same-sex married couples are entitled to the same federal benefits bestowed on straight married couples. But because some federal agencies, such as the Social Security Administration, look to the state of residence (where a couple lives) to determine whether a couple is married and eligible for benefits, same-sex couples living in nonrecognition states will not qualify for *all* federal benefits. We will explore this further below.

Who's Federally Married, and Who's Still Single?

The Supreme Court's DOMA ruling means that the federal government can no longer treat same-sex married couples as single, but instead, they will be treated just like married straight couples. This new rule applies to every federal agency, including the IRS, the U.S. Citizenship and Immigration Services (USCIS), the Social Security Administration, as well as the military, and it will extend to every benefit offered to federal employees.

What's less clear at this point in time is what happens to same-sex couples in marriage equivalent registrations (such as domestic partnerships or civil unions) and same-sex couples that are legally married, but live in nonrecognition states.

It's going to take a few months or even longer to clear up all of these grey areas, but for the most part, we expect things to go like this:

- For any federal rule that looks to the "state of celebration" of the marriage (where it was solemnized), all married couples will receive federal benefits, regardless of where they live.

- For any federal rule that looks to the "state of domicile" (where the couple currently lives), federal benefits will not be extended to married couples living in nonrecognition states until the rules are changed, either by Executive Order, agency rule making or congressional action.

- Couples registered as domestic partners or in civil unions most likely will not receive federal benefits, even if they are treated just like married couples under their state laws, until there are contrary rulings from the relevant federal agencies or changes in the applicable law.

For these reasons, a couple for whom federal recognition is crucial should seriously consider marrying if they are only state registered. And, if the benefit they are looking to receive is based upon their state of domicile (where they live), rather than the state of celebration, they should consider moving to a recognition state if they don't already live in one. We realize that moving out of state isn't a simple decision to make, but if the benefit is truly critical, it may be the most prudent thing to do—especially as it make take several years before all states recognize same-sex marriages.

Immigration

To my mind, the plight of binational same-sex couples has always been one of the worst consequences of the prohibition of same-sex marriage and the denial of federal benefits. Paying higher taxes is one thing, but not being able to live in the same country as one's partner (let alone husband or wife) would be unbearable. This type of legal discrimination has wreaked havoc on the lives of far too many same-sex couples—which is why the lifting of this oppressive regime is so very welcome.

Within a few days of the Supreme Court's DOMA decision, the U.S. Citizenship and Immigration Services (USCIS) started issuing "green cards" to the spouses of lesbian and gay Americans, and in one dramatic instance, the scheduled deportation of one gay man's spouse was stopped just hours after the Supreme Court issued its ruling on DOMA.

The best feature of this important development is that for immigration purposes, it's the place of celebration that counts, not the state you live in. Thus, if you are legally married anywhere, either in the United States or overseas, you now have the right to file a petition to allow your spouse to remain in this country. The same goes for seeking a fiancé visa if you haven't yet gotten married. There are some serious complexities to these rules, especially if your spouse is already in the United States, so it is generally recommended that you work with a local immigration lawyer who knows the applicable rules and procedures. You will want to be sure you are ready to demonstrate that your marriage is not a sham, and there may be some lingering discrimination as to how these rules are applied. But the law is on your side, for the first time in United States immigration law history.

Employment Benefits From the Federal Government

If either of you is a federal employee, being in a recognized marriage can mean a lot in terms of employment benefits. Fortunately, the U.S. Office of Personnel & Management is taking the position that if you have a valid marriage, your spouse is entitled to benefits, even if you reside in a nonrecognition state. This rule should apply to health insurance and retirement benefits. If either of you works for the federal government, you should ask about applicable benefits so you can get the goodies you are now entitled to.

Remember, at this point, only *married* couples will receive federal employment benefits. We don't know if or when domestic partners or civil union partners will be treated as married, so if receiving these benefits is crucial for you, it may make sense to get married as well—even if you are already state registered. Keep in mind that you can travel to and get married in any state that allows same-sex couples to marry, without having to establish residency there. Consider it a kind of premarital honeymoon vacation!

Tax Issues

On June 26, 2013, the U.S. Supreme Court struck down a key section of DOMA, which cleared the way for federal recognition of same-sex married couples. But the Court's decision did not address specifics, such as whether the IRS and other federal agencies would recognize same-sex married couples living in nonrecognition states.

On August 29, 2013, the U.S. Treasury Department ruled that legally married, same-sex couples qualify for federal tax benefits, regardless of where they live. Under the ruling, federal recognition for tax purposes applies whether a same-sex married couple lives in a jurisdiction that recognizes same-sex marriage (such as California) or a nonrecognition jurisdiction (such as Texas). Now, same-sex married couples can move freely about the country, including to a nonrecognition state, and their federal tax filing status will not change.

Same-sex married couples that are legally married in any U.S. state, the District of Columbia, a U.S. territory, or a foreign country will be recognized as married under all federal tax provisions where marriage is a factor. This includes provisions governing:

- filing status
- personal and dependency exemptions
- standard deductions
- employee benefits
- IRA contributions
- the earned income tax credit, and
- the child tax credit.

You will report your filing status as "married," and you can either file jointly or separately. You will be taxed based upon the tax rate that applies to married couples, and you will share in the deductions just like any other married couple. Unlike the complicated rules that applied before the DOMA decision, you won't need to complete special forms or follow complex procedures—you can file the same forms and use the same process as straight married couples. For some folks, their taxes will increase, but at least the procedures will be simpler.

What's still complicated, however, is what happens for those couples who are treated as "married" by the laws of their state, but are civil union or domestic partner registrants, rather than legally married.

The Treasury Department made it clear that federal recognition by the IRS will not apply to civil unions or domestic partnerships. So, if you are state registered, either as a civil union or domestic partnership, then you will file your state tax returns as married, but you still have to file your federal returns as single people. That is presumably how you've been doing it before the DOMA and Treasury Department rulings, so the same messy rules we told you about before will continue to apply to you. Depending on the rules of your state, you may have to create a dummy federal return to determine how to prepare your state return, as many of those returns are derivative of the federal forms. Then you'll have to create a new federal return as a single person, and that's the one you'll file.

If you're living in an equitable distribution (noncommunity property) state, such as New Jersey, you each report your own income on your state tax forms or you can file a joint return combining both incomes, and you will be subject to the state marital limits on deductions, which can affect your tax rates and deductions. And, under state law, neither of you can take advantage of being considered a single head of household. For your federal return, you will each report your own income, and you will do so as a single person—or as a single head of household, if it makes sense for your own situation.

The most complicated situation arises for those who are state-registered domestic partners and live in a community property state, such as California. In this situation, each of you will have to report 50% of your total community property income, plus any separate property income you receive, on both your state and federal tax return. You can do that either by filing jointly or separately on your state return—for which your filing status is married. But on your federal return, your marital status is still single (or single head of household), and yet you each still have to report 50% of the total community property income (and 100% of your respective separate property income). The amount of taxes you will owe may go up or they may go down, depending on how much you each earn. For your federal return, there's a form you can use to determine how much of the community property income you should each report.

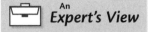 **Expert's View**   **Tax Considerations for Same-Sex Spouses and Partners Post DOMA**

In June 2013, the U.S. Supreme Court opened the door to federal recognition of same-sex marriage when it struck down a key section of the Defense of Marriage Act (DOMA). In August 2013, the U.S. Treasury Department ruled that for federal tax purposes, the IRS now recognizes all legally married same-sex couples, even those living in nonrecognition states.

The Treasury also ruled that marriage equivalent registrations (domestic partnerships and civil unions) will not be recognized for federal tax purposes. Thus, there are two camps at play here: those who must file as married (either jointly or separately) and those who still file their returns as single taxpayers (or as head of household). If you are in the "clearly married" camp, you can proceed just like any straight married couple, for better or worse, and be treated just like your married friends and relatives.

But for those in the marginal camps—couples in domestic partnerships and civil unions—you will have special tax preparation burdens. If you are in a marriage equivalent registration, you will file your state returns as a couple, but file singly with the feds. This will make it especially complicated to figure out how to report income and deductions and how to determine the tax basis of property you have sold.

In the past, there was great uncertainty as to how state-registered partners in community property states should report their income. The IRS finally issued some guidance on the impact of California community property laws on same-sex partners; in 2010 the IRS issued an advisory memorandum stating that registered partners in California filing returns as single persons must split their community property income with their partners for reporting purposes. For now, these rules still apply, even if these couples are not considered married for federal tax filing purposes.

Even where your relationship is recognized by your home state, you may face serious tax problems—or you may receive some tax benefits, depending on your income situation. As a married couple, you may hit limits on loss deductions or other deductions, compared to how single taxpayers are treated, and you may lose some valuable deductions. Your filing status would change from single or head of household to married.

It's essential that you work with a tax preparer who is up to date on all of these rules, and knows how to navigate the complicated pathways of state and federal regulations.

Chris Kollaja is a tax partner at A.L.Nella, a San Francisco CPA firm. He specializes in tax planning for lesbians and gay men, and recently married Tom, his partner of 20 years.

Gift and Estate Taxes

For unmarried people (including unmarried same-sex partners living in recognition states), there are potential tax consequences whenever one person transfers property or money to another person. Heterosexual married couples and (thanks to the DOMA decision) same-sex married couples are now exempt from nearly all taxes on any transfer of money and property. Same-sex couples who are living together as cohabitants or in a marriage equivalent registration do not enjoy these tax exemptions. For tax purposes, any property or money that those partners transfer between one another will be subject to the same tax rules as would apply if they were two single, unrelated individuals.

This problem can present itself in a number of ways. For example, if you and your partner sell a house that you own together, there may be questions about who bears the capital gains obligations and whether there was a gift between one of you to the other—especially if you owned the property unequally or have been contributing unequal amounts to the property's expenses. The problem can also arise if one of you owns a property separately and then you decide to share ownership with your partner—either voluntarily during the course of your relationship or semi-involuntarily upon a breakup. Unless you're married, you don't have the benefit of the tax-exempt spousal transfer rule, and you may have to report the transfer as a gift. Keep in mind that no taxes are owed until the gifts over your lifetime exceed $5,250,000—but if a lot of property is involved or either of you is really rich, this could become a real problem.

There are two other details to bear in mind. Transfers of community property income or assets probably aren't reportable (or taxable) as gifts, since each of you technically owns 50% of those assets already. And, any transfer of less than $14,000 per year (per person) is exempt even from the reporting requirement for potentially taxable gifts.

The same rules apply for estate taxes. Now that the 2013 estate tax limit is $5,250,000, very few of our readers are likely to have an estate tax problem under federal law. But the exemptions can be lower for your particular state, so be sure to check on the state tax rates. Whichever rule applies, the same principal as applies to other tax rules apply here. If you are married, and living in a recognition state, any bequests to your spouse will be tax free, under both state and federal law. If you're married, but living in a nonrecognition state, at this point you should assume you are not exempt as married spouses under state law, but you will be under federal law. And if you are in a civil union or state-registered domestic partnership, most likely you will be exempt from any taxes on a state level, but you will not be exempt on the federal level.

Health and Retirement Benefits

The place of celebration rule also applies to health and retirement benefits. If you're legally married (regardless of where you live), you will be treated just like straight married couples. You will no longer be taxed on health insurance premiums or benefits provided to your spouse—as was the case before a key section of DOMA was ruled unconstitutional. But if you're domestic or civil union partners, you will probably be taxed by the IRS for those benefits conferred to your partner by your state law since you are still technically single for federal tax purposes. Some employers are covering this extra tax for their lesbian and gay employees, so you should check with your employer to see what their rules are.

Retirement benefits are filled with nonrecognition land mines, since, for the most part, they are regulated by federal law called ERISA (Employee Retirement Income Security Act). Once again, if you are legally married, this should no longer be a problem, as you will be treated just like any straight married couple. That means that even if there is a divorce or death, the employee's ex-spouse (or surviving spouse) will be entitled to his or her share of the retirement account. It also means you can transfer retirement assets from one spouse to the other upon divorce or death, and you can split up the accounts without incurring a federal tax penalty. This applies to 401(k) as well as regular IRA accounts.

If you're covered by state marital law because you're in a domestic partnership or civil union, you will be treated as married under your state's laws. This means you may have to share your retirement accounts at the time of a divorce, and you are free to transfer retirement benefits upon death without incurring any state tax penalties. However, you probably won't be treated as married by the federal authorities—at least not for now, and thus, such transfers could trigger significant federal taxes and/or penalties. You should double-check with your accountant and read up on the ever-changing rules, but as with all other federal benefits, if a lot of money is involved, you might want to consider getting married.

If you're facing a breakup and you aren't married or registered, then you probably won't be getting any of your partner's benefits—so this won't be a problem from a nonrecognition point of view. But if you're state registered and thus entitled to benefits under your state's rules, you will probably have to find some other way to transfer those benefits—or allocate some other asset to balance out the retirement fund allocation. If you aren't able to do so, then you may be facing a significant federal tax penalty.

Other Federal Benefits

Some federal agencies only recognize marriages that are valid in the state of domicile (where the couple lives) for the purposes of granting federal benefits. For same-sex couples, this means that as long as you are married and live in a recognition state, you will be entitled to receive all the same federal benefits that straight married couples receive. If you're married but live in a nonrecognition state, you won't qualify for all federal benefits.

The Social Security Administration, for example, determines marriage based on where the couple lives. This means if you're legally married *and* live in a recognition state, you're eligible for Social Security benefits based on your spouse's work record, including death benefits if your spouse predeceases you and he or she was the higher earner (so long as you were married for at least ten years). If you're legally married, but live in a nonrecognition state, you're not eligible for any Social Security benefits based on your spouse's work record.

The benefits for your children will depend on who is the legal parent—but if you are a presumed parent because of a marriage to your spouse, that should suffice to make you a legal parent in the eyes of the federal officials. It's still uncertain if presumed parentage based upon a marriage equivalent registration will be sufficient.

The same rule goes for receiving other federal benefits, such as those under the Family and Medical Leave Act, Small Business Administration loans, or any other special benefit that federal agencies bestow on married couples: If you're married and live in a recognition state, you will qualify for the benefit.

Hopefully, the rules will be revised to extend all federal benefits to married couples living in nonrecognition states, but if you are one of those unfortunate couples, you should keep close tabs on the rulings issued by the federal agencies that matter most to the two of you.

Following are some of the key rules to be aware of for federal agencies that use state of domicile to determine marriage.

Social Security: So long as you are married and live in a recognition state, you and your spouse will have the same protections as straight married couples. Generally, you must have been married for at least a year, and you probably won't be covered if you live in a nonrecognition state. Couples that are state registered in a domestic partnership or civil union and live in a recognition state should be covered by Social Security protections, but the law is a bit vague so we won't be sure of this for a while.

Medicaid and Supplemental Security Income: If you are married and live in a recognition state, your spouse's income and assets will count against you in determining whether you are qualified for these benefits, as they are only meant to help low-income individuals and families.

Medicare: The rules for Medicare are especially complicated for legally married couples. Your marital status can affect when you apply and what benefits you receive, and at this time, it's uncertain whether state-registered partners will be treated as married spouses. If you are close to 65 years old, you should take a look at the Social Security Administration website (www. ssa.gov) to see how your marital status affects your Medicare coverage.

Bankruptcy: Married couples can file taxes jointly or separately, but the assets of your spouse might be taken into account if either of you files for bankruptcy. This is especially problematic if you live in a community property state.

Family and Medical Leave Act: As a married couple, you are entitled to receive the benefits of the FMLA, so long as you live in a recognition state.

Several of the national LGBT legal organizations have compiled excellent websites with detailed answers to many of the questions presented by the recent federal recognition of same-sex married couples. Lambda Legal is a great resource for getting the latest information on these tricky legal issues: www.lambdalegal.org/publications/after-doma.

⚠ **CAUTION**

Don't forget that there are potential negative consequences of federal recognition: If either of you is receiving any benefits that depend on a low income level, your spouse's assets and income will now be recognized by the federal government and taken into account to determine if you still qualify. Your marriage could disqualify you if your spouse's income or assets push you above the relevant income threshold. This can be especially burdensome for those receiving discounted HIV/AIDS medications.

Factoring Federal Issues Into Your Decision Making

Now that same-sex married couples living in recognition states are treated as married by all federal agencies for purposes of receiving *all* federal benefits, those couples needn't worry about nonrecognition issues. Unless one of you is receiving a federal benefit that you might lose by having your spouse's income attributed to you, this will be a good thing. Take note that for some married same-sex couples, their total income tax burdens will increase, just as what happens for some straight married couples. We encourage couples to run their figures by an accountant, simply because it's good to know what is likely to happen and so you won't be surprised.

The real problems arise for those who are in marriage equivalent domestic partnerships or civil union registrations, and for those who are married but living in nonrecognition states. If you are registered in a state that allows you to marry or recognizes your marriage (such as California), then you should consider getting married if receiving federal benefits is important to you. It will probably take a few more years before we know for certain whether you are going to be treated as federally married, and unless you are up for being the test case, getting married is the easy solution to this problem.

The biggest problems remain for those of you who are married but living in nonrecognition states, if the federal benefit you need is awarded based upon the state of domicile (rather than state of celebration). Again, you may not wish to be the test case—but unless you are able to relocate to a recognition state, it may not be so easy for you to solve this problem. If this is your situation, then you should assume you will be treated as single both by your state government and the federal government, and plan accordingly. It's going to be a difficult situation until these nonrecognition problems are resolved, but better to be aware of these barriers and try to minimize their impact on your lives, than to pretend that all such problems have ended with the demise of DOMA. And please, join the political effort in your state to turn things around.

Interstate Nonrecognition

After the California Supreme Court ruling in May 2008, I counseled a gay couple before their summer wedding. They wondered whether they should prepare a premarital agreement. Their relationship was going fine and there didn't seem to be any major legal complications; I explained the problems that existed then of federal nonrecognition, and they felt comfortable proceeding with their wedding notwithstanding some minor issues. But then, just before the end of the meeting, one of them mentioned that he was a finalist for a new job in Utah and was also being considered for a different job in New Hampshire.

This raised complexities of a whole new order. New Hampshire was, at the time, a marriage equivalent state and, as such, it would probably recognize a California domestic partnership, but it was then still a DOMA state so a marriage wouldn't be recognized there. Utah, the home of the Mormon Church, doesn't recognize either status—and isn't likely to change that position any time soon. We talked about the various scenarios that were likely to play out. The following options emerged just in the first hour of our discussion:

- Register as domestic partners and get married in California, and hope for recognition if they move to New Hampshire, knowing there would be none in Utah.

- Register and marry after signing a detailed premarital agreement setting out the financial terms of their relationship, and provide that this agreement would remain in effect regardless of where they lived or whether their domestic partnership or marriage was recognized anywhere else.

- Remain unmarried and unregistered, have a private commitment ceremony and sign a written agreement about financial terms, then wait until they knew where they going to live before making decisions about marriage or registration. Then they could see how that state's laws would affect their specific situation and write an agreement that would be valid there.

At the conclusion of our meeting, the couple decided that given all the uncertainties about where they were going to live, it made sense to have a commitment ceremony now, but forgo the marriage license and domestic partner registration, and postpone legal marriage or domestic partnership decisions until they knew where they would be living and could evaluate the laws that would apply to them. That way, they needed to consider only how they would be treated under the laws of one state instead of three.

This seemed a prudent solution for that particular couple, but many couples cannot wait for the future to unfold before making their decisions. And as it turned out, these two ended up feeling they couldn't wait either. They called me back a month later to say that because of the impending vote on Proposition 8, which would ban same-sex marriages, they were going ahead with a legal marriage, and then would either register or write an agreement (or both) afterwards, once they decided where they were going to live. As a result, their marriage was subject to the ballot initiative litigation. Ultimately their relationship was validated by the court, despite the state's losing marriage equality for the next five years.

This story demonstrates one of the ways interstate nonrecognition can affect you. Because each state sets up its own rules of registration or marriage, its own rules about whether it will recognize a legal partnership or marriage entered into in another state, and its own rules about how it will handle (or refuse to handle) the dissolution of an out-of-state same-sex relationship, the practical decision about whether marriage or registration will work for you becomes confusing and confounding. Add the element of uncertainty about how the laws may change in the future and where you'll be living, and you've got a complicated decision to make.

Also, it's one thing for you and your partner to have a nonrecognition problem because you decide as a couple to move to a nonrecognition state for an educational, career, or family opportunity. In that situation, you can plan ahead and work together to reduce the impact as much as possible.

On the other hand, a breakup that finds one or both of you living in a nonrecognition state can create a much more severe problem—one that is often out of your control. Depending on where you got married, you could even find yourselves unable to obtain a divorce in the state where you live, so that one of you is forced to relocate simply in order to end your relationship legally.

Worst of all by far, you could face a situation where your partner takes advantage of homophobic laws to deny obligations of the relationship, including trying to cut off your legal connection to a child you have been raising together. It might seem unlikely to you, but it happens all too often.

Full Faith and Credit

One term that needs to be clarified is that of "full faith and credit." Most folks use this term to refer to the notion that one state's court should honor the rulings of another court—or accept the validity of a marriage entered into in another state or a foreign country. In fact, full faith and credit only applies to court "judgments," which are orders such as adoptions, divorces, or financial awards issued by a court. A marriage is not a judgment; rather, it is considered a legal action. The rule that applies to marriages is called "comity," and states have more flexibility in deciding whether to honor other states' marriages. That is why the multiplicity of state-enacted DOMA laws are likely to be effective when it comes to not recognizing another state's marriage or domestic partnership—until, at least, there is a United States Supreme Court ruling that throws out these discriminatory state laws.

States That Have Weighed In

The most painful instances of nonrecognition have arisen in the context of breakups, where courts have refused to grant divorces to couples who married in Canada or in another U.S. state, on the basis that getting divorces is a "benefit" of marriage. Here are some examples of cases around the country dealing with relationship recognition.

Florida. A lesbian suffered a stroke while on a gay-friendly cruise in Florida. The local hospital refused to honor her civil union registration status, so her partner could not be with her while she was dying.

New York. A New York City court recognized the validity of a Canadian marriage for purposes of establishing coparentage and ruling on a property claim brought by the nonbiological mom. Some New York courts have also extended public employee benefits to same-sex couples. In May 2008, Governor David Paterson directed state agencies to amend their policies to recognize same-sex marriages from other jurisdictions, and a growing list of state agencies now extend marital benefits to couples who married in states where it is permitted. It's fair to assume that New Yorkers will find their out-of-state marriages recognized, but it's not a certainty—and it's not certain whether civil union and domestic partnership registration will be treated as equal to marriage. And these marriages still won't be granted any state-level tax benefits, as only the legislatures and courts can mandate tax changes.

Rhode Island. Although the attorney general issued an opinion declaring that the state could recognize same-sex marriages from other states, a later court opinion by the state supreme court held that a same-sex couple legally married in Massachusetts could not divorce in Rhode Island. Eventually, Rhode Island legalized same-sex marriage, but for years there was uncertainty.

Virginia. A lesbian from Vermont moved with her civil union partner to Virginia and then, when they broke up, tried to use Virginia's rules prohibiting same-sex parenting to deny the nonbiological parent any access to the child they had coparented after the child's birth in Vermont. The Virginia courts upheld the nonbirth-mother's legal connection to the child and honored the Vermont rules of coparentage, but the litigation took years.

Maryland. The Maryland attorney general has issued an opinion calling on agencies to recognize same-sex marriages, domestic partnerships, and civil unions from other places, but for years, it remained uncertain how broadly this advice would be followed there.

Texas. In 2009, a state district judge ruled that two men who married in Massachusetts could legally end their marriage in a Texas court. But in August 2009, an appellate court in Dallas reversed that decision and ordered the trial judge to dismiss the case on the basis that because Texas doesn't recognize same-sex marriage, a Texas court can't dissolve one through divorce.

Factoring State Nonrecognition Into Your Decisions

Does this confusion of rules mean that the task of making a decision is impossible? Absolutely not. If you follow the bouncing ball, you can get a general sense of the most likely outcomes and avoid—or at least be prepared for—negative results. Here are some FAQs about interstate nonrecognition.

What if you live in a state that expressly bans same-sex marriage, and you travel to a marriage equality state or to Canada to get married? Your state agencies and courts probably will not treat you as married when you return home; the same is probably true of private institutions (such as banks or title companies). When state forms, tax returns, and the like ask for your marital status, the legally correct response is to not check off either box. Instead, write in that you have obtained a marriage license and were lawfully married, but that you are uncertain as to the validity of your marriage in the state you live in. It doesn't really fit in a simple "check the box" format, but it's the truth. If you don't want to thrust yourself into the fuss that may result from such an unconventional response, the safest option is probably to describe yourselves as single.

Nonrecognition also means that if you break up, your state divorce court may not be willing to end your relationship. If you married in California or D.C., you should be able to get divorced there. In the worst-case scenario, one of you may have to move to a recognition state in order to obtain a divorce.

What if you live in a state that bans same-sex marriage and you get legally hitched through a domestic partnership or civil union, not a marriage? If your state expressly bans not only same-sex marriage but any type of same-sex legal relationship, then the answer is the same as above. But some states that have DOMA laws do not have any law relating to nonmarital same-sex relationships, so it's possible your relationship might be recognized. And states that have recognized same-sex marriages, including New York and New Jersey, are likely to also acknowledge marriage equivalent relationships.

What if you live in a state that doesn't have any laws or rulings, and you travel to a relationship recognition state and get married or otherwise legally partnered? In that case, you may end up a test case if you break up and want the state to grant you a divorce, or if you seek any of the benefits that come with legal marriage in your state.

What if you live in a state that recognizes your partnership or marriage and you are considering moving? Read up on the laws of your new home state before you move. You may even want to consult an attorney in that state in advance. You may need to execute new documents (such as powers of attorney or a property agreement) to be certain that the basic agreements you have made as a registered or married couple will stay in effect. You also may be at risk of losing some key federal benefits.

The key to coping with these problems is to not rely solely on your partnership or marital status to protect your relationship. Nothing substitutes for legal documents like a will, medical directive, and power of attorney (all discussed in Chapter 9), or for a formal adoption of a child you are raising together. This advice applies to everyone, but is especially important if you live in or may end up in a state that doesn't recognize your status.

Miss Manners Says You're Married

In a recent column, etiquette expert Judith Martin, aka Miss Manners, was asked by a same-sex husband what to do about the fact that, although he and his spouse were legally married in Iowa, their marriage was not recognized in their home state—specifically, whether he could call his spouse a "husband" in his nonrecognition home state. Miss Manners noted that it would be crazy making to have to reconsider one's marital status every time a border was crossed and was unequivocal in her answer to the question at hand: "You got married, and you are each other's husbands." She added politely: "Miss Manners congratulates you."

Special Issues for Transgender Partners

Transgender and intersex people face unique challenges when it comes to legalizing their partnerships. The difficulties of legalizing one's transition are exacerbated when relationship issues are also at stake, and interstate nonrecognition can be a factor with both of those issues.

Changing Your Gender Legally

Depending on where you live and on how you proceed with your transition, you may or may not be able to change your gender legally. Some states have well-established laws that allow you to obtain a court order to change your birth certificate and other official documents if you meet certain requirements. Some states require sex reassignment surgery to qualify for such a legal order, whereas others are not so explicit. Some states have not enacted laws about gender change, but in practice allow you to change your legal gender on certain documents such as a driver's license or birth certificate, based upon a letter from your surgeon. And in some states, there is no right at all to change your legal gender on your birth certificate or on any other legal document. Making matters worse, it is not at all certain that every state will honor an out-of-state court order or revised birth certificate.

There are separate rules for changing your gender for federal purposes, such as your Social Security records. These procedures usually require a surgeon's letter and, in some cases, a court order. If you can't get a court order in your state, it can be arduous to change your federal identity.

However, things may be changing somewhat. The State Department recently eased its rules so that it is now possible to have your gender identification changed on your passport without proving that you have undergone surgical sex reassignment. Instead, a physician's certification will be sufficient. For anyone in the midst of a gender transition, the State Department will issue a limited-use passport that is valid only for a short period until the transition is complete and a passport can be issued in the person's new gender.

Gender Identity and Marriage

If you have legally changed your gender through a court process, then you should be able to register or marry using your new legal gender. If you and your partner are legally opposite sexes, you can marry anywhere. Whether you can enter into a domestic partnership or civil union will depend on the state you live in. The chart in Appendix A tells you which relationship recognition states limit registration to same-sex couples and which don't—it's about half and half. But if you live in a state that does limit registration to same-sex partners, you will no longer be eligible. On the other hand, if you are legally of the same sex, you will be able to marry, partner, or register as civil union partners wherever that is allowed.

You may identify publicly as a gender that does not match what your birth certificate or another legal document says. If you're someone who passes for the opposite sex in all aspects of your life, you might be tempted to just identify yourself to the city clerk as your presenting gender and obtain a marriage license on that basis—especially if you've been able to get a driver's license or another "official" document. Even if this has worked for other purposes, you can't marry or register based on your presenting gender. Rather, the gender assigned to you at birth or through a legal court order determines what you can and cannot do in terms of registration or marriage.

Going ahead with a marriage based on your presenting gender may cause problems later regarding the validity of your marriage or registration. The most likely problem scenario for transgender partners is that the nontransgender partner challenges the relationship on the basis that the partners weren't actually of the appropriate sex to enter into the marriage. For this reason, it is prudent to sign a private agreement with your partner, stating that neither of you will renounce the marriage or partnership, or claim that you were misled about the other's gender. You should also have the standard protective documents (see Chapter 9), to be certain you are both protected in case your legal relationship is invalidated upon a breakup or death.

📁 An **Expert's View**   **Issues for the Transgender Partner**

Where You Marry Matters

The legal landscape of the United States varies greatly from state to state. If you and your partner constitute a "heterosexual" couple (for example, a transgender man and a nontransgender woman) it is best to marry in a state that recognizes the ability of people to legally change their sex. Generally speaking, avoid states with negative case law that denies the ability of transgender people to transition and marry members of the "opposite" sex. If you are a same-sex couple (for example, two transgender women or a transgender man and a nontransgender man), it is best to marry in a state that recognizes same-sex marriage.

💡 TIP

Make sure you marry in a state with laws that support the family you are creating. If you have your heart set on a particular location that does not have favorable laws, you can obtain a marriage license in a more optimal jurisdiction and then celebrate with a ceremony or party in the location of your choice.

Gain Legal Recognition of the Transgender Partner(s)' Gender Identity First

In certain states, such as California, it is possible to obtain a court order recognizing a change of gender. Such orders constitute legal recognition of your gender identity by the state where the order was issued. I highly recommend seeking such a court order. Obtaining a new or an amended birth certificate can be helpful, but shouldn't be necessary. (For immigrants who will be using marriage to adjust their statuses, obtaining new or amended birth certificates is strongly suggested, if possible.)

💡 TIP

Find out what's involved in the marriage application process from the city or county clerk's office where you will be applying for a license. If possible, make sure the required identity documents accurately reflect both partners' names and gender identities.

Prevent Confusion Later by Putting It in Writing Now

One of the methods sometimes used to challenge marriages involving a transgender person is a claim that the nontransgender spouse was not aware of their partner's transgender status at the time of the marriage. To prevent any possible confusion about this issue later on down the road, I recommend that both partners sign and notarize a "Memorandum of Understanding" in which both partners acknowledge that each has a full understanding of the transgender partner(s)' transgender status.

Ben Lunine is a female-to-male member of the transgender community who works as an attorney at the Transgender Law Center in San Francisco. He provides direct legal services as well as training to transgender individuals and their families, and to government agencies, private employers, and community-based organizations.

Another set of issues can arise if you married or entered a legal partnership on the basis of your legal gender at that time, and then you change your gender legally. Technically, your gender change does not invalidate your previously lawful marriage or registration, and so far this has not been a problem. Chances are no one will notice your history so long as you are not in a family conflict, but if your partner wants to try to invalidate the marriage, he or she may argue that you are no longer eligible for the relationship you entered into. Again, a private contract can protect you in this situation.

Unfortunately, there is no single set of rules that answer all these questions for transgender folks, across all state lines. Therefore, it's a good idea to consult a local attorney—or a national or local transgender advocacy group—to learn how the specific rules in your state will affect you.

Recognition ... Of What You Can and Can't Control

We are living in changing times, and our current legal status is far from perfect, no matter how far we have come. It is inherent in being lesbian or gay in this era that making major life decisions is complicated and fraught with risk and uncertainty. It will take political action to remove the discriminatory laws, but learning the facts and taking strategic action will enable you to reduce the negative impact of the homophobic laws. ●

Marriage Material

t's the age-old question: "But is s/he marriage material?" For the first time, lesbians and gay men must face this fundamental question in a literal way. And the stakes have changed; with legal marriage and partnerships, the rights and obligations that come with commitment are much more significant. This chapter is designed to help you focus on the primary concerns (both legal and nonlegal) that should factor in to your decision about whether or not to legally partner with your current beloved.

Most conventional approaches to this task presume that you are just getting to know your partner, but for many of you reading this book, that is not the case. Many of us have been cohabiting outside of any legal structure for years or even decades, a history that will dramatically alter the decision-making process. For some of you, that history will provide the benefit of intimacy, familiarity, and existing structures. For others, asking these questions will raise some touchy subjects, and possibly even highlight lingering doubts and dissatisfactions.

Applying Logic to Picking a Partner

If the high rate of straight divorces and gay breakups is any indication, neither opposite-sex nor same-sex couples have a great track record at picking partners. Choosing a partner isn't a simple task, and the evaluation process relies in part upon hard-to-learn skills like intuition and emotional intelligence. In addition, as we all know so well, romantic love and physical passion are powerful forces, and when someone draws you in, satisfies your deepest desires, and appears to meet your every need, it is not easy to engage in rational decision making.

You can take some comfort in knowing that according to some experts, if your romantic needs are being met, then there's a decent chance that your lover is indeed marriage material—even though you might not be able to document that in any rational way at the outset. This is especially true if you've been living together for a while. If these experts are right, then trying to do this rationally might seem to be a waste of time. But there are three very important reasons why you can, and should, make a serious attempt to analyze carefully whether marrying your partner is the right thing for you to do.

First, unlike many of our heterosexual friends and relatives, we know that we can have satisfying long-term relationships outside of marriage—indeed, same-sex partners have been living that way for centuries. Most heterosexual couples in our country, even in these post-sexual-revolution and postfeminist days, still cling to the notion that marriage is the inevitable culmination of a serious long-term relationship. While not everyone elects to follow the mantra my grandmother used to repeat, "No chuppah, no shtuppa," the accoutrements of marriage still seem to exercise a powerful influence over all of us, both gay and straight. (The chuppah is the tent under which a couple stands in a traditional Jewish wedding ceremony—and you probably can figure out the meaning of the second Yiddish word for yourself.)

The second reason for considering marriage logically is this: While it's unquestionably true that many opposite-sex spouses face difficulties in their marriages, the rapid evolution of same-sex relationships as formal legal partnerships poses some unique challenges for us, especially for couples who've been together for a while. It's my sense that our long-term relationships actually are different than most opposite-sex marriages, in ways that directly affect our decisions about marriage.

We certainly aren't ever going to find ourselves facing an unwanted pregnancy, which insulates us against the impulsively bad marriage. Moreover, recent studies have established that we are more likely than opposite-sex couples to partner cross-class, cross-race, and cross-age—in other words, we usually don't end up marrying the girl next door, or our high school sweetheart, or the guy we were introduced to in church by our mother. And, to the extent that fewer of us have children than our straight counterparts—though we parent in greater numbers every year—we are free to organize our lives in unconventional ways.

Many of us also haven't been socialized to pair up in any conventional marriage-oriented way, and some of us have been actively discouraged from expecting or seeking that type of relationship. We've often been mistreated by our own families and even by some of our partners, and so we may be anxious about stepping into long-term commitments and thin-skinned when it comes to facing the challenges of relationships. All of these potential complications should caution us to think carefully about the commitments we do make.

Finally, there can be practical and legal reasons why getting married isn't a good idea for you. Those are discussed in "Legal Barriers to Commitment." The less legalistic factors are discussed in "Things to Consider Before Saying 'I Do.'"

Part of the attraction of marriage is that getting married or legally partnered is actually different than living together, both legally and emotionally. But since it can have both positive and negative effects, we should feel free to analyze the option of marriage in a reasoned manner. As far as I know, no straight couple ever got married just because they legally could, and neither should you.

Selecting a Mate: The Historical Backdrop

A brief detour to look at how mates were chosen in the past—based on logic and money much more than on love—may be beneficial. In many pre-20th-century European and Asian cultures, decisions about marriage were made by parents and extended families. In most instances, the important factors in the selection were strengthening bonds with other families, economic security, and the potential for establishing business and property linkages. A financial payment or "dowry" was paid by the bride's parents, financial contracts between the families were signed, and the legal and financial relationship was fixed in place, sometimes even before the intended spouses met one another.

There was an assumption that over time the couple would form a loving bond, at least to a sufficient degree to stay together. The partners were not expected to be best friends or passionate lovers, and these low expectations often were met. (Some historians now suggest that the rising expectations of long-lasting romantic passion within marriage is precisely what has led to so much disappointment and divorce.)

Even in the 19th and early 20th century, middle- and upper-class American households gave great importance to the opinions of extended family about a young person's choice of spouse. The initial connection may have been romantic, but before either partner would commit to legal marriage the families would meet. Relatives might weigh in, and a parent's disapproval or withholding of financial assistance could quash an engagement. The whole concept of a period of a publicly announced engagement was, in part, an open invitation for input from friends and family, as well as a trial period for the couple.

It wasn't just social practices that were different: The couple's own psychological framework also was a world apart from contemporary perspectives. Marriage was viewed as a merger of each person's goals and long-term life directions, in a decidedly gender-unequal manner. It was the husband who earned the money and established the couple's "place" in society, and a wife's choice of a husband would forever determine her future economic and social status. A foolish decision could result in social ostracism, poverty, personal misery, or exclusion from community—and because divorce was hardly ever available, the consequences of this mistake would most likely last a lifetime. On the other hand, winning the hand of a husband who was advancing in his career, acquiring or at least retaining substantial financial capital, and standing proud in the eyes of the local society, would garner the socially and financially dependent woman a lifetime of enviable social status and financial security.

It's rare these days for Americans to engage in any sort of arranged marriage, undertake formal background investigations, or even pay much attention to public or family input. Far fewer lesbians or gay men would approach their choice of partners this way. Even so, while it is most likely that love and passion will remain at the top of our selection criteria for some time to come, most of us would admit that when one is considering a transition from the realm of cohabitation to that of legal partnership or marriage, some additional criteria beyond love and passion should be added to our list. Some of these additional factors are purely legal.

Legal Barriers to Commitment

In some cases, there are specific legal reasons not to marry. If you're in any of the categories below, you'd probably be wise to wait until you work out your legal issues before tying the knot.

People Who Are Already Married or Registered

If either of you is still legally married to or in a marriage equivalent domestic partnership or civil union with someone other than your current partner, you are not eligible to get married until you terminate the other legal relationship. If you were married or registered in Canada or in any of the marriage or marriage equivalent states, and you haven't obtained a divorce, you are still legally married. If you are domestically partnered or registered as a civil union partner in any state whose rules say that such registration triggers all the rights and duties of marriage, then you are still in that relationship for legal purposes, even if you've long ago ceased living together.

In these times of rapid change, inevitably there are going to be some in-between situations. I've counseled clients who married in Massachusetts after misstating their state of residence; clients whose domestic partnership terminations were improperly processed because they got lost in the mail or weren't properly filled in; and clients who married based on one partner's lying about his gender. Each of these situations required a different approach to figure out and then legally establish the clients' actual status.

If you're unsure about your legal status because you got married under some kind of false pretenses, because something about the process didn't go right, or because you're not sure you effectively terminated a legal relationship, consult an attorney. In some instances, you may need to process a divorce, an annulment, or another nullification of your previous relationship before you can marry or register with your current partner. This is true even if you live in a nonrecognition state and want to marry an opposite-sex partner. You are still legally married, so you must find a way to get unmarried before you remarry.

If you only discover this problem after you've married your current partner, you may be able to get a divorce or an annulment "nunc pro tunc," which is a fancy way of saying it's retroactive, so that you don't have to remarry your current spouse.

Those Who Don't Meet State Qualifications

Every state has well-defined rules for marriage and partnership. The most common requirements are:

- Both parties must be of the age of majority or have consent from a parent or guardian.
- The parties must not be related by blood within the degrees stated in the law, or in some states, must not have been raised together in a blended family.
- Both parties must be legally competent.
- The parties must be free to marry—that is, not be married to or in a legal partnership with someone else.
- In some relationship recognition states, the parties must live together.
- In some relationship recognition states, the parties must be of the same sex; of those, a few make an exception when one partner is 62 or older, if marriage is otherwise allowed.

If you don't meet these qualifications, don't get married or register. It will only cause problems later, either when you try to take advantage of the benefits of partnership or marriage, or, more likely, if you and your partner break up. The fact that you weren't qualified to marry in the first place could void your relationship and deprive you of important legal protections.

Those Who Can't Be Out

It is prudent to assume that if you enter into a legal relationship, you are making your sexual orientation public. Marriage records aren't sorted by sexual orientation, but they are public records, so someone who suspected you of being gay could check in that way. In some of the relationship recognition states the names of registered domestic partners are publicly available, and because you must be of the same sex—or over 62—to register in many of these states, your registration can effectively out you. In fact, in California, the registration list is more accessible than the marriage list—a quick phone call to the Secretary of State's office will get you confirmation over the phone of anyone's domestic partner status, whereas marriage records are kept by each county separately.

Some states allow "confidential marriage," which means that your names won't be disclosed to the public. If you're interested in that, check your state's laws. But even with a confidential license, don't forget that you are likely to be asked often about your marital status. In many states, your spouse may have to be involved and even sign papers if you are buying a house, taking out a loan, or even investing in a business. If you aren't ready to be out to your boss, your mortgage broker, your real estate agent, and your business partner, then getting married would be unwise.

Binational Couples

Perhaps the most significant consequence of the Supreme Court's DOMA decision is the opening up of the immigration pathways to the spouses and fiancés of lesbians and gay men. After decades of harsh treatment by the INS (now the U.S. Citizenship and Immigration Services (USCIS)) and the near-universal exclusion of partners in same-sex relationships, the federal government is finally treating lesbian and gay spouses the same as straight couples. So long as there are no other barriers or legal impediments, married lesbian and gay spouses are entitled to green cards and eventual citizenship. Indeed, the deportation of a married gay man was stopped just hours after the United States Supreme Court issued its decision on DOMA.

As mentioned in Chapter 4, the USCIS looks to the validity of the marriage in the state where it was celebrated and doesn't consider where the couple lives. Thus, even if the couple lives in a nonrecognition state, the immigration benefits bestowed on married couples will apply. In fact, the first gay spouse to get a green card was living in Florida—a state that does not allow or recognize same-sex marriages.

There still may be complications for some same-sex spouses. Marriage validity must be proven to the government's satisfaction, and there is some concern that the USCIS will be particularly cautious in honoring our marriages. In the past, many lesbian and gay individuals have been somewhat casual in their approach to immigration law—such as by arranging a marriage with a straight friend to try to "go legal" inappropriately. There also may be problems for lesbians or gay men who come from homophobic countries, where their personal histories may complicate their applications for fiancé or spousal immigration petitions. Thus, when processing your visa application, it makes sense to work with an immigration attorney who is familiar with the rules and practices that apply to same-sex couples.

Military Spouses

The last few years have resulted in dramatic, positive changes for lesbians and gay men serving in the military. "Don't Ask Don't Tell" has been officially repealed, and lesbians and gay men are now entitled to serve openly in the United States military. It will take some time for the military culture to adjust to this momentous shift in social customs, but the authorities have been remarkably conscientious in removing the long-standing barriers.

And, now that much of DOMA has come to an end, military spouses are entitled to the same benefits as straight married couples. Most likely it will take a while for all the programs to be revised to cover same-sex spouses, and there may be some uncertainty for those who are state registered but not married. But in general, you can count on receiving all the same benefits as your straight colleagues—including health care, housing benefits, and retirement benefits.

Couples Planning to Adopt

For many years, same-sex partners were able to adopt children from other countries with relative ease by finding a gay-friendly adoption agency in the United States and remaining closeted with regard to the adopting country. But in the past few years, this has become exponentially more difficult, and it is now close to impossible for open lesbians or gay men to adopt children from overseas.

The rules may ease up again in the future, so if you're interested in adopting internationally you should keep your eye on the news. If you are really dedicated to the idea of doing an international adoption, it's best that you not get married until after the adoption is completed. You'll have to disclose your marital status on any adoption application, and if you are married to a same-sex partner, you will be disqualified. It is far better to complete the adoption while you are single and then have your partner adopt your child.

It's also possible that being married to a same-sex partner could affect your ability to complete a domestic adoption. If you live in or plan to adopt from a state that is open-minded about same-sex couples adopting, it won't be a problem. But if not, being married will be the equivalent of coming out to the adoption agency in your state or in the child's home state.

People Receiving Needs-Based Government Benefits

If either of you is receiving government assistance for which you qualify based on your income or net worth, you should seriously consider deferring legal partnership. In most states, even those that don't recognize same-sex relationships for other purposes, your partner's income or assets could disqualify you from receiving that benefit. This is certainly hypocritical, but in fact, it could happen, because many benefit programs look to any financial support you are getting.

If you live in a relationship recognition state and you receive state disability income, a state-funded scholarship, housing assistance in a local or state program, or even private insurance benefits based on your family income, those benefits will be threatened by your marriage to someone whose net worth would disqualify you. Even first-time homebuyer subsidies may disqualify applicants if either spouse has owned a home before.

If you are receiving assistance through federal programs, the demise of the federal nonrecognition of same-sex marriage that occurred in June 2013 means that the government can deny or terminate your benefits on the basis of your marriage. Many of these programs defer to state law definitions of marriage, or involve both state and federal funds. We don't yet know whether being in a marriage equivalent registration will have the same consequences.

In some instances, cohabitation alone can lead to disqualification, so it is equally important to learn the disqualification rules that apply to cohabitation with a high-net-worth partner, to make sure you are not going to lose benefits even if you remain unmarried.

People Who Might Lose Alimony or Other Support

You may be receiving payments that will terminate if you remarry, such as alimony from a prior marriage, pension payments from a deceased spouse's former employer, Social Security survivor benefits, or even income under a restrictive trust. Often, the terms of such payments state that the payments will end upon marriage. Unless they specifically refer to opposite-sex marriage, you'll lose your benefits if you do marry, but you have a strong argument that the termination provisions don't apply to a same-sex partnership that isn't a marriage. But some courts have found that a marriage is a marriage and so is a marriage equivalent relationship—and ended the benefits. If you are receiving any payment of this kind, talk with an attorney about the risk of losing this income if you legally partner or marry. Remember, even those who disdain your gay marriage may well use it against you to cut off your benefits.

People Who Owe Major Debts

In most states, getting married can make you liable for some or all of your partner's debts—sometimes even debts that were incurred before you met. In California, for example, either partner's creditors can seek repayment from community property money—and all of both partners' earned income is considered community property unless you have a premarital agreement that says otherwise, so you could find your money being used to pay your partner's old debts. And some states that don't consider premarital debts to be shared have rules that debts either of you incur during marriage are joint, unless you have entered into a premarital agreement.

Debts can cause problems both during a relationship and, especially, if the relationship ends. Before making decisions about marriage, make sure you understand your state's rules about marital debt and know whether your earnings can be tapped to pay these debts, and what would happen if you and your partner split up.

A PAINFUL EXAMPLE: I recently mediated a case where the couple each had some credit card debt before they got together. They registered as domestic partners and purchased a house, then used a home equity line of credit (HELOC) to pay off their debts, without having any clear agreement as to how the new HELOC obligation was to be split between the two of them in the event of a breakup. They then each accumulated more debt, both believing it to be their own separate debt even though they live in a community property state, California. When they broke up, one partner thought the debt should be allocated based upon who had incurred it, regardless of what the law said—while his partner wanted to follow the state's marital law rules, which would have pushed half of "his" debt on to the shoulders of his partner. Eventually they reached a compromise, but had they learned something about their state's rules about joint property and debt, they might have made different decisions that would have made their separation smoother, with less misunderstanding and rancor.

I think it's important that each of you know as much as you can about your partner's financial situation, beliefs, and habits. It's fine to date over-indebted folks or even live with them (though I wouldn't recommend co-owning property with them), but there are hardly any persuasive reasons to throw in your legal and financial lot with such partners. And if you do jump into this particular quicksand, be sure to have a written agreement that identifies premarital debt as separate and allocates debts to the person who incurs them. I am always an optimist that folks can reform their bad financial habits, but I also think it's better to live together, unmarried, until they are able to do so. There's more about that in "Things to Consider," below.

It's true that if you co-own a house with a nonmarital partner you face some of the same risks married spouses deal with, but at least in this situation you can refuse to increase your credit line to pay your co-owner's debts, and in most states you can shield your half of the property's equity from the other owner's creditors. Once you are legally partnered, you may not have this same sort of insulation.

People With Other Liabilities

There are legal liabilities other than debts that you should pay attention to. These include:

- liability for unpaid taxes
- professional liability for people in high-risk, uninsurable professions, such as midwives, and
- professional liability for people developing real estate or practicing law without carrying professional liability insurance.

In most states, spouses can partially shield each other by entering into premarital agreements and then keeping their assets completely separate.

They can also provide that if one spouse gets dinged for the other's liabilities that spouse will reimburse the other—but that only helps if there is money for the reimbursement. And, while you can protect assets designated as separate, having someone take only your partner's half of your house may effectively mean that you aren't able to stay there either. And some states don't allow you to put these terms in premarital agreements.

Single Parents Who Want to Be Sure to Stay That Way

In many relationship recognition states, having a child while you're in a legal relationship with your same-sex partner means that both of you are automatically legal parents under that state's laws—and this is the result that most people want. But some people enter into parenthood with the intent to be and remain single parents. If that's your situation, you may want to also remain legally single.

Staying single will only achieve your goal in some situations, however. If you are currently the sole legal parent of a child whose conception you planned on your own, then in general the only way a nonrelated person can obtain visitation with your child is with your consent. So, if you have a partner who came on the scene well after the child was born, and you do not marry or enter into any other legal relationship, your partner generally won't be able to claim that a parent-child relationship has been established.

However, if you do marry or legally partner, the other person becomes a stepparent with some limited rights to seek custody or visitation. And, in some cases, if you and your partner stay together for a significant period of time and your partner acts in a parental role, a court might acknowledge the relationship between your partner and your child.

In some states, if you and your partner plan to conceive and raise a child together, then your legal status is irrelevant—acting upon your intent to coparent makes you both legal parents.

Remember that your child is a person with opinions and feelings, too. If you allow a bond to form between your child and a partner and then the relationship ends, try to do what is right—that is, what will meet your child's needs best—in terms of allowing contact between your ex and your child.

Uncertain Jurisdiction and Nonrecognition

People who live in states that don't offer any form of legal partnership to same-sex couples and don't recognize same-sex relationships from other states are another group that should think long and hard before heading off to a relationship recognition state and getting married or legally partnered. In Chapter 4, we explained that problems with jurisdiction—the court's power to make decisions about your relationship—can create havoc when you live in or move to a nonrecognition state. We've explained the inconsistencies that every same-sex married couple must endure and the tax and other problems that the inconsistencies can cause. These include the uncertainty whether you will be considered married in your home state while you are together and whether you will be able to dissolve your partnership or marriage if you decide to. The question is whether you are willing to take on this legal risk.

If your partnership is not recognized, then you will miss out on the benefits of partnership or marriage, including those affecting your kids or your partner's health. And the worst-case scenario is that you would not be able to end your relationship. In the minds of some judges, granting a divorce in a same-sex marriage is a way of recognizing that relationship—and some judges will refuse to entertain a divorce case for a same-sex couple. If that's the case, you won't be able to get a divorce and neither of you will be free to marry someone else, unless you return to the state where the relationship was formalized, live there for as long as it takes to establish residency, and then file the necessary paperwork to get the divorce. (The only exceptions to this so far are in California and D.C., where registered domestic partners and married spouses can use the courts to divorce even if they have moved to a different state.)

You may have an even worse problem if you and your partner are in conflict, because living in a nonrecognition state means one partner can try to deny that the relationship is valid in order to avoid paying support or sharing assets.

My own position and that of many other lawyers is this: When we're asked by couples living in nonrecognition states whether they should marry or partner in any of the relationship recognition states or abroad, most of us say pretty unequivocally that we don't think it's a good idea. You would be better off protecting your kids and your partner with private agreements and powers of attorney or an adoption, than relying on a marriage or partnership of questionable validity. But now that some federal benefits are being extended to all married couples, there are situations (such as those involving federal tax benefits and immigration) where there are good reasons to marry.

That covers the legal, logical, practical elements you should think about before getting legally married or partnered. But there's another dimension to the question as well.

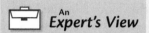 **An Expert's View   The Meaning of Commitment**

With all the legal work-arounds that had been provided to gay and lesbian couples over the years, the primary reason for any couple to marry has always been to signal their commitment in a permanent and public way as a sign of their love. So, with gay and lesbian marriage, I'm finally able to talk directly with my clients about the real reasons two people form a couple in the first place—out of love and commitment.

Sexual attraction is a wonderful thing, but it changes over time. So does one's financial status, or health, or career, or spirituality, or one's emotional capacities. But throughout all these changes, a couple's loving commitment, best affirmed in the act of marriage, can be an anchor for them, a grounding in dedication to live their lives selflessly and to work as hard as they possibly can for the best and highest good of their spouse. Marriage is a promise that one makes to one's husband or wife but also a promise one makes to one's own higher self, a promise that love will be the standard by which one lives one's life.

As gay and lesbian couples, we can contract our way legally into a shared life, home, and even family. But only the act of marriage affirms that higher commitment to love, and in my opinion, this commitment to love is the only reason to take that step. So far, it is a joy to see how thousands of couples have told the world of their deep and abiding love in this way, and it is my fervent hope that there will, in the future, be many, many more to come.

Robert H. Hopcke is a licensed Marriage and Family Therapist in private practice in Berkeley, California. Over the past 20 years, he has been the author or editor of numerous articles and books on gay and lesbian issues, including *Jung, Jungians and Homosexuality* and *Same-Sex Love: A Path to Wholeness*.

Things to Consider Before Saying "I Do"

It may seem odd for a lawyer to give you plain old relationship advice. So here's my disclaimer: I am not Dr. Phil, Dear Abby, or a qualified relationship counselor. I don't even play one on TV. But I have seen hundreds of couples enter into and dissolve relationships of all varieties, and in the process I believe I've learned about some of the things that are important to consider before taking the plunge into a legally binding relationship with your partner. (Most of these same issues also arise in choosing to live with someone in a nonmarital relationship, but in light of everything we've learned so far, the stakes in electing to marry or legally partner are much higher.)

The other reason for offering this advice is that the questions discussed in this section are often the very ones that clients bring into my office. Most people don't make important life decisions based solely on practical criteria, and very often the legal and nonlegal questions are inextricably tied together for clients—so we end up discussing both. After listening to clients tell me stories for 25 years and after engaging with all variety of experts on the subject, I've developed my own list of issues and topics that most people should probably consider in thinking about the "marriage material" question. Remember, these are just issues to consider. After you've done that, Chapter 6 has the steps you can follow in making your final decision.

I am convinced that every relationship can be improved and every intimate partnership can benefit from an open evaluation of risks and concerns, so long as it is done with a positive and proactive approach at the right time and in the right way. It isn't easy, and it requires a full embrace of the project by both partners, but once your hearts and minds are open, I am confident that you will be able to tackle these difficult subjects.

This exercise may or may not work for couples who've been together for many years—essentially, because you've probably already done it. Feel free to skip ahead if that's the case for you.

A Walk in the Woods—Or Two

I also believe that there are two steps in this process. The first is to consider for yourself, on your own, whether your prospective spouse is marriage material. These are the things you might consider while taking a long walk in the woods by yourself, or talking over your concerns with a friend. The second is to talk with your partner about them, and explore your concerns, questions, fears, and hopes together—the kind of conversation you might have when you take a long walk in the woods together.

It's not a linear thing where you'll first do the just-you step and then the both-of-you step. Most likely you'll go back and forth between them. But in the categories below I'll make a distinction between the two walks.

Home

Whether you own or rent, live in an urban townhouse or on a couple of acres, have kids and pets or live alone, home is an enormously important place. For many people, home means security, tranquility, and family. And often, a home is the single largest and most valuable financial investment a person will ever make. When you're thinking about partnering permanently with someone, questions about your home life are important, and so are questions about how to manage the financial aspects of this valuable asset.

It's entirely possible that you and your partner, in utter good faith and with loving hearts, could view a given issue completely differently. One partner may view the retirement housing he or she anticipates as fully adequate, while the same arrangement may be another person's last resort. One partner's notion of a safety net can look like scarcity to the other. That is why it's so important to talk about your future together and anticipate as many possible contingencies as you can.

Questions to Consider for Yourself

Thinking about your own perfect home situation, ask yourself what elements of it feel nonnegotiable for you. What is your vision of the home you are going to share together? Does it need to be in one particular city or neighborhood? Does it need to be big and fancy, or do you prefer small and simple? How were you raised, and what are the economic and lifestyle expectations you bring into the relationship?

Do you feel that you need to stay living where you are, or are you open to the idea of moving to a different house, a different neighborhood, or even a different state? What factors would be important enough to uproot your current life—a great job, a parent in need—or are you dead set against moving? If so, how likely it is that something might come up that would cause your partner to want to move?

Questions to Consider With Your Partner

Housing issues are one of the most frequent areas of conflict when couples separate, so it's crucial that you develop clear understandings on the subject early in your relationship.

It's especially important to talk about it if your incomes or your housing situations are very different now. How are you expecting to share expenses? What about home equity if only one of you owns the house? Who will pay for repairs and improvements?

Are you both tolerant of how the other partner organizes (or fails to organize) domestic space? Is there an expectation that one of you is going to be the domestic spouse, taking care of the cleaning and organizing?

Do you have the same boundaries and limits about entertaining or hosting out-of-town guests? Do either of you join a lot of organizations and host lots of meetings at your home, or do you expect to nest into a private space with few intrusions? Are you in sync about this?

Does one of you have a greater attachment to your home than another? It's important to talk about what would happen to your home if your relationship ends—can you agree about who has the first right to buy the other person out? How you will determine its market value? These are questions you'll cover in a discussion of a prenup (see Chapter 7), but they can be useful topics to bring up in these "marriage material" conversations as well.

Money

Money is an enormous and complex issue for most couples and tends to be the topic people most want to avoid during the premarital romance (and sometimes during the marriage). But it's crucial that you look honestly at whether you are financially compatible. There are so many questions—none of which are easily answered by any of us, but all of which need to be considered.

Questions to Consider for Yourself

Now that you know the basic rules of marriage, are these conventional economic rules in sync with the way you are currently living your lives and the way you want to design your future? Or are your financial arrangements dramatically at odds with the fundamental marriage rules, such that getting married could force you to adopt certain financial and legal practices that you really don't want to follow?

Are either of you considering relocating to another state for a new job prospect? Are you willing to consider saying no to a fabulous job offer, or do you expect your partner to follow you anywhere to further your career?

My experience tells me that none of us is particularly good at admitting our financial weaknesses. Thus, while talking about these issues is crucial, observing the behavior of one's beloved is equally important. If credit card bills are racking up beyond your partner's financial capacity, face the truth. I believe that you should observe what your partner earns and spends for at least a year before making any legal commitments. Everyone has their own bottom line about what they feel is acceptable financial management—at least for a partner with whom you are legally bound. My advice to clients is not to marry anyone who has a car that costs more than they make in a year (even if it is leased or financed) or anyone who has used more than half of their home equity to cover credit card debts.

Once you've made these observations, do you fully respect and trust the manner in which your partner manages income and expenditures, or do you think you'll need to act independently when it comes to monetary decisions? How will it feel to have someone watching how you handle your money, and will you feel the need to totally control your partner's decisions?

Questions to Consider With Your Partner

How well do each of you handle money, and more fundamentally, how do you each handle money, and how do you think about it? How responsible are each of you in balancing available income and spending? What standards of living have you been raised with, and what are your aspirations? Are your habits compatible? Is one of you a saver and the other a spender? If so, are you able to accept each other's habits and values without judgment?

Will you keep your assets and debts separate or commingle them? (My partner and I use what I call the "perforated" approach to financial security: We hope to be together forever, but just in case we end up apart, we want each of us to be financially self-sufficient.) How will you make joint decisions about expenditures? If you are able to save, how do you invest your money and make investment decisions—and what do you do if your decisions turn out to be unwise?

What are you able to earn in the real world of today's changing economy? What sacrifices will it take for you to increase your earning capacity, if that's your shared priority? What are your savings plans and retirement strategies? How well do your long-term financial goals mesh? Are you hoping to stop working, and if so, when? If you are heading to or older than 50 years old, have you already made realistic retirement plans? Or is your secret retirement plan marrying your richer partner—and if so, how does your partner feel about your plan?

Are you planning to merge your finances and engage in joint decision making about spending, and are you willing to be jointly responsible for each other's debts? Are either of you taking care of a child, a parent, or a friend, and if so, how is that obligation going to be integrated into your family finances?

It's very important that you and your partner share information about money. Ask for and be willing to provide disclosures of income, assets, debts, spending habits, and beliefs about money. A client once asked me if I thought it would be tacky (or even illegal) for him to obtain a credit report on his partner or ask a private investigator to investigate his partner's financial situation. I told him it probably isn't illegal, but I also counseled him that if he believed such an investigation was necessary, he should probably think twice about marrying his boyfriend.

The key here is compatibility, not uniformity. Your financial styles need not be identical, but they must complement each other, be acceptable to each other, and not be likely to lead to mistrust or disapproval.

The Question of Children

Most experts believe that couples raising children together should commit strongly to being together long term, and that marriage is the best way to express that commitment. It sends a clear signal to your families and your children that you are making a commitment, and makes it less likely either person will leave the relationship impulsively. That raises important questions about your plans.

Questions to Consider for Yourself

When it comes to children, the work you need to do alone is to sort out your own feelings about having children and your expectations of your partner. Are you hoping to raise children? If your partner isn't as enthusiastic as you are about it, how will you resolve the disparity? If your partner is adamantly against it, is that a deal breaker for you? What about if you run into a strong difference of opinion about how many children you want to have, or how you want to conceive them?

If you already have children, think about how you want your partner to be involved with them—what role do you expect your partner to take? Are you open to your partner's becoming a legal parent in the future, if that's possible?

Consider these issues for yourself, but most of the work on this topic is work you'll do together.

Questions to Consider With Your Partner

If both of you are to become parents, are you ready to make what is truly a lifetime commitment to raising your child as a family, even if eventually you divorce and live apart?

If one or both of you already are raising children, how will your marriage affect those relationships? Are you in agreement about the stepparent's role in parenting? Is the legal parent prepared to share parenting responsibilities? Do you have the same expectations about parental rights?

For lesbians choosing donor insemination, there's the question of which partner is to be the birth parent. What do you want to do about a donor: anonymous, identity release, or known? If you are using a known donor, what will his relationship with the child be? Do you need a donor agreement? Should the other partner donate eggs for in vitro fertilization?

Do either of you feel strongly about adoption or using a surrogate to carry a child, or about using or avoiding medical intervention in the process?

Gay men face other questions: Should you adopt? Should you use a surrogate—and if so, who should provide the sperm? And what if only one partner can be the legal parent because you live in a state where coparent adoptions are not allowed? How do you choose? Should you relocate to a state that allows adoptions, or can you live with an arrangement where one parent is dependent on the goodwill of the other to maintain a long-term relationship with the children? These are just the legal issues. Obviously, there are innumerable other things you and your partner will talk about when you plan for children—issues like discipline, religious upbringing, education, and the like. Most of the baby-making methods for lesbians and gay men are not cheap, and so you'll also need to discuss finances and whether you both feel the same about what's a reasonable amount of resources to devote to creating a family. Finding out whether you're on the same page is a valuable exercise.

Extended Family and Community

Don't underestimate the way that getting married will transform other people's expectations of you, and to what extent it can pull you into conventional family roles even if that hasn't been your relationship up until now. It's important to understand how you each relate to your friends, family, and larger community.

Questions to Consider for Yourself

What is your relationship like with your family of origin? Do you expect your partner to participate in lots of family events with your parents, siblings, and other relatives? How has that gone so far—does everyone get along? Does your family like your partner, and vice versa? Are you willing to meet your partner's expectations in terms of his or her family? Do you like them and vice versa?

What about your friendship circle? Do you have a lot of close friendships that you spend time maintaining? Is your partner supportive of that, or jealous of the time you spend with others? Do you enjoy spending time together with your partner and others? Do your friends and your partner like each other? Are any of your friends hesitant about the relationship? Do you like your partner's friends? What do they tell you about your partner—not literally by talking about your partner, but by what kind of people they are?

Questions to Consider With Your Partner

Do both of you have the same expectations about your relationship—as a couple—with your family and friends? Are you planning to see your in-laws on a weekly basis, or are you a couple that will mostly socialize with friends and each other? (Spend a day with your straight married friends or siblings, and you'll be amazed at how irritated many of them are at the extended family obligations and interactions. One of the "privileges of oppression" is being left alone by your in-laws, and getting married may change that.) Do you have the same expectations about how much you will socialize as opposed to spending time just the two of you together?

Are both of you comfortable being identified publicly as each other's partner, and of being considered "married" by others? Is being treated in this way something that will be positive for each of you individually, and for you as a couple?

Intimacy and Emotional Support

If these terms seem somewhat abstract, it's because this is a broad category, encompassing what it means to each of you, in the deepest sense of the term, to become legally committed partners or spouses.

Questions to Consider for Yourself

Trusting that emotional support is available in your relationship is one of the most important steps toward making a commitment. Emotional support represents that intuitively felt sense of being seen, appreciated, honored, respected, and cared about. Do you trust that your partner will be there to support you in both good times and bad? Do you find it easy to talk to your partner even about difficult subjects? Do you ever feel shut down or ignored when you try to bring up topics that are important to you?

Is your partner a cheerleader for your career and other endeavors? Do you feel that your partner admires and respects you, and do you feel the same?

Are you someone who needs a great deal of assurance and wants to be part of a team effort, or do you need a great deal of personal space and separate time? Does your partner meet your needs or give you your space? Is it easy to meet your partner's emotional needs, or give the space that's required?

Questions to Consider With Your Partner

For some partners, marriage means joining a social framework that feels alien. To others, it means claiming a social position that matches your vision of your relationship. Will getting married lead to a reframing of the underlying assumptions of your relationship, especially if you've been together for a while, or are you merely signing up for certain practical benefits? How will you work out the emotional dynamics of autonomy and cooperation in your marriage?

If either of you is committed to a religious or spiritual practice, how does your spiritual practice shape your daily activities and personal values? Do you share a common spiritual foundation? If you are planning to raise children together, how will each partner's approach to and choice of religion play out when it comes to raising your growing family?

How satisfying is your sexual life together? Does it seem likely that it will sustain you even during the rockier times? Are you in sync about sexual exclusivity? Nonmonogamy is always an option (and has a long tradition in the relationships of gay men), but the limits of outside sexual activities and the degree of information sharing needs to be resolved. For some couples, the transition from cohabitation to marriage implies a change in the terms of such agreements—is this true for either of you?

As touchy as it can be, talk about your current habits and attitudes about alcohol, recreational drugs, smoking, and diet. Do either of you abuse any substances? Is either of you in a recovery program that would make it difficult to live with someone who uses substances, even responsibly? Do you agree on what "responsibly" means, or do you have different ideas about what's an okay level of drinking or drug use?

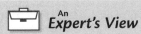 **An Expert's View**   **The Spiritual Dimension**

Choosing to be married means you will spend the rest of your lives choosing each other again. At every crossroad, in the midst of debilitating disappointment, in the presence of incomparable joy—love and commitment will demand that you choose each other again.

You choose based on your commitment to one another and your dedication to your own growth and development.

Make every effort to keep romance alive. Make love that is loving. Revel in the mystery of your own soul's journey and the soul journey of your beloved.

When you know a truth, tell it. Telling each other your own truths, no matter how hard they are to hear, is the most intimate act you will experience.

You must enter into this union respecting each other. Familiarity has the potential to atrophy a relationship but when it is subject to respect, it will deepen your companionship.

How will you know when you are ready to make the biggest decision of your life? You may never be ready but you must be willing. Willing to enter fully the journey of self-revelation, willing to enter the fire of honesty, and willing to relinquish your deepest self to the highest good—to love another as your own soul.

Rev. Dr. G. Penny Nixon served MCC San Francisco for 11 years and is currently the Senior Minister of the Congregational Church of San Mateo, UCC.

What about your roles in the family? A recent study revealed that while many gay couples like to think of themselves as beyond traditional gender role assignments, in fact there is quite often a delegation to one partner of those duties (cooking, cleaning, maintenance of social relations) that would conventionally be seen as the wife's role. The person in the "wife" role might also defer career opportunities in order to meet the family's more immediate needs, or take the emotionally passive role in arguments or conflicts. Are you likely to fall into gender-different roles (especially if you are raising children), and how might those affect your relationship? It's not that taking on these roles is a bad thing—it's just that knowing what you're getting into, and having agreements about what part each of you might play in your family life, is a good thing.

Living and Working as a Team

Marriage frequently means taking on joint projects that extend over years, such as raising children, buying or renovating a house, or building a business together. This will require you to accommodate each other's needs and work collaboratively on projects and responsibilities over the long haul, and to collaborate on an almost daily basis on practical and financial matters.

Questions to Consider for Yourself

Do you believe you and your partner will collaborate well on major projects? What about small day-to-day details? Do you trust your partner to take care of business on behalf of your partnership, or do you feel the need to double-check or supervise everything your partner does that involves you? Are you comfortable with your own level of responsibility in the relationship, and do you feel trusted?

Have you traveled together? It's a great relationship tester, as the unpredictability of being in a foreign environment can bring to the surface anxieties and irritations that otherwise might be kept hidden for a while. What was it like to be in a different environment together? Were you able to make decisions effectively, and did you feel safe and comfortable with your partner?

Questions to Consider With Your Partner

How does it go when you do try to work on projects together? Do you find yourselves easily in agreement about how to proceed and what needs to be done? Or is there bickering or disagreement about the best way to do something? If one of you has skills or knowledge in a particular area, is the other person comfortable deferring?

When you and your partner find yourselves in a situation where you can't both get your way and your options feel limited, do you find ways to compromise, or do you end up in a major battle?

Planning for the Future, for Better or Worse

Finally, there are some "bottom line" commitment questions. In light of the legal complexities and emotional consequences of ending a marriage relationship, marriage is not something you want to jump into for the short term or with an attitude that if it doesn't work out, you'll just get divorced. Are you sufficiently confident in the likely duration of your relationship that legalizing it in this way makes sense?

Have you shared your full medical histories so that you both know what to expect in the future, to the extent that's predictable? Are you prepared to take care of your partner "for better or worse," even in the event of a serious health or financial crisis that creates dependency that didn't exist when you first got together? If you are in a relationship with someone who is more than ten years older or younger, these questions have special resonance. Are you each ready for the responsibilities that will come with that situation?

No one likes to talk about the possibility of one's own divorce, or about one's own death or the death of a partner. But even though it might seem macabre, unless you engage with your partner about these hard subjects you will not be able to develop strategies for minimizing the negative consequences of unwanted events. Facing the possibility that your relationship might end should be part of your agenda.

Think about your partner's relationship with exes—are they on good terms, or did they have toxic breakups? If the latter, what was your partner's part in that? Do you have reason to think things would be different if you break up, or do you need to take steps to protect yourself from a bad breakup? Ask yourselves whether there are things that you know would cause you to leave the relationship? Is infidelity a deal breaker? What about another kind of dishonesty or deceit?

This is a long list, and each time I counsel or represent a partner in a premarital agreement or a dissolution, I add a few more items. Chances are you will have your own list to review—which is exactly what you should be doing at this point, as you move toward making the marriage or partnership decision.

The Value of an Engagement Period

The standard method of addressing these questions is through the engagement process. It's a way of saying "yes, but then again, maybe not" to your partner, family, and friends, and it's not a bad way to manage this decision-making process. No one has to know why exactly an engagement was called off, so you can maintain your privacy about what you have learned during the engagement period. It may seem old-fashioned, and you certainly don't need to buy an expensive ring and announce your engagement in the local papers. But don't be shy about benefiting from this particular social ritual, especially if you have not been dating or living with your betrothed one for any length of time.

For still more questions that may help you assess whether you're ready to make a permanent commitment to your partner, see *The Hard Questions: 100 Questions to Ask Before You Say "I Do,"* by Susan Piver (Tarcher/Putnam), and *101 Things I Wish I Knew When I Got Married: Simple Lessons to Make Love Last,* by Linda Bloom and Charlie Bloom (New World Library). ●

Ten Steps to a Decision

E ver since domestic partnership and marriage (in 2008 and again in 2013) became available in California, I have spent much of my professional time counseling couples who are considering some kind of legally recognized partnership. Once I finish explaining how marital laws are most likely to affect them, many find themselves totally stumped as to how to make the critical decisions. In particular, those of us who have been in relationships for years may have already organized our social and financial lives as unmarried partners, with a public identity and a private arrangement that doesn't quite fit into the marriage box. The sudden prospect of marriage can be downright confusing for some couples, who are uncertain whether it is the right direction for them.

They ask me what they should do, and I advise them to do what is right for them—reminding them that there is no universally correct answer. But this response is less than satisfying to most clients, who would prefer a road map that would lead them directly to the "right" decision.

It's certainly true that opposite-sex couples can also find it difficult to figure out what is best for their relationship. But they have the luxury of weighing their options in the context of a legal and social environment that has been relatively constant. True, there have been many changes to the marital rules in the past 50 years, but those changes happened relatively slowly—certainly as compared to changes in the realm of same-sex relationships. The rules for opposite-sex couples apply across the country—there are no nonrecognition issues to contend with. And, for the most part, the marital rules are consonant with the basic social arrangements of many, if not most, couples.

As a result, the external forces are fairly stable, and opposite-sex couples can focus their attention entirely on what is unfolding within the internal realm of their relationship. We, on the other hand, have to manage our personal pathfinding across a landscape that is constantly changing, often very dramatically—and that most likely will continue to change for some years to come.

The complexity of the laws and the unpredictable ways in which they are changing complicates the decision-making process. Which legal and nonlegal factors should be given the heaviest weight? How does one prioritize the competing pressures and new opportunities? When is there enough information or certainty regarding the laws to justify taking one path, and when should one stand back and wait for greater legal or personal clarity?

While there often is no single and certain right answer, it's possible to make wise choices and avoid major missteps. But because it can be so difficult to navigate this terrain, it's necessary to reflect a bit on the decision-making process itself. This chapter focuses primarily on the methods of resolving your decisions—the how of it.

The Ten Steps to a Decision

Recognizing the difficulties today's legal landscape imposes on my clients, I've developed a simplified ten-step "recipe" for your decision-making process; it's intended to provide a rational framework and a basic set of directions. Consider these "steps" as landmarks on your roadmap for staying sane and calm as you make your decisions—or at least, sufficiently sane and calm to maintain your relationship in the meantime. The steps are set out in the following list, and then considered in detail.

If, in the end, you elect to not legally partner or marry, that certainly doesn't mean you have to break up. Be sure you complete the legal tasks that every unmarried couple should do, but don't get caught up in any false notion that in the absence of marriage, your relationship is not legitimate.

Fred's Ten-Step Recipe for Partnership Decision Making

1. Don't rush the process, and don't skip any of these steps.

2. Pay attention to your doubts.

3. Listen to input from all sources.

4. Talk to your partner about what marriage or legal partnership means to you.

5. Learn how the laws of marriage will change your relationship, and determine whether any of the unavoidable legal consequences are unacceptable to either of you.

6. Determine whether and how any of the unacceptable consequences of marriage can be minimized.

7. If you are still undecided, work together to figure out the most important factors for each of you.

8. Make your own tentative decision in light of all these factors, and then spend some time living with your decision to see whether it's the right one.

9. Finalize your decision. If you've decided to legally partner or marry, implement the premarital tasks you've concluded need to be done. If you've decided not to, take the other important steps to protect your relationship.

10. Plan your event if you're having one and then, at the appointed time, celebrate your commitment!

1. Don't Rush the Process

Our legal system allows partners to enter into marriage or its equivalent on almost a moment's notice at a cost of less than $50, but imposes rules of divorce that take six months or longer and can cost thousands of dollars to complete. Wouldn't it make more sense if it took longer and cost more to enter into a marriage, and then, were easier and less expensive to get out of it (especially if there are no young children)? Some historians have suggested that the "easy entry/slow exit" approach was designed to encourage reckless men to quickly marry the women they impregnated, and then make it hard for the dads to abandon their wives and kids. Maybe this was a convincing justification centuries ago, but it certainly doesn't make sense when it comes to our marriages.

Given how complex our legal and personal lives are these days, it's my recommendation that you give yourself six months to a year to make your decision about marriage or legal partnership. Also, depending on where you live and what resources are available, accept that it could cost you as much as $5,000 to deal with the legal issues, especially if you decide that a premarital agreement is necessary. (See Chapter 7 for more about premarital agreements.)

Please, don't base your decision on worries about the availability of marriage rights. After the California Supreme Court lifted the ban on same-sex marriage in May 2008, a state constitutional amendment banning same-sex marriage qualified for the statewide ballot. Rightly fearing that approval of the amendment would close the door to marriage, many couples felt compelled to schedule weddings immediately—even though domestic partnership would still be available if the amendment passed, and even though the possibility existed that the marriages solemnized during this period eventually might be voided by the court. Some of these couples had been together for decades (and some were state registered already). In other cases, however, personal and political pressures trumped rational decision making.

2. Pay Attention to Your Doubts

As just discussed, the new options for legal commitment have the potential to create a dangerous rush to the proverbial altar. They may also create an implication that those who are hesitating are old-fashioned spoilers. But if you're one of those hesitant folks, don't ignore your concerns: Many legal uncertainties still exist, and you're right to consider your choices carefully. And in fact, no one should marry in haste—you must attend to not only your legal concerns but also the question of whether you are truly ready to make a commitment to this person at this time.

Consider all the questions in Chapter 5. Make sure you spend a healthy amount of time with your partner, and also away from your partner, so that you can take accurate stock of your innermost feelings. If you experience anxiety or a sense of foreboding, or if there are long-range worries that simply don't go away, pay attention to these concerns, as they are sending you an important message.

That's not to say that if you have doubts you shouldn't ever marry this person. It may be that you are a slow decision maker, or that a few counseling sessions together would foster useful communication about this commitment. But don't ignore your gut.

Marriage Education 101

It probably sounds hopelessly old-fashioned, but there may be some value in the conventional "marriage education" classes offered by churches and community groups—especially if they could be redesigned to meet our community's needs. Part of their focus is on the financial ramifications of a legal partnership, but they also address issues of emotional compatibility, extended family relationships, and decision making about raising children. Most valuably, they provide a forum for facing and discussing the hard issues you may have wanted to avoid, at a time when you are still free to say "no thanks" if the partnership doesn't seem quite right to you.

---

3. Listen to Input

Take the time to talk about your decision-making process with your friends, coworkers, and family. Ask for their honest opinions about your relationship, your partner, and whether you are ready for this big step. People who love you may be reluctant to express concerns about your partner or your relationship, and it may be hard for you to hear those concerns, but the people who know you well are the best sources you have for an outside look at how things stand, so encourage them to be straightforward with you. And then listen to and consider whatever they say.

It's also interesting to find out what other people think about marriage and its place in our world. I did my own minisurvey in June 2008, when marriage seemed to be on everyone's mind in California. I queried couples on whether they were considering marriage and why, and got a variety of responses.

A lesbian couple together more than 20 years described the powerful feelings of legitimacy and societal acceptance they felt the moment they received the government's "blessing" when they married in Canada several years back. By contrast, a woman in a relationship of more than 12 years declared that she and her partner both felt that marriage was completely unnecessary and irrelevant, and would impose an archaic structure of unrealistic expectations and emotional constraints that they didn't want. Another friend, this one an attorney, revealed to me that he felt that getting married was essential to ratifying and preserving the inner sense of commitment and connection he felt toward his boyfriend, who, by contrast, perceived it as a sentimental ritual of no real significance.

That's one couple gung ho for marriage, one couple equally committed to saying no, and a third of divided opinion—quite illustrative of the range of reactions I was hearing.

Having been excluded from marriage for so long, we are all beginners in this classroom in a certain way. Yet everyone has some degree of expertise, and so, talking and listening to others is a great way to figure out what is best for you. Find out what other people think about marriage and consider whether it affects your own view. And don't omit straight folks or older couples—many of them have enjoyed happy marriages or endured miserable ones (sometimes a few of each), and can offer different perspectives.

4. Talk to Your Partner About What Marriage Means to You

In addition to talking with others, it goes without saying that you and your partner should spend some time talking about what this decision means to each of you. If you read the previous chapter and put it into action, you're well along this path.

Many of us have incorporated the absence of legal and social recognition into how we structure our relationships, often in ways we aren't immediately aware of. Consider this: If you are never going to be held liable for your partner's debts, it doesn't really matter how close he is to bankruptcy, and if you are never going to be accepted by your partner's parents as a full legal partner, what does it matter what they think of you? If there is no legal obligation to support your partner financially, how crucial is it that she finish graduate school? All of these questions take on a new and deeper resonance when you consider how marrying or entering a legal partnership changes the stakes.

Until now, one feature of same-sex relationships is that there was never a point where one partner asked "will you marry me" and had to wait for the answer and deal with the consequences of an answer other than an enthusiastic "yes." Exploring this territory can expose doubts that have rested quietly beneath the surface for a long time, and reveal unsettling anxieties about the future. Or it may reveal a depth to your commitment that you weren't aware of. For these reasons, it is essential you make it possible for your partner to speak the truth to you and that you do the same.

5. Know the Relevant Law

Chapter 3 provided you with a general understanding of the laws of marriage, but trust me, your education is only beginning. It is crucial that you educate yourselves—either by doing research on your own or by consulting with a local attorney who understands marriage laws in your state and can advise you what marriage would mean in the context of your actual life. Many marriage rules may not affect you directly, but there may be some that will have a dramatic effect on your lives.

If either of you finds yourself in one of the especially problematic situations discussed in Chapter 4, it will be well worth the time and expense of spending an hour or two with an attorney. Just about every couple would benefit from learning about the tax consequences of getting married. In most instances, this sort of knowledge won't be the thing that makes your decision for you, but you will know what you are getting into and that knowledge is important.

EXAMPLE: For some couples the decision-making process can be especially compli-cated. Consider the situation that Alan and Ben are facing: Alan is the single father of a five-year-old son, and he receives some county assistance for medical and child care costs because he adopted his son through a foster-adopt program. Ben's income is much higher, and he has savings from a prior job. They are considering becoming domestic partners, which would make their future savings presumptively shared under

Oregon law. That is okay with them, but registration also could disqualify Alan from receiving county assistance, in light of Ben's higher income. In order to make their decision, they will need to compile a comprehensive list of all the benefits and downsides of registration, and then make the best agreement given all the circumstances—and then determine whether they need a preregistration agreement as well. At the same time, they need to evaluate whether Ben should become a legal coparent of Alan's son, and the financial and tax consequences of doing so.

6. Strategize to Avoid Unacceptable Consequences

It's possible that there are certain marital rules that you want to avoid, and you certainly want to stay away from the many negative consequences of nonrecognition. For some couples the biggest tax problems can be avoided by careful planning or by shifting assets or making gifts. Partners with significant financial assets, family trusts, or similar arrangements should consult with the attorneys who drafted the legal instruments to determine how they can preserve these family arrangements in the context of their new marriages. In some situations, a change in your estate plan or retirement fund designation will be necessary, in order to prevent your marriage from disturbing well-designed plans for either partner's financial future.

You can also plan to manage your financial relationship using a premarital agreement. A legally enforceable agreement can be a good form of protection against some of the nonrecognition uncertainties. Your private agreement can specify that even if your partnership or marriage is not recognized by your state, the financial terms of your agreement will still apply. Moreover, your agreement can be designed to cover the various contingencies of relocation or a change in your own state's policies in the future. The details of preparing a premarital agreement are covered in detail in Chapter 7.

Exploring and managing these challenges is probably not going to be romantic, easy, or cheap. It draws you into a world of accountants and lawyers, and forces you to deal head-on with the homophobic laws at the heart of the nonrecognition problems discussed in Chapter 4. But the consequences of not doing it are even less romantic and, certainly, more expensive.

7. Determine the Factors Most Important to You

Figuring out your own subjective criteria for deciding whether to marry should be the easiest task on the list, because no research is needed and no expense is incurred. On the other hand, weighing honestly what is truly most important to you and your partner can be surprisingly difficult—especially because few of us have given the question several decades of thought, like most heterosexual people have.

Talk to some of your straight friends and you may be amazed to learn how much time they have spent pondering the pros and cons of marriage and whether each prospective spouse who entered their lives was marriage material. You, on the other hand, may have thought this day would never come, and so it's not how you've been organizing your search for Mr. or Ms. Right.

It's also possible that your feelings will swing back and forth as you face the true meaning of legal commitment. A friend of mine broke up with his boyfriend when he saw how the boyfriend reacted when my friend's father needed a lot of attention and care. Another friend's partner faded from the scene when that friend became ill himself. An embarrassing scene at a party where your partner has too much to drink or a refusal to compromise when making important plans together can trigger serious doubts when you're considering marriage. Research on the emotional dynamics of unmarried opposite-sex couples shows a tendency to overreact to such events, because each partner is constantly evaluating the other one as potential marriage material. In the past, same-sex couples have been free from this social framework, but don't be surprised if you have intense reactions to this process, now that you are on the marriage track.

Your evaluation process also will be affected by your past experiences in relationships, previous relationship dynamics, age or personality differences, and major life changes either you or your partner are going through. For example, if you were always the caretaker in the past and now you've realized that is not what you want to be doing, you will be more attentive to that downside than you were in your earlier years. If you were recently left by someone who was going through a midlife crisis, you may be extra cautious around indecisive or volatile people.

All of these factors, and the factors described in Chapter 5, should be part of your decision-making process. It's up to you to prioritize them and decide what's most important to you and where you can compromise.

8. Make a Tentative Decision

Let me share with you how I make important decisions. Oftentimes, I have to acknowledge that I can't really "decide" unequivocally in the abstract once and for all. So, I make a tentative decision and "wear" the tentative decision for a few weeks or months, acting as though I've made the decision. With the tentative decision as my temporary "cloak" I take stock of how it feels and how it is likely to feel over the long term. It's a strategy I've used to evaluate quitting a job, leaving a lover, buying a house, or taking on any new project. It allows me the time to experience the prospective decision safely and to figure out whether I need to make adjustments to my plan. It also bestows on me the freedom to change my mind before I've taken any irrevocable actions.

After you've surveyed the data and considered your feelings and needs, it is time to make your tentative decision. You will settle on one of three possible decisions. You'll either decide to make a legal commitment to your partner (analogous to "engagement" status), decide not to partner legally but to stay together as a couple, or decide that the process has brought you to the end of your relationship.

This last possibility can be a painful turning point in any love affair. If this is your tentative decision, I'd encourage you to spend some time either in individual or couples counseling to help you figure out your best course of action, rather than making any precipitous decisions. Don't let the marriage movement undermine the solidity of your nonmarital relationship.

One of the necessary ingredients of this trial period involves a certain amount of time not talking about the decision with your partner, so you can be sure that you are making a decision that is right for you and you alone. Many of us find it hard to hold on to our own emotions in the face of our partner's strong feelings, and so, some time holding your thoughts to yourself can be very useful.

I also encourage my clients to spend some time together talking about these issues, away from the daily grind, to give each partner a chance to reflect and talk in a more relaxed setting. Sometimes that means taking a long walk in the woods or wherever is your favorite place; sometimes it requires a weekend away from jobs, children, and daily household demands. What counts is that you give yourself the setting you deserve to make such an important decision.

9. Make Your Final Decision

Once you have sat with your tentative evaluation for a while, you'll find you are ready to make a final decision.

If you and your partner have both concluded that you want to make a legal commitment, I encourage you to make an event of it—something that you can look back on in later years. My partner and I made our decision to live in the same city—after two years of managing a long-distance relationship— on a walk around historic Walden Pond, the site in Concord, Massachusetts, made famous by Henry Thoreau. We had several hours by ourselves to reflect on our past as well as the future, and the location provided a perfect backdrop for what turned out to be, thankfully, the right decision.

Your decision having been made, you can attend to practical matters. For some people that means meeting with an attorney to draw up and sign a premarital or preregistration agreement, or a cohabitation agreement if a legal partnership is not for you. (See Chapter 7 for the details of preparing a prenup.) For others, telling family and knowing they're on board is an important step. Some people decide to buy a new home as a shared investment in their future, and increasingly, partners are changing their names to create shared last names.

Completing the process of finding a lawyer and negotiating a premarital agreement can easily take two or three months or more. Make sure you give yourself enough time to take care of these tasks in a careful way, so that they don't feel like "assignments" that keep you from enjoying your life and your plans.

If you've decided not to enter a legal relationship now but are committed to staying together, your tasks are different. Because you won't have the legal protections of marriage or legal partnership, it's critically important that you do have the written documents that protect your relationship in other ways. Chapter 7 contains a section about written agreements for unmarried couples, and Chapter 9 addresses estate planning when you're not married or partnered. Make sure you review those sections carefully and take care of these important documents.

10. Plan Your Event, and Celebrate!

If you have decided to take the legal plunge and you want to mark the change in your relationship with an event, then once you are far enough along on the premarital tasks you will be able to start planning your wedding, partnership ceremony, or whatever you want to call it. Don't be overly burdened by thinking about how others celebrated their marriages, unless you have some family traditions that are important to you. Be your own couple with your own values and priorities. If you want to have a big party, go for it—but don't feel obligated to channel Martha Stewart or out do your older sister. I recently read a report on how many couples were still paying off the expenses of their wedding long after they had gotten divorced, and I'm sure you don't want to find yourselves in that position. What counts is that your celebration is meaningful for the two of you.

You may want your event to reflect the political aspects of your right to get married or legally partnered. I recently bumped into one of my clients on the subway commuting home with her partner. I had drafted their premarital agreement, and she proudly showed me their recently printed wedding invitation that included a quote from the California Supreme Court's ruling on same-sex marriage. They wanted every one of their guests to be aware of the cultural and legal significance of their personal commitment. I also gave a talk at a backyard wedding about the political history of the marriage equality movement, so that all of the guests would appreciate the meaning of the event. In the summer of 2008, many couples eschewed the traditional gift registry and instead "registered" with organizations fighting Prop. 8, the constitutional amendment banning same-sex marriage in California, encouraging their friends to make political donations in lieu of wedding presents.

The Question of Announcements

Ten years ago, I remarked that when *The New York Times* started running gay marriage announcements, we would know that our community had truly become part of the mainstream. Well, here we are. Many newspapers have slowly followed in the steps of the "newspaper of record," but you'll have to decide what degree of public recognition is better for the two of you.

Privacy is still an option, so don't feel obligated to tell your news to everyone in your town. Instead, an announcement mailed to your friends might be the preferred approach. Whatever you do, give it the dignity that this event truly deserves.

I'm certainly not an expert on wedding ceremonies, and there are plenty of books, planners, and opinionated mothers to help you make your plans. Just be sure you and your partner decide together on the wedding that reflects your own unique relationship. And by the way, congratulations on implementing your decision, whatever path you have chosen!

To Prenup or Not to Prenup

When California amended its domestic partnership law in 2005—and again when the California Supreme Court temporarily opened the door to legal marriage in 2008—my lawyer colleagues and I were deluged with calls from clients with questions about the new law. The number one question was "Do I need a prenup?" These days, couples in marriage equality and relationship recognition states are asking the same question as we all come to grips with the new legal possibilities.

As I had to explain to each caller, the answer depends on each couple's personal situation. But the short answer is that couples who want to accept all of the rules of marriage don't need a prenup. Conversely, any couple wanting to arrange their finances in a way that's different from the default rules should have a written agreement stating exactly what their financial arrangements and plans are.

What's a Premarital Agreement?

There are various names for the type of agreement we're considering here. The most common are "prenuptial agreement" (from the Latin word for marriage, *nubere*) or "premarital agreement." There are also postmarital agreements—agreements entered into after the parties are already married. When two people are entering a marriage equivalent domestic partnership or civil union, the agreement is called a preregistration agreement or pre-civil-union agreement. For the sake of simplicity, we'll use the term "premarital" or "prenuptial" interchangeably to refer to any agreement made prior to entering into a legal partnership or marriage relationship, and "prenup" for short. At the end of the chapter, we'll discuss nonmarital agreements for couples who are living together—typically called cohabitation agreements. Whatever the label, prenups have had a long and rather controversial history.

Background

In many other places it has long been relatively commonplace to select a "separate property" marriage, but premarital contracts only became acceptable in this country within the past century. Most European countries have long been open to premarital contracts and separate property arrangements. This may be because in those countries wealth often comes from inheritance and there is a strong bias toward keeping that wealth within the biological family. But in this country, only the richest couples bothered with such contracts until recently, so the rules were designed to protect the needs of the upper class—and in most instances, the richest of the rich.

To this day, some countries (including France and Germany) allow couples to select either a shared property or a separate property arrangement when they marry. There's no requirement that the couple hire lawyers to draft private contracts—the parties simply meet with a notary and fill out a separate property designation—and there seems to be little stigma if a spouse insists on keeping his or her assets separate.

In England and the United States, the laws of marriage have been far less flexible. Premarital agreements directing distribution of assets at one spouse's death have typically been honored, but agreements controlling the distribution of property in the event of a divorce have a far shakier history. In England, even nowadays, prenups are viewed as tending to encourage divorce and are sometimes disregarded altogether. That was also true in the United States until the first half of the 20th century, and some states prohibited married couples from making premarital agreements until as late as the 1960s.

Current Status

Even now, courts are suspicious of prenups, and every state regulates the procedures for forming a prenup as well as the circumstances under which the contract will be enforced. Why this tight control? It all goes back to the concept, described in Chapter 3, that marriage is a "status relationship." Legislatures and family law courts believe that the status imposes baseline obligations that should be inescapable, such as the obligation to support a spouse during a marriage. And other obligations should be subject to alteration by contract only in circumstances where the contracts are truly fair and where both partners really know what they are getting into—and what they are letting the other spouse out of.

Underlying the strict regulation of prenups is a belief that lovers rarely comprehend what the future might bring, and that the dewy-eyed optimism of romance can cause couples to discount what can happen if things go wrong. There isn't a gay exception to this tendency, and for this reason, the world of marital contracts is a wholly different universe than that of business contracts, where supposedly rational and equally empowered parties are free to take advantage of one another. Courts will rarely second guess an otherwise valid contract between business partners, but are much more inclined to do so when it comes to an agreement between spouses—even same-sex spouses.

Basic Legal Rules Governing Prenups

Given this background, it should not be a surprise that courts won't always enforce the terms of a premarital agreement—meaning, if one partner challenges the terms, the court may not support what the prenup says, but may order a different division of property or allocation of support. The usual reasons for nonenforcement are:

- The judge considers the prenup fundamentally unfair (the legal term is "unconscionable").

- The judge believes that one of the partners didn't have all the relevant information when the agreement was signed.

- The judge believes that one person unfairly pressured the other into signing the agreement.

- The judge believes that enforcing the contract would result in one spouse's going on the public dole.

Some states are more likely to enforce premarital agreements than others, and implementation of rules has been inconsistent. In an effort to impose some order to this system, many states have now adopted the Uniform Premarital Agreement Act (UPAA), which establishes minimum standards for prenups. The UPAA sets forth the following rules:

- A prenup is presumed to be invalid unless each partner has an independent lawyer review the agreement before it is signed.

- Each partner must make a full disclosure of all assets owned and debts owed before the agreement is signed, including separate as well as jointly owned assets.

- The agreement must not encourage divorce in any way.
- The agreement must meet basic standards of fairness.
- If the couple doesn't get married promptly after signing the agreement, it is void.

In California and some other states, a couple must wait seven days after completing their agreement before signing it, so that no one is handed an agreement on the day of the wedding. This isn't part of the Uniform Premarital Agreement Act, but it's a good practice, allowing both partners a fair opportunity to reflect on what they have agreed to before they sign.

Postmarital Agreements

The rules for a *post*marital agreement are even tougher, because in most states, spouses have a fiduciary duty to look after the other's best interest—which makes it hard for either spouse to justify taking away any substantial marital rights. In some places, any postmarital agreement that disadvantages one party is presumed to be invalid and the advantaged party has to prove the legitimacy of the agreement. And it's not yet clear in most states whether a postmarital agreement can include a waiver of spousal support (alimony). In other words, you can make tough demands on a prospective spouse, but once you get married your negotiation options are severely limited.

Thus, you should assume that the way to make it most likely that your agreement will stand up later is for each partner to fully disclose all assets and debts, for each partner to have an independent lawyer review the document (especially if there is any waiver of spousal support), and for each partner to have at least a week to review the final draft of the agreement before signing it. Those are just the minimum requirements. Even if all these rules are followed to a "t," a waiver of spousal support—a very common provision, especially in same-sex prenups—can be ignored by a judge if the judge concludes that enforcing it would land someone on welfare or otherwise be seriously unfair.

How These Rules Help Both Parties

Not all states have adopted the UPAA, and some have adopted modified versions. And, the rules in some states allow parties to sign agreements that fall below these standards. I've worked on more than a hundred prenups over the past 15 years, and I've come to the conclusion that these fundamental rules are important and should be followed, even where state law doesn't impose them as requirements. Here's why:

- It's essential that each partner spend some time alone with a lawyer whose only loyalty is to that partner, so that each spouse can ask difficult questions and explore fears and concerns in complete confidentiality.

- It doesn't make sense to enter into a prenup unless you really know each other's true financial status. It's not fair for your partner to ask you to give up the right to spousal support if you don't know how much your partner earns or what other resources are available. The same applies to savings or debts—no one can negotiate fairly without the basic facts.

- The agreement must be made fair, taking into account all the potential worst-case scenarios, such as unemployment or disability.

- Given the potential long-term consequences of an agreement, having a week to think about it before signing is just plain sensible.

Just because prenups are disfavored by some judges doesn't mean that you shouldn't be able to rely on your agreement if it's done right. There's no such thing as an "ironclad" prenup, but so long as you abide by all the rules and create an agreement that a judge will be able to see was truly fair when entered into, it's very likely that both of you will honor the agreement—thus avoiding any future litigation. And, if one party does decide to try to challenge it, chances are quite good that the agreement will be upheld.

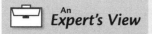

An Expert's View   Mediating Your Prenup

Here's the deal. If you and your partner do nothing in terms of marrying or registering and you live together, one set of rules applies to you whether you know them or not. If you register as domestic partners or marry, a different set of rules applies to you, whether you know them or not. And if you're going to move in together, register, or get married, you might as well make your own rules, or at the very least understand the general rules that apply to you in the absence of an agreement.

The most important suggestion I offer is to start early, so that you have the luxury of time to work things out with each other. Negotiating an agreement the week before a wedding or commitment ceremony is almost always excruciating.

In many instances, mediation or a collaborative process is the best way to handle discussions like this, because you're both present and there is less room for miscommunication. I've seen too many couples traumatized because one of them went to a lawyer who simply presented the other with a proposed agreement. If you work with a mediator or in a collaborative process, you will discuss questions such as: Where do you want to live? How will you handle the day-to-day finances of your lives? Do you have, or do you want, children? Do you want to pool everything, or only some things, or nothing? What are your thoughts about retirement? You will discuss all the categories of assets and debts and then decide what's "mine," what's "yours," and what's "ours."

Your mediator (or collaborative attorneys) will help you think about how your ideas today might play out over the long term. The end result is your own agreement, which the two of you have created to fit your particular situation.

Martina Reaves has been a full-time mediator in Berkeley, California, since 1986 and has mediated family, partnership, and neighbor disputes ever since, including many same-sex dissolutions.

Essential Ingredients of a Prenup

There are certain elements that are common to nearly every premarital agreement. These include:

- introductory paragraphs that state the couple's names, addresses, employment status, and plans for marriage, as well as identifying each person's lawyer
- a section defining key legal terms used in the agreement
- substantive paragraphs that state the couple's agreements, describing how they will treat the basic elements of marital law (see "What You Can Include in a Prenup," below)
- "boilerplate" or standard paragraphs about things like what state's laws govern the agreement, how the agreement will be interpreted if it's ambiguous, or a commitment to try mediation if there are conflicts, and
- signatures, notary statement, and attorney acknowledgments.

In addition, every prenup must include financial disclosure forms that are attached as exhibits, generally in the form of lists that detail each partner's assets and debts, as well as any property or debts belonging to both partners jointly. You don't need to list every item of furniture you own, but any major assets or valuable belongings need to be included in the disclosures.

What You Can Include in a Prenup

You can deal with a lot of issues in a prenup. There may be some areas where you're willing to accept your state's laws, and you don't have to address those; if you don't address a particular issue, your state's law will apply. Here's a list of the issues that you should consider covering in your agreement.

How you will deal with assets or property you each had before marriage. In most states, assets and property owned before marriage are considered the separate property of the owner spouse. However, some states allow for distribution of all assets at divorce, even those owned prior to marriage. And even in states that don't, it's possible to change the character of the asset by contributing marital funds to it, such as using marital income to pay the mortgage on a premarital house. Your prenup can provide that regardless of how you treat it and what funds you contribute during marriage, assets owned by either partner prior to marriage will remain the separate property of the original owner.

For those of you that lived together before you decided to legally partner or marry, this can raise tricky questions. One of you might want to apply the rules of marriage retroactively and have the agreement say that even separate property purchased during the premarital relationship is jointly owned. The other partner may want to share only the postregistration or postmarital assets. This can be hard to resolve if you really see things differently.

Whether you want to reimburse each other for contributions made to the other person's separate property, or vice versa. Let's say one of you owns a rental property that you identify as that person's separate property, and you expect to contribute marital assets—for example, earned income—to the upkeep of the rental property. You may have already agreed that the property will remain separately owned despite the contributions, but you also need to decide whether the contributions must be returned to the marital pot if the property is sold or if you divorce. You must make the same decision for contributions of one person's separate property assets to a marital asset (as when you put your separate savings into a new roof for your jointly owned house).

How you will deal with income earned during marriage. Your agreement can state whether income earned by each spouse is considered marital property or the separate property of the spouse who earned it. Once the money is spent, it isn't there to fight over, so these provisions basically cover any savings that you accrue during the marriage from either partner's earned income. "Earnings" include things like stock options. Remember, in some states, having the money in an account in just the name of the partner who earned it doesn't protect it from being divided in the divorce, so it's best to address the issue explicitly in your agreement.

How you will deal with property acquired during marriage. You can decide whether you want to treat property you buy during marriage as jointly owned or whether you want to rely on how the property is titled, or who paid for it, to determine ownership. This includes real estate as well as valuable personal property like automobiles, jewelry, and art. You can treat different categories of property differently if you wish—for example, sharing all furniture and other items you buy for the home but designating real property as owned according to who's on the title.

How you'll deal with a business, a professional practice, or intellectual property like books, music, or artwork. If either of you is an entrepreneur, professional, or creative artist, your agreement should state how you'll deal with creative works as well as royalty or licensing income. Oftentimes you'll come into the marriage already owning such an asset, which then grows in value due to your postmarital efforts. Rather than having to deal with an asset that is part shared and part separate, it is often prudent to allocate it completely to the person who created it.

Whether and how you'll share retirement benefits. Retirement benefits earned through employee benefit plans before marriage belong to the person who earned them, and most people confirm this in their prenup. Keeping the same agreement about benefits earned during marriage is the simplest way to deal with retirement benefits for same-sex partners, but most retirement benefits are governed by federal law and so dividing them up is now possible. This is often the most fair way, especially if one of you is has significantly higher income or much greater savings. If one of you has a job that offers a cushy benefit program and the other one is self-employed, not sharing the retirement benefits can result in the lower-earning partner losing out in a way you might not intend. You'll need advice from your attorney and tax adviser about the best way to handle this in your particular situation so that you can address it in your prenup.

You can also address the issue of continued health insurance coverage—and a prenup can really help in this area. Same-sex spouses are now eligible for COBRA continuation coverage after a spouse loses a job or following a divorce. Alternatively, if the employee spouse is the higher earner and the other spouse doesn't have available insurance, your prenup can provide for the employee spouse to pay for the other spouse's insurance for a certain period of time—or until the other spouse is able to get insurance of his or her own—whether or not the insurance is no longer available through the employee spouse's job.

How you'll treat inheritances and gifts. It's very likely that one or both of you will receive gifts from others during your marriage, or even an inheritance.

Your agreement can state whether gifts given to one partner are that partner's separate property (as the law says) or are marital property. Many prenups also provide that gifts spouses give to each other become the separate property of the person receiving them. You can also make commitments about what you intend to bequeath to each other at death, but you must then follow up by putting the bequests into a will or trust document.

How you'll deal with debts. Like premarital property, premarital debts are usually considered the obligation of the person who incurred them—but in some states, marital income can be tapped to pay premarital debts. Therefore, your agreement should spell out your plan about such debts, as well as how you'll deal with debts incurred during your marriage. It's difficult to prevent a creditor from coming after both of you, but you can provide that if one of you is stuck paying the other's debts, at least that person will be reimbursed if there are funds available.

Whether you can claim alimony. If you don't include anything in your agreement about alimony (also called spousal support or maintenance in some states, and partner support for civil union partners and domestic partners), your state's laws will govern support in the event of a divorce. You can use your agreement to waive support entirely, set out a formula for how support will be calculated, or determine a set amount that will be paid in one lump sum. In many agreements, the partners agree that support will only be paid if the difference between the partners' incomes reaches a certain percentage level, or if one of the partners loses a job, has an income reduction of a certain percentage, or has assets that are less than a designated value.

How you'll deal with taxes. Your agreement can indicate whether you will file jointly, separately, or whichever way is more beneficial at the time.

What a Prenup Can't Do

There also are some things that you cannot do with a prenup.

You can't use a prenup to establish parentage. Your child is a separate human being and two adults cannot enter into a contract that defines a third person's legal status or rights. So you can't establish parentage (or nonparentage) by agreement—you must use an adoption or another legal parentage proceeding.

You can't use a prenup to set child custody or support. Whether you already have children when you marry or they come into your life afterwards, you can't use your prenup to regulate anything about how you'll share custody or arrange financial support if you divorce. Child custody decisions depend on the best interests of the child at the time, and child support is set by state guidelines. You can enter into agreements about financial support at the time of a divorce, but you can't do it in advance.

You can't use a prenup to opt out of divorce court. While you can use a prenup to determine how you'll divide your assets if you divorce, you cannot waive the requirements of going through a court divorce. This doesn't mean you have to actually show up in court or argue in front of a judge—if you resolve all the issues in your divorce by agreement, you can usually get a divorce based on paperwork alone. You can use your prenup to commit to trying mediation first to resolve any dispute.

You are limited in how much you can insulate each other from financial obligations. Remember, your creditors won't be signing your premarital agreement, so you may not be able to protect each other from all debts, even if you call them separate. In some states, a valid premarital agreement that is followed by a strict segregation of finances can offer fairly strong protection against some creditor's claims, but not all of them, and that's not the case everywhere. The only way to ensure you won't be sued for a partner's debts is to not get married or partnered, keep all your assets separate, don't co-own a house, and don't apply for any joint credit cards or loans.

You may not be able to give up inheritance rights. In some states, you're not allowed to give up the share of a spouse's estate to which you're entitled by law (see Chapter 9 for more about these "statutory" or "forced" shares). And if you want to waive your right to receive death benefits under your spouse's retirement plan, you may have to sign a specific waiver form with the administrator of the retirement plan after your marriage.

You can't make agreements about personal behavior. As much as you would like to do so, you can't condition the financial terms of your prenup on personal agreements about monogamy or other elements of your intimate relationship. Just as a divorce will be handled on a no-fault basis, your agreement also cannot allocate finances or property based upon a finding of fault.

The Process of Creating a Prenup

With this history and these rules as a backdrop, you can see why you will have a lot to learn and a lot of decisions to make.

Knowing the Rules and How They Apply to You

Your first task is to learn about marital law in your state. To learn the general rules, try any or all of the following sources:

- **Websites.** www.findlaw.com has a useful Marriage and Family Law Center that lists marriage (and prenuptial agreement) rules for each state, at http://family.findlaw.com/marriage/marriage-laws/state-marriage-laws.html. Ironically, many of the sites with the most information about marriage are the ones about divorce—because that's the point at which marital law becomes relevant to most of us. Some good sites are www.divorceinfo.com, www.nolo.com, and www.divorcenet.com.

- **Books.** Probably the best place to start is with *Prenuptial Agreements: How to Write a Fair & Lasting Contract*, by Katherine E. Stoner and Shae Irving (Nolo), which includes detailed information about state laws as well as requirements for prenuptial agreements. (There's a companion eGuide for California domestic partners.) And again, you'll find useful information in books about divorce, including *Nolo's Essential Guide to Divorce*, by Emily Doskow.

- **Lawyers.** There's no substitute for advice from a lawyer about your state's laws and how they apply to your specific situation. You may want to see a lawyer together to get this education, or you may each want to consult a separate attorney. See "Orchestrating the Agreement Process," below, for details about these choices. Then consider the issues you want to address in your prenup, and see whether you understand what the law would do.

A Bit More About Lawyers

If either of you own a business or are involved in a business or property that is co-owned with others, sorting through the applicable laws will be a bit more complex. The same is true if either of you has stock options, significant prerelationship debt, or thorny tax problems. Sometimes an estate planning lawyer can help you in the analysis, but in most cases, you'll be better served by an experienced family law attorney—and specifically, an attorney experienced in LGBT family law. Many mainstream family lawyers aren't aware of the tax and other nonrecognition problems that same-sex couples face. You can work with someone who has experience helping unmarried opposite-sex couples, but it's essential that your lawyer has experience with couples whose marriages are not federally recognized.

Understanding the legal rules allows you to decide what is right for you. Here are some examples of how understanding the law can help your process.

In the first example the rules are simple: In the absence of a prenup, for example, if one spouse saves $100,000 from earned income during the marriage and the other incurs $20,000 in credit card debt for household expenses during the marriage, and then they divorce, most likely the spender will be entitled to $50,000 of the other's savings and they will each be on the hook for half of the credit card debt. (This would definitely be the case in California, Nevada, and Washington, the community property states, and would be very likely in other states that favor an equal distribution.) In other words, they each will walk away with $40,000—half of the $80,000 left over after they withdraw all the assets ($100,000) and pay off the total debt ($20,000).

This couple can see clearly what the law would do, and needs to decide only whether that's the outcome they would want, or whether they want to provide in their prenup for a different outcome.

Here's an example of where applying marital rules can be quite complex. A client of mine bought a house with her girlfriend before they registered as domestic partners. She put in $100,000 of her inherited money for the down payment and they took title as joint tenants (in equal shares). After they registered my client put in another $75,000 for renovations using the rest of her inheritance, while her partner paid about two-thirds of the mortgage out of earned income. In this example, nonmarital law applies to the preregistration purchase (with uncertain results as far as whether my client gets her down payment back), while marital law allows reimbursement of the inherited funds but not the earned income spent on the house during the marriage.

In this case, it wasn't clear what would happen if the partners broke up and couldn't agree on how to divide the value of the house, and when they did, their case went to court. For my client and her partner, a prenup would have allowed them to make their own decisions about what a fair outcome would be, and avoid the uncertainty of a court process.

Another area frequently addressed in prenups is alimony. Predicting likely outcomes in this area is challenging, in part because the rules in most states are vague, and also because it is impossible to know what each partner's income and financial needs will be in the future. If the couple has children who are still minors at the time of a divorce, child support obligations take precedence, and these burdens can dramatically alter what each spouse is entitled to receive as alimony. Again, it is exactly this uncertainty that leads many couples to want to establish their own plans.

Most people need to look at several different possible scenarios that are realistic for them, in order to decide what they want to do. I ask clients to imagine that one partner gets a promotion, or loses a job and can't find an equally good-paying one for five years, or fails to get an expected inheritance just when planning to retire. Then, under each scenario, we try to imagine what the earnings and expenses are likely to be.

Note: If there's any chance you'll be relocating to a state that doesn't recognize your marriage, your agreement should state that it will still be enforceable as a private contract.

Orchestrating the Agreement Process

Once you've completed your legal education and talked about what you want, the practical steps that you'll need to take are the same for most couples, following a pattern roughly in this order, though the various stages may overlap to some degree.

STEP 1. Establish Relationships With Lawyers

There are several different ways of working with lawyers to negotiate an agreement. If your financial situation is complex or if it's important to you to discuss as a couple what you want your agreement to say, you may decide to meet jointly with a lawyer at the outset. That lawyer will not represent either person, but will work with both of you together to explain the legal rules and how those rules might apply to you. That lawyer can draft an agreement on behalf of both parties, much as a mediator counselor would do. If that's the way you go, each person then should hire an independent lawyer to review and approve the agreement. This means there will be three lawyers involved in preparing your agreement.

If you don't choose to meet with a lawyer together, you'll each hire an attorney and one partner's lawyer will prepare the initial draft of the agreement based on what that partner conveys about the agreements reached. The second partner will then review it with an attorney as well.

Joint Representation Is Not Recommended

You may talk to lawyers who will offer to do the agreement on behalf of both of you without either partner having it independently reviewed by another lawyer, but my advice is not to do that. Even if your state laws don't expressly require separate representation, there's a good chance the agreement will be thrown out if you don't have separate counsel. This is not an area where you want to skimp on fees; you'll actually be wasting your money on an agreement that may not be worth anything at all.

Make sure that your lawyer has experience in LGBT family law. You can get referrals from your local LGBT center or LGBT organizations, from friends who've already done prenups, or from lawyer directories. Make sure you talk to the prospective lawyer and that you feel comfortable that he or she is a good fit. Also make sure you get a clear agreement about fees and that the lawyer is available to do the work in time for your planned ceremony, if you're having one.

STEP 2. Start Talking With Each Other About the Issues You Want the Agreement to Cover

Having learned something about the rules and how marital law would apply to you, your next task is to figure out the ways you may want to deviate from the rules. This involves each of you assessing your own current financial situation and trying to anticipate the future and decide whether you can afford to renounce marital benefits—or whether you can afford to adopt marital rules.

If you're the lower-income or lower-asset partner, do you have sufficient pension or Social Security income to provide for your own retirement? If you are currently living in a house that is owned solely by your partner, do you own property of your own that you could move into in the event of your partner's sudden death? Are you each putting away enough savings? If you are the richer partner, how do you feel about sharing some of your wealth with your partner, either during the relationship or in the event you divorce? Are you willing to be "burdened" by the marital rules or do you want to ask that your partner give up some or all of those benefits?

Creating an agreement also involves deciding how you are going to handle money while you are together. If you are merging your finances, then you are (at least legally) pooling your financial decision making and sharing your risks. You'll make spending (and saving) decisions together as a couple. By contrast, if you agree from the outset that you are going to lead separate financial lives, you will sink or swim independently as a result of your own private decisions. As a couple you will surely engage in certain joint financial endeavors, such as buying a house or raising children, and oftentimes the line between your shared and separate dimensions will be difficult to define.

Over time, you are likely to merge your finances to an increasing degree, and this likelihood needs to be integrated into your agreement as well.

If your incomes and assets are relatively similar, then you are lucky in a way, as you'll make decisions mostly on a practical basis, looking at what will be most advantageous to both of you. But if one of you has a significantly higher income, more savings, a separately owned house, or a likely inheritance, then this discussion may trigger some sticky relationship questions, particularly around the dilemma of need and entitlement. Many of my clients have been self-supporting for a long time, and they aren't entirely comfortable with the notion of being supported by someone else. Learning that California law may entitle them to some degree of support, even after a breakup, can raise expectations and reorient their thinking. Not surprisingly, such raised expectations can trigger some awkward discussions, especially if their partner does not share this way of thinking.

If you find yourself in real conflict about any issue, be prepared to spend a significant period of time talking, reflecting on your reactions, and reevaluating your goals and concerns. If the dynamic really begins to unravel it might be helpful to meet with a counselor or spiritual adviser. If the problems are more legal in nature, you might want to meet with the lawyer or lawyers who are going to write up the agreement to help sort out your thoughts and concerns.

Some couples find it helpful to work through a draft of their agreement themselves, using the book *Prenuptial Agreements: How to Write a Fair & Lasting Contract*, by Katherine Stoner and Shae Irving (Nolo). This can nudge you to focus on issues you otherwise might wish to avoid and also enable you to provide a draft to your lawyer to use as the basis for the formal agreement.

What's Fair?

Most people negotiating a prenup would say that their goal is to reach an agreement that is fair to both parties. One of the principles I stress is that this is a mutual caretaking process, not just a self-protective undertaking. I believe that if you are entering into a loving marriage or partnership, one of your priorities should be to take care of each other even if your relationship ultimately does not work out. If you can fully integrate this caretaking approach into your discussions and be motivated more by that than by a desire to look out for your own interests, it's more likely that the process will go smoothly and result in a fair agreement.

But what does it mean to be fair? This is one of the most intractable dimensions of this process, because there are so many different views of fairness. You might be focusing on where you each stood before your relationship began, and whether either of you helped the other one in ways that could create some sort of obligation, such as if one of you quit work to be a parent or moved across the country to enable a partner to take a new job. Or you may feel that because you registered solely to take advantage of insurance benefits, neither partner's economic condition should change at all. One partner may believe that "fair" in a marriage means that everything is shared equally, regardless of who earned what, while the other may believe each person is responsible for his or her own financial well-being.

In short, fair means different things to different people, and it's crucial that you spend time talking about its meaning for you. (And remember, you can't structure your agreement to have different outcomes depending on the reasons you break up or on whether a partner has an affair. Sorry, but the judge doesn't want to get dragged into your drama!)

Don't forget that this agreement is a contract that you can always change in the future. If your circumstances change—you decide to raise children, or one or both of you makes a career change—you can always amend your agreement, as long as you do it in writing with the same formalities you used for the original agreement.

STEP 3. Explore Tax Issues

Find out whether you are likely to face any tax problems as a result of the choices you want to make. Meet with a tax accountant or attorney who is familiar with the tax concerns of same-sex couples and find out how tax rules affect your situation.

Even though our legal marriages are recognized by the federal government, taxes are a topic of vital importance for same-sex couples. Even partners who would otherwise be comfortable sharing their assets and debts under marital law—especially those with significant assets—may find that a prenup benefits them.

EXAMPLE: If one partner earns $1,000,000 a year after taxes and manages to save half that amount, under the law of many states, his domestic partner would be entitled to $250,000 at divorce—his half of the $500,000 in marital property earned by the high earner. In community property states, the nonearner is viewed as having "received" half of that money as soon as it is earned. In noncommunity-property states, the partner wouldn't get any of that money unless it's transferred during the marriage as a gift or he gets it in a divorce. In either case, if you multiply this amount by ten or 15 years, quite a pot of gold will have been transferred. At the point that the money does change hands, regardless of the reason, the transfer previously could have been seen as a taxable event under federal tax law and therefore subject to additional income tax—even though the wealthy partner already paid taxes on the income before saving it. Now, just as for an opposite-sex married couple, they would be protected from being retaxed because all marital transfers are tax free.

In the past, a prenup could have helped this couple avoid these tax burdens by providing that the earner would keep all his money to himself, and then, only if he died or they broke up would he transfer some percentage to his boyfriend. The hope was that by the time one of those events happened, the federal government would have recognized gay marriages or other circumstances might have changed—for example, perhaps the lower-earning partner would himself be so rich that he could decline the transfer.

However, in 2010, the IRS issued rulings that suggest the agency won't be double-taxing these earnings but instead will acknowledge the state-mandated rules of community property for same-sex couples in California and Washington. Same-sex married couples no longer have to worry about this problem, but if you're in a civil union or domestic partnership, you will.

STEP 4. Initiate the Agreement Drafting Process

If you're going to use two attorneys rather than relying on a joint attorney to do the drafting, you'll need to decide which lawyer is going to be the drafting attorney and who is going to review the document. Tell the lawyers which items are agreed on and which are still unresolved. Instruct the drafting lawyer to prepare the first draft of the agreement, which that lawyer's client will then review and approve to share with the other partner and the other lawyer.

You will then need to talk through any remaining issues with your partner, communicate your decisions to the lawyers, and the two lawyers will finalize the language of the contract. Sometimes, the two of you need to do the emotional work that is necessary to bridge any gaps or confusions; other times, the issues are more appropriately left to the lawyers to resolve. Sometimes, the two lawyers will convene a collaborative meeting with all four of you present to discuss any difficult issues in a safe environment. In some situations, you may be able to resolve everything in one meeting, though sometimes, a follow-up meeting or a phone call or two will be necessary.

STEP 5. Compile Asset and Debt Lists

Each of you must provide your attorney with detailed lists of your assets and debts and any joint assets and debts, listing real estate, bank and investment accounts, valuable personal property, and all of your credit card and other debts. Estimate the value of each asset and identify any loans encumbering assets. Determine what you are likely to earn this year and figure out what other assets you have or have a share in, such as family assets or investments. Disclose all of this information to your partner and the lawyers.

STEP 6. Negotiate Final Terms

If there's anything left over from Step 4, you must conclude all of your negotiations and settle all the details so that the attorneys can complete a final draft of the agreement for the two of you to review and sign.

STEP 7. Take Care of the Details and Formalities

Once both of you and both lawyers approve the agreement, you can finalize your asset and debt lists with current balances and attach them to the document. Then the lawyers add the notarization form and attorney certification and compile the document, and send a final version to you and your partner. In some states, you must wait a week after you receive the final version of the agreement before you sign it. Some lawyers like to have both partners come to their office for signing, to be sure that it gets signed and notarized properly. Both lawyers also sign the agreement, acknowledging that they have reviewed it. You should do all of this with two different printouts of the agreement, so that you end up with two originals. Each of you should keep one of the originals, and each lawyer should retain a complete photocopy.

STEP 8. Follow Up

In some instances, there are further tasks to be done, such as amending your will or trust documents, changing the deed on a property, or signing a release of retirement fund assets. Don't forget to complete these tasks, or the enforceability of your agreement may be affected.

If you don't marry or register soon after you sign the agreement, it will become invalid. If you decide not to get married and you want an agreement that will structure your financial affairs as an unmarried/unregistered couple, then you need a cohabitation agreement, which is a very different sort of animal. A lawyer can convert the terms of your premarital agreement into a cohabitation agreement, but it's important that you do that, rather than relying on an agreement prepared in contemplation of a marriage or registration that didn't happen. See "Making Agreements If You Choose to Remain Unmarried," below.

If anything changes dramatically in your lives in the future, like you move to another state, sell your house, or bring children into your lives, you should contact your attorneys and discuss whether you need to revise the agreement to reflect these changes.

If you should ever divorce, it will be the rules of the state you live in then that govern your divorce, not the state you lived in when you married or registered. For that reason, if you've moved from the state you live in when you sign your agreement, you should have your agreement reviewed by a local attorney after you move, to be sure that it meets the standards of your new state. If you've done it right this shouldn't be a real problem, unless you've moved to a state that doesn't recognize your partnership or marriage at all. In that situation, you may need to recraft the agreement as a nonmarital agreement—but it still can contain the same substantive terms.

Previous Agreements

Many couples who have been living together for some time already have oral or written co-ownership agreements or asset sharing agreements (sometimes called cohabitation agreements). Unfortunately, those agreements probably won't be valid once those couples get registered or married. Most likely, your cohabitation agreement did not explicitly waive marital rights, and you probably didn't meet the procedural requirements described in "Basic Legal Rules Governing Prenups," above. You can keep the substantive provisions of your agreement, but you will have to go through all the steps of the premarital agreement process in order for your new agreement to be valid as you head into your marriage or other legal relationship.

The Emotional Dimensions

As tricky as the legal questions may appear, they are actually the easy part of the process for most couples. The much harder piece is dealing with the emotional dimensions. Why is it so difficult? Very few of us believe we will ever divorce, and we certainly don't think we will be the one who is left. We also find it hard to comprehend that we may become disabled, unemployed, or broke, especially when we're younger. A pollster once asked a set of recently married couples how many marriages end in divorce and they correctly answered "half." But when the same newlyweds were asked the chance that their marriage would end in divorce, they all responded "zero." And yet, it's impossible to negotiate a premarital agreement without facing the possibility of divorce; in fact, it's the main point of preparing a prenup.

Despite my constant exhortations, many of my clients resist opening up these discussions. It's my sense that, if asked, they would say that their hesitance is because they believe one or both of two things:

- Simply speaking the possibility of a bad outcome (like divorce or death) will make it more likely to occur.

- Working out in advance how you'll deal with possible future events reflects a lack of trust that your partner will "do the right thing" when the time comes.

Instead, what I've observed is that once the discussion commences, the landmines turn out to be located in an entirely different place: The exposure of each partner's sense of what is fair and generous and, often, the revelation of some previously hidden negative feelings about the relationship or the other partner. Painful as it can be at first, if properly managed, these revelations can strengthen a relationship and bring couples closer together in very powerful ways. The metaphor I use to explain this to my clients is this: Until you know where the riverbank of each partner's "edge" really is, you can't build a bridge to connect the two sides of the chasm.

Quite frequently, dealing with these difficult issues openly brings couples closer and leads to a mutually satisfactory resolution. For example, I recently drafted a prenuptial agreement for a moderately successful woman who was taking a few years off to be the primary parent for the couple's two young children. She asked her partner for an agreement calling for a few years of retirement fund contributions to make up for what she would have otherwise saved, and a few years of support to get back on her feet should they break up after she'd been on the mommy track for a while. The discussions were delicate at times and the higher-earning girlfriend at first did not see why she should ever be put in what she perceived as a "husband" role. But the two of them continued talking about the reasons for creating and managing mutual dependence in support of their having the family life they wanted together. And within just a few weeks, they had worked it out and signed the agreement. Both of them felt their relationship was stronger and healthier as a result.

The Lessons of Experience

Here are some of the lessons I've learned in more than two decades of counseling couples as they consider the type of commitments they want to make.

You can't make a meaningful agreement unless you can realistically envision breaking up or having your partner die. These are not comforting thoughts but you have to approach them as real-life possibilities and not abstract concepts. You must be willing to consider what your life will be like if your partner rejects you, or if you find yourself needing to leave the relationship. You have to be able to imagine what your life will be like if your partner dies while you are still together, either sooner or later, and what your partner's life will be like without you there.

Personally, I'm a worst-case scenario person. I find it oddly comforting to think through possible tragic events and imagine how I will recover from them, both emotionally and financially. I dive into the darkest emotional corners and conjure up how I will emerge back into the light, and by taking that painful mental excursion, I become aware of what I will need to do to be equipped for this recovery. The process also helps me recognize that I will recover from even the most painful circumstances, which makes it much less frightening to consider that they might happen.

You must contemplate the possibility of other unwanted changes in your life. These include disability, unexpected events that destroy the prospect of an inheritance you were expecting, or a severe decrease in your pension plan as a result of misconduct by the administrator or an imploding economy. You have to take seriously the possibility that you could lose your job and not be able to find another one, or that your financial investments could tank completely, and accept that you might become economically dependent. Only by envisioning these events can you think strategically about how you are going to take care of yourself—and how the two of you are going to take care of each other—in the long run.

You have to acknowledge, and accept, how hard it might be to divide your shared assets with your partner if you are the wounded party in a breakup. Many, many people feel fine about taking care of a partner while the relationship is intact and can even imagine splitting up assets if the relationship ends by mutual agreement. But those same people often balk when they think about sharing with a partner who has betrayed them sexually or left them precipitously for reasons they don't understand. You can't use your prenup to plan just for this—the terms you agree to must apply regardless of the reason for the separation. This means you must figure out how to accept that the terms you are agreeing to in a time of mutual care and generosity could be hard for you to swallow later.

You must be prepared to deal with emotional issues. We all walk around with a ton of psychological baggage, and entering into the conversations that are required to create a prenup can trigger an array of anxieties and concerns. You might have an unexpressed desire to be taken care of regardless of your net worth, or conversely, a deep fear of being "on the hook" for anyone else's care. In ways that are rarely acknowledged, the marriage movement itself has inspired a new way of looking at our relationships. This has been especially true for economically dependent partners who may now be asking "Why shouldn't I have the same protections and benefits that my straight sisters have?" "Why shouldn't I have a right to half of the house, the savings account, and the future income of my high-earning same-sex husband?" On the other side, many of my higher-earning clients find themselves resentful of the caretaking assumptions imposed on them by the marital system. Many of the gay and lesbian "husbands" have never thought of themselves in this role, and articulating such expectations can seriously disrupt the equilibrium of a relationship. Be ready to have these conversations, even if they challenge you emotionally in ways you might not have expected. (See "Acknowledging the Risks of the Process," below.)

You must be willing to talk about finances. Talking about money is enormously challenging for most of us, even more than most other subjects (even parenting and sex). The topic raises questions about earning, managing, saving, and spending—as well as questions about values and self-worth—in ways that are convoluted and complex. For almost everyone, thinking and talking about money can stir up embarrassment, anxiety, and resentments. Many of us have opinions that are subtle, highly personal, and not easily explained, even to a loved one. But you'll never complete your prenup if you're not willing to have a meaningful conversation about these topics.

You must be prepared to show up for a true negotiation. To some people, the notion of sitting in a stuffy room arguing over the financial provisions of the divorce you don't ever expect to have is unbearable. If there is an inequality between partners with regard to negotiation skills or familiarity with legal and financial matters—as is often the case in financially unequal couples— then each step of the process, from hiring the lawyer to reading the drafts to talking about one's priorities, can be difficult. And if there are other—or related—relationship problems looming in the background, the negotiations can be seriously stressful. Nonetheless, both of you must take a deep breath and commit to the process—that's the only way it will be successful.

You must be willing to abandon your plans if the process isn't working out. In some instances it is simply too early to be negotiating a prenup. You may find that while your financial agreements have been working out just fine until now, you're not able to agree on what you would do in the context of marital rules, and you may end up deciding to put off marriage for a time, or not to marry at all. This doesn't mean that your relationship has to end, by any means. (See "Making Agreements If You Choose to Remain Unmarried," below.) It just means you would be wise to delay the legal commitment.

Acknowledging the Risks of the Process

One of the things I always say to clients when they come in to talk about doing a prenup is that while most people find that the process of negotiating a prenup brings them closer and strengthens the relationship, it's also possible the process itself will expose or even create very difficult rifts in their relationship. This can be true for both newly minted couples and those who have been together for a significant time.

Here's an example. Some years ago, I was helping a client, Arthur, negotiate a preregistration agreement. He was living nearly rent free in a house owned by his partner in the Castro district of San Francisco. Arthur's partner wanted

Arthur to give up any claims over the house and for any postseparation support, and when Arthur first walked into my office he was ready to agree because he was grateful to his partner for the current living arrangement.

I explained to Arthur that while the proposal was beneficial to him in the short term it could be disastrous in the long run. He would be giving up the chance to buy in as a part owner of the house now, as well as the possibility of buying his own place using the down payment and low interest rate assistance his public-sector employer provided. If he failed to invest in property in one of these ways and he and his partner broke up after 20 years, Arthur could be homeless at age 65—not an attractive prospect in a town with very high housing costs.

Arthur went back and told his partner that he wanted to "buy in" to the house, and proposed a way to make that happen. The boyfriend reacted badly, and in the course of the next two months all sorts of deeper issues of gratitude, dependency, and blame bubbled up, in turn raising issues about their divergent class origins and family backgrounds. These underlying issues were always there, but Arthur and his partner had successfully avoided talking about them in the past.

In the end, they parted ways, and while I would like to think that this was a pot ready to boil over and that my advice merely released the "cover" off their avoidance tendencies, I'm not sure. Had they not considered marriage, maybe they would have stayed together a few more years, relaxed into a closer and more financially balanced relationship, realized they needed some kind of safety-net housing plan for each of them, and entered into a fair agreement. But because the issues arose before their relationship had "seasoned" a bit longer, the process led to an unraveling of their partnership.

At the same time, this is a situation that could have easily been negotiated with very little actual financial impact on the wealthier partner, but his attachment to his own version of what generosity was and his assessment of Arthur as greedy didn't allow for a meaningful discussion of how to take care of the vulnerable partner.

These things do happen. But I've helped facilitate nearly 150 such agreements just in the past ten years, and in all but a very few of them the partners have worked through their issues and decided how to customize their arrangements. And from the conversations I've had with these clients after they have completed the process, they universally tell me that the clarification and resolution that emerged from these discussions has been healthy for their relationships.

Making Agreements If You Choose to Remain Unmarried

It's possible that you will decide not to marry or register right now, either because you're pretty sure it's not a good idea for you or because you don't feel it's quite time yet. If that's the case, you can still enter into written agreements that will govern your financial life together and even make provisions for what will happen if you separate. Such an agreement might be called a "cohabitation agreement" or a "living together agreement."

Just as you can with a premarital agreement, you can use a cohabitation agreement to establish your shares of ownership in a house or other property, make arrangements about how you will or won't share your income, and even provide for support in the event of a breakup. If you don't do this, as an unmarried partner generally you have no rights to anything titled in your partner's name, and vice versa. If you own or owe anything jointly the legal system will presume that you own or owe it equally. If you break up at any point in the future, you each will walk away with whatever is all yours and 50% of anything that is shared, and neither of you will owe anything further to each other. (There's more about some of the common reasons couples prepare cohabitation agreements in "Avoiding the Ugly Gay Divorce When You're Unmarried" in Chapter 8.)

The process of preparing a cohabitation agreement is not unlike that of preparing a prenup, although you don't have to be quite as formal about it. It's just as important to make sure you research the rules for unmarried couples in your state, and consult a knowledgeable lawyer about any questions you have. You'll find sample agreements and more information about cohabitation agreements in *A Legal Guide for Lesbian & Gay Couples*, by Frederick Hertz, and Emily Doskow (Nolo).

The main distinction between a cohabitation agreement and a prenup is that you have more flexibility with a cohabitation agreement. You aren't bound by any of the "status" rules of marriage, and thus you are free to create your own arrangements. And because you aren't opting out of the marital rules, it's almost certain that your agreement will be enforced by the local court. There are some states that won't honor cohabitation agreements. If you live in one of those, you may need to arrange your property and asset ownership documents in a way that accomplishes the same goals as an agreement.

The Bottom Line: Costs of a Prenup

And, you ask, what is all this going to cost and how long will the process take? In my experience, the average cost of a prenup (including both parties' attorneys' fees), is about $5,000. But that is just an average: Some really well-organized couples with very simple financial lives, who know what they want and don't change their minds during the process at all, can get it all done for significantly less. Other couples, who have very complicated lives, have difficulty handling the emotional hurdles, or have trouble deciding how they want to deal with various assets or possible future situations, can spend more than $10,000 on the two lawyers combined. This isn't a cheap process—but not doing it can be far more expensive in the long run.

How long it takes to complete your prenup depends on how organized you are, how prepared you are in terms of your education and your prelawyer discussion process with your partner, and how efficient the lawyers are. I've done agreements in just over two weeks, start to finish, including meeting with my client and drafting the agreement, having it reviewed by her partner's attorney and revised and finalized, compiling the asset and debt list, and setting up the tasks of signing of the agreement. Adding the seven-day waiting period that is required in California, the clients were able to sign the agreement and get married within a month of the first call.

An Expert's View | **Financial and Property Issues for Same-Sex Couples**

Whether or not you can enter into a legal relationship where you live, it is essential that you protect the agreements you and your partner have made regarding your financial assets.

The importance of consulting with knowledgeable professionals cannot be stressed enough. You should find an attorney familiar with the law for same-sex couples in your state and find an accountant or tax lawyer when you are purchasing property together or transferring property between you, to make sure there are no unintended legal or tax ramifications.

Couples in legal relationships will receive state-based protections and be able to obtain legal dissolutions in the state where they entered the legal relationship and, in some cases, in other states that may recognize the legal relationship. Even so, you may wish to enter into a prenuptial agreement in order to determine for yourselves how your assets will be treated. If you decide to enter into a legal relationship and do not want the state to dictate a division of assets, then in most instances you need to enter into a prenuptial agreement before you get married or partnered.

The most important thing to remember is that unless you have such an agreement, the state-imposed rules of dissolution or divorce will be imposed on you—even if you were not aware of them and even when they are in conflict with what you thought was fair or what you believe you orally agreed to. If you live in one of those states that recognizes your partnership, then signing up for a legal partnership means the laws of marriage apply to you!

Joyce Kauffman practices family law in Cambridge, Massachusetts, and specializes in legal issues affecting LGBT families.

Far more typically, it takes partners about a month to get focused on the task, do their preliminary research and find qualified lawyers, and get the ball rolling. Then, it takes another month for the couple to meet with their lawyers (or the joint attorney who is drafting the agreement), gather their documents, and figure out what they want the agreement to say. Then, usually it takes a third month for the lawyers to draft and review the agreement, allowing time for the clients to figure out how they want to handle any sticky wickets that come up. That's a three month period—presuming that no one goes on vacation or experiences other delays.

Three months, $5,000 or more in attorneys' fees, and a lot of sometimes challenging conversations—no wonder so few folks, straight or gay, sign a premarital agreement. But if the marriage rules don't work for you, or a lot of money is at stake, it's a process you should undertake. Talk to anyone who has gone through a horrible and expensive divorce, and you'll hear good reasons to define your rights and responsibilities in advance, in a way that's consistent with your values and your shared vision of your relationship. ●

Avoiding the Ugly Gay Divorce

Being in proximity to anyone going through an ugly divorce can be excruciating—and having your own relationship end in horrible conflict is even worse. A nasty breakup has few parallels in terms of emotional strain, wild emotions, and destructive behavior, and you want to take whatever steps you can to avoid it. In my view, there are two fairly straightforward ways to avoid the ugly divorce. The first is to maintain and strengthen your relationship to avoid divorce in the first place. The second is to structure your lives and your relationship in such a way that if you do end up parting ways, your divorce is less likely to be an ugly one.

The Lessons of Experience

Once again, a disclaimer. I am not a licensed therapist, and I have no experience as a social worker, couples counselor, psychiatrist, or psychologist. I have, however, had the opportunity to spend significant time over the past 25 years listening to and working with therapists, psychologists, psychiatrists, and psychoanalysts, and I've tried to absorb as much as I could of the useful information and skills that these professionals bring to their jobs. Nowadays, I participate in a study group consisting of five lawyers and five therapists, in which we discuss cases and try to share information that will be useful to the other professionals, about the interaction between the legal and psychological dynamics we observe in our particular clients and in the community. I have also pored over psychologically-oriented treatises and articles on relationship issues—and, I admit, I'm fascinated by fiction that delves into relationship dynamics.

I started laboring professionally with gay and straight unmarried couples more than 25 years ago. In the first decade I primarily worked on drafting co-ownership and cohabitation agreements for happy couples constructing their relationships in the absence of legal marriage, and advocating for partners in adversarial conflicts over their money and property at the end of their time together. In other words, I worked with couples at the beginning and end of their relationships. In subsequent years, I found myself handling some nasty breakup litigation between ex-lovers arguing over co-owned residences, claims for support, and conflicts over businesses. I now work with couples in mediation, trying to help them resolve their conflicts outside of the courtroom.

Regardless of the nature of the legal relationship between my clients— whether they are gay and unable to marry, opposite-sex but unmarried by choice, married, or domestically partnered, when I deal with partners ending their relationships, the breakups might as well all be marital divorces. Breaking up is breaking up, and it's hard to do.

Each and every one of these couples' stories is unique, but what is striking is how frequently a few core issues arise—no matter the makeup of the couple and no matter what phase of the relationship they are in. Over and over I hear similar tales of woe—each told somewhat differently and each viewed, of course, through the lens of the reporter's own narrative. While my clients often have trouble articulating the moral of the story they are telling, a high percentage of the underlying disputes fall somewhere on a continuum of one of these three issues:

- One partner doesn't want to "take care" of the other by providing support (whether financial, practical, or emotional) in the present or promising it in the future, and the other partner wants to receive that care.

- One partner feels that the other doesn't honor the contributions (usually nonmonetary) made by the first partner to the relationship, or one partner feels that the other overstates the value of certain types of contributions. In the same realm lies the dynamic where one partner feels the other could not have achieved career or life goals without the relationship, whereas the achieving partner disagrees.

- Partners have different feelings about how much they want to operate as "a family," in the sense of sharing (or not sharing) resources and making financial decisions together.

How these three core dynamics manifest is different for each couple, because each individual has a unique set of emotional blueprints that sets that person's priorities and defines what words, actions, and events mean. I would never pretend that I understand every nuance of these relationships or the interpersonal dynamics of each couple—especially when the relationships are in conflict. I also know that I encounter a limited sample of couples, those who come to a lawyer for help, and certainly there are many, many happy couples out there who never need the assistance of a lawyer. But I strongly believe that what I am seeing are typical concerns. And it is in the territory of these dynamics where the lessons for a lasting relationship—and a healthy separation, if it happens—can often be found. I also believe that if you can identify these dynamics early on in your relationship and deal with them constructively, there's a good chance the quality of your relationship will improve.

Things You Should Know About Divorce

An experienced divorce lawyer once offered me a list of the legal rules and realities that come as the biggest surprises for spouses when they consult her for divorce advice. I think her list also offers some great up-front lessons for avoiding an ugly divorce:

- "No fault" really means what it says. Only a few states allow you to argue that your property division or support award should be affected by the other spouse's bad actions, and it rarely makes much difference in the financial outcome. In most every courthouse, the split will be based solely on property laws.

- Rules about shared debt obligations can be absolutely brutal to a more frugal spouse, who may be on the hook for a share of debts incurred unilaterally by the other spouse.

- Business interests owned prior to marriage may not be joint property, but retirement funds earned during the marriage are most often treated as joint assets regardless of which spouse accrued them.

- The name on a title or on the bank account may not mean very much when it comes to the legal divorce.

- Long-term patterns of financial dependency can lead to spousal support obligations—if you have paid all the bills for a decade, the rules of support can keep you on the hook for many years postseparation.

- Getting a divorce is rarely simple or inexpensive. Even an uncontested dissolution can take six months to a year and cost $2,500 or more in court fees and legal fees (although it is possible to do it less expensively).

None of these are reasons to not partner or marry. Instead, they are reminders of what you must do to protect each of you in the event that your marriage or partnership does not last.

Divorce Stories

There are almost as many ways to divorce as there are couples going through the process. Here are a few examples.

The Good

Consider the tale of Ellen and Sharon. They owned a house together for nearly ten years, and they had used up much of the equity by taking out credit lines to pay for various expenses, including Ellen's student debt. They always kept track of how the funds were used, and they had an oral agreement as to who would ultimately be responsible for the obligations. When they mutually decided to part ways last year, they were able to sort out the debts and arrange for Sharon to buy out Ellen's share of the house. It was painful for Ellen to accept how little equity she had left, but both of them accepted that the numbers were what they were, and they were able to move on without acrimony or resentment.

Arthur and Kevin also avoided the ugly gay divorce, by recognizing early on that they weren't inclined to share their finances. Even though they registered as domestic partners, they always thought of their lives as financially separate, and they wrote up a short "affirmation" of these principles years ago. Arthur was devastated emotionally when Kevin announced he was leaving the relationship, but money was never a source of conflict. Each of them had built up retirement savings and each had continued working full time, and so when Kevin, the higher earner, offered to cover Arthur's moving costs, it was accepted as a thoughtful gift, not the payment of an obligation.

The Bad

Doug and Martin lived together as unmarried, unregistered partners for more than ten years, never pooling their money or buying anything major, preferring to rent a little cottage in Berkeley and save for a country house in Sonoma. For years, Doug was the "boss" in the relationship, being slightly older, far better educated, and used to being in charge. Martin appreciated the guidance and support that Doug provided in the early years of his career, but eventually resentments began to grow. Doug thought of the two of them as somewhat discontented but basically married for life, whereas Martin always had doubts about the relationship.

Eventually Martin's string of casual affairs became too much for Doug to handle, and a tirade of anger (stoked by a bit too much to drink) brought the troubled relationship to an end. Given the absence of children or a house to fight over this could have been a simple breakup, but it wasn't. Martin blamed Doug for his lack of career advancement and ended up claiming he was entitled to the entirety of the savings account that had been put in both names. Doug, in response, argued that Martin had never paid his 50% share of the household expenses and so not only should Doug keep the entire account and all the furniture "they" had purchased, Martin also should pay thousands of dollars in back rent. Exacerbating the conflict, Martin filed a domestic violence charge against Doug, which soon was dropped by the prosecutor, and Doug demanded that Martin reimburse him the $1,500 he had to pay his lawyer to get out of the criminal charges.

A year later they were still at war, having each spent more than $10,000 in lawyers' fees and gotten nowhere. After a day of mediation they both finally gave up—the savings account had been spent on the lawyers' fees. They each kept whatever furniture they'd walked out with and dropped all their claims. Not really a "resolution" in any sense of the term, but an ending—and a bad one.

The Ugly

Sandy and Fran's breakup was explosive, and trying to sort it out legally took more than two years. They'd been together for nearly 20 years and registered as California domestic partners five years before their relationship ended. Over the years, Sandy gradually cut back on her high-tech consulting business as she took on more responsibilities for the couple's partially disabled son and for her own aging parents. She also was writing a memoir of her experiences as a lesbian parent. Meanwhile, Fran signed up for extra shifts as a physician and spent much of her inheritance renovating their expensive house and paying for their child's education, moving more and more into a typical "husband" role.

For years, they each harbored growing resentment over the other's contributions to their complicated lives, with Sandy convinced that Fran valued only monetary contributions and Fran increasingly frustrated by Sandy's perceived sense of entitlement and superiority. Everything blew up when Sandy announced she was taking a three month "sabbatical" to attend a prestigious writer's retreat and would be closing her consulting business upon her return, in order to devote full time to her writing. After a month of arguing and even a few shoving matches Sandy moved out and lawyers were hired.

Resolving this dispute was neither simple nor inexpensive. From a legal perspective, Sandy and Fran were unmarried for 15 years and "married" under California law for five years. They had competing claims for a greater share of their residence, because Sandy had put in the down payment and Fran had paid for the renovations. Fran insisted that Sandy immediately ramp up her consulting business to generate income, but Sandy contended that the years of part-time work had rendered her skills obsolete. Every element of the custody schedule and every piece of furniture was grist for the dissolution mill, worsened by an underlying struggle over who was the better parent. Only after more than a year of expensive legal battles did they pull back from active conflict, more out of fatigue than resolution.

Eventually they met with a mediator and after two days of negotiation they sorted out the essential items, sold the house with each receiving less in proceeds than they felt they deserved, and subsequently muddled through the duties of coparenting with contention and bickering for years—an ugly process and an ugly result for both of them as well as their son.

Don't Become the Bad or the Ugly

We all have witnessed, or even experienced, just these sorts of dramas in our own lives or the lives of our friends. Sometimes it seems that circumstances lead inevitably to extreme conflicts. But is that really true? Or can anyone avoid an ugly divorce? And how is that accomplished?

In my opinion, the best way to ensure that you have a good divorce is to have a good relationship, while staying open to the possibility that even the best of relationships may come to an end. Remember, even good relationships do eventually end, either in death or divorce, and the healthy and balanced relationships are the ones more likely to end well when the end point does arrive.

So the first and best work you can do to ensure you don't end up in a battle royale is to improve the quality of your relationship—first, to reduce the likelihood of your relationship ending, and second, to minimize the risk of an ugly divorce if you do break up.

Improving Relationship Quality to Avoid the Ugly Divorce

Despite my many years of experience, I am still baffled as to why certain breakups are so much more rancorous than others. The amount of money at stake doesn't explain it, nor is there any particular issue couples deal with that leads more frequently to nasty divorces. When I asked a therapist colleague to explain why the nature of a divorce is so unpredictable, she encouraged me to recognize that a divorce is not something that happens after a couple has broken up; rather, it is the final chapter of their relationship. In other words, the same dynamics that have driven your relationship while you were together are likely to also drive your divorce.

The divorce can be the final opportunity for partners to achieve certain goals they have not been able to meet while they were together—and sometimes they're not such nice goals at all. If either partner (or both) has been carrying resentment over some relationship dynamic for years, then the breakup will be the final chance to "right" that wrong. For example, if one feels like a victim in the relationship, then the dissolution process can offer a stage to play out that drama. If one partner's self-perception is of being the excessively generous but underappreciated provider, then the divorce negotiations will be framed by the resentful partner's desire to take back prior generosity.

I don't always get the chance to expound on my views about the nonlegal aspects of relationships. But if I did, I would offer every client the following six lessons, developed out of my experience with clients over the years. If you can embrace each of these six lessons, I think you have a good chance of staying together and, if you do break up, of doing it in a fair and relatively amicable way.

LESSON ONE: Take Your Partner Into Account

As obvious as it may seem, you are not the only one in the relationship, and your partner's point of view is just as important as yours. Both partners' views need to be taken into account on issues large and small, from how you organize your vacation time to who handles the household tasks to how the responsibilities of raising children are shared.

Time and time again I see that when resources are limited—whether tangible resources like money or intangibles like time, affection, or attention—it becomes more difficult to appreciate and respond to a partner's point of view, needs, or desires. But those are the times that it's most important to make sure that both partners have the chance to be completely heard, and that neither partner clings to a nonnegotiable version of how life should be lived.

LESSON TWO: Face the Difficult Issues

When I meet with clients who are breaking up, over and over again they tell me that, in retrospect, the conflicts that drove them apart were there from the beginning—they just didn't realize how major they were at the time and they repeatedly ignored them, hoping the problems would disappear.

Given this hindsight, a primary strategy for reducing the likelihood of divorce is to make a conscious effort to deal with concerns before they become divisive. This is not to say that one must become an obsessive "house-cleaner" searching for every little dissonant chord or irritating behavior and then hauling off to therapy for a year. And there are instances where conflicts will in fact evaporate by not talking about them, as a small percentage of problems will recede or be resolved over time. But these are the rare exceptions and in my opinion it's best to err on the side of engagement rather than avoidance. The key is to understand what issues are truly vital for each of you, and pay the appropriate amount of attention to those.

As we've seen already, one of the hardest issues to talk about is what would happen in the event of a breakup. But in order to avoid the ugly divorce, you need to take the time during your relationship to make mutually acceptable plans about the level of financial protection you each need in the event of divorce. If you haven't done a prenup, make the agreements on your own, and write them down—taking the time to do some thoughtful planning that will help both of you feel more secure.

LESSON THREE: Don't Act in Haste

When clients are uncertain about the consequences and meaning of a proposed action, I always advise them to postpone the decision if at all possible. I regularly watch couples move too quickly, out of frustration with their own or their partner's inhibitions or concerns, and this is almost always a mistake. The kitchen renovation really can wait until later; the domestic partnership registration can usually be postponed; and even the new house you've been longing for can wait another year or two. True, if decades go by and you are still living in separate rental quarters because you can't resolve the proportional ownership of a new house, you may need some professional help. But barreling through a difficult juncture just because you lack the patience to deal with your partner's point of view is rarely a recipe for happiness.

EXAMPLE: Consider the following drama, which shows up in my office in various versions on a regular basis. Rose has owned a house for ten years and she wants to refinance to do some bathroom repairs and renovation. She has bad credit—yet she can't afford to do the work she desperately wants to do without a new loan. Toni, her girlfriend of about three years, has recently moved in, and is paying Rose $500 per month as rent. They've figured out that if Toni goes on title they can get a lower interest rate. Toni is also willing to contribute some of her construction skills, which could save them half of the renovation expense.

A friend of Rose's suggested that she should have a co-ownership agreement, but Rose doesn't want to deal with "legal" stuff and she is sure that Toni will be "reasonable." Toni is in love, loves the house, and wants to help Rose out, and she assumes that Rose knows what she is doing. Adding time pressure, the interest rate on Rose's current mortgage is about to increase significantly and they've already locked in a great rate on a new mortgage based upon Toni's better credit rating. They take out the loan and add Toni to title without resolving anything about their co-ownership arrangement.

Within a year both women are stressed out and only now are they are trying to work out their agreement. Toni thinks she should just continue paying $500 per month even though she's now a co-owner, legally speaking. Rose regrets adding Toni to title and is starting to worry whether she will lose the house if they break up. They never bothered to figure out what Rose's prior equity or Toni's labor or credit rating contributions were worth. There is a wide variety of ways to address these concerns, but now taking on this task is fraught with fear and resentment.

Rose and Toni eventually find a way to allocate their interests in the property and sign a co-ownership agreement, but the process is painful and full of conflict—and within a few years their relationship comes to an end. Chances are they could have approached the task with far less acrimony had they tackled the subject earlier on.

The rule of not acting in haste applies to the status of the relationship itself. It's never a good idea to register or marry just for tax or health insurance reasons. And I always encourage clients considering a breakup to make an effort to stay together for a while even when things are rocky and they feel completely pessimistic. I say that for two reasons: First, you actually might decide to stay together; but even if you don't, you are far less likely to have an ugly divorce if you move through the transitions more slowly. If you are raising young children together or if one of you is especially vulnerable financially or medically, you have a special obligation to consider your decisions carefully.

LESSON FOUR: Do More and Acknowledge More

Most of us share a fundamental human flaw: We notice the reality that is closest to us more clearly than that which is any distance away. We vividly remember when we wash the dishes or make dinner, but we don't always notice with the same clarity when our partner stops at the store for something we need or spends an evening helping our son with his homework.

If not held in check, this tendency can mean that we start to feel that life is out of balance, even when an objective look at the situation would tell us otherwise. That is why it's not just important to contribute as much as you can to the relationship, but also to recognize what your partner contributes. And this is true on a day-to day-basis when it involves picking up the dry cleaning or washing dishes, and also on a larger scale, when one partner supports the other financially for a few years and later is the one in need of care because of health problems.

A related tendency is for one person to create conditions or tests without communicating these explicitly to the other partner. For example, you might feel that because you are doing most of the grocery shopping, your partner should take on some other household responsibility. If you are beginning to inwardly impose such conditions, make them known. If they're significant, like your belief that you're earning equity in the house because you're contributing to the mortgage, put them in writing and be sure you and your partner are on the same page.

LESSON FIVE: Live Your Own Lives

It's vital that partners in every long-term relationship maintain a degree of self-sufficiency. Each of you should keep up your independent friendships and create a realm of work, hobbies, or community activities that is yours alone. Of course, it's a delight to invite the other partner into "your" world from time to time, but don't suffocate yourselves by cramming yourselves into a one-room life. I strongly encourage couples to create some degree of separate financial spheres as well, so that each of you can manage some money, make tough decisions, and face the consequences alone—and then keep track of your own approach to the material world. You will reduce the likelihood of falling into patterns of excessive dependency and maintain your ability to think and act on your own.

LESSON SIX: Honor Your Agreements

Make every effort to integrate your personal agreements and the realities of your relationship into your legal arrangements. For example, if your agreement is that you're both owners of your home, both of you should be on title. If you are coparenting, then both of you should be legal parents. The more dramatically your legal paperwork is at odds with the truth of your relationship, the more likely it is that things will go awry if you break up.

Then, if you do find yourself in a breakup, honor those same truths. It is possible that you might discern an opportunity to take advantage of homophobic laws or rules to gain an advantage over your partner. This happens most often with partners who try to prevent a nonbiological parent from maintaining a relationship with a child they're helping to raise, but it could occur with financial issues as well, especially in those states where legal partnerships are not recognized. In my view there's simply no excuse for this. Honor the truth of your partnership, even when the law does not recognize it.

Finally, honor the love that has existed between you and your partner by leaving your accusations of fault and betrayals out of the divorce process. In the past, a spouse who wanted a divorce had to prove that the other spouse was at fault in some way—and judges divided assets accordingly. Now, every state has some version of no-fault divorce, where parties can simply agree that they've encountered "irreconcilable differences" and go their separate ways. Take advantage of these rules, respect the fact that you once cared about your partner, and divide your property and deal with your children fairly, without bringing your interpersonal dramas into your lawyer's office or the courtroom.

Structuring Your Lives to Survive Divorce

While I truly hope that every one of your relationships is satisfying for decades to come, I would be remiss if I didn't encourage you to devote some attention to planning for the possibility that your relationship might end in dissolution.

It's really quite simple. Start by visualizing in concrete terms what your life would be like after a breakup. Where would you live and work; how would you support yourself; how would you take care of your health; and how would you relate to your children? The answers to these questions may change over time, but as you consider entering a legal relationship and at various times throughout your partnership, it's vital that you answer these questions based on a realistic observation of conditions as they exist at that time.

Some of these questions are the same ones you consider when preparing a prenup. If you've prepared a prenup or are in the process, then you've already done some of that visualization. This chapter just comes at it from a different angle.

Dealing With the House

One of the biggest sources of tension when a relationship ends is what will happen to the family home. Ideally, if you are homeowners, you have been working toward a mutual goal of building up enough equity that if you separate you can afford two houses or condominiums, however small, so that neither of you has to leave town or rent a room somewhere. Planning for this future should help you refrain from draining the house equity on non-necessary purchases, over-renovation, refinancing to pay off credit card bills, or the like. If you are renting, monitor your spending so that you can build up some savings to pay for moving to a new place, or for covering your rent during a difficult time of transition. If it is financially impossible to achieve these goals, then make sure you will have a place to land with family or friends if things go poorly in your partnership.

Managing Money

Ultimately, your goal is to manage your money, debt, and employment prospects together in ways that acknowledge that each of you might be on your own in the future. Becoming financially dependent on someone else is a big risk. As successful as your partner may be at the moment, there are no guarantees for the future—and whether your partner will continue to support you after a breakup is always an open question. Unless you are sure of receiving a very sweet inheritance soon, be careful about stepping off the employment ladder completely, even when there appears to be enough money. Chances are you were self-sufficient when you were single; don't lose that autonomy just because you make a commitment to someone else.

Health Care

If you have been covered by your partner's health insurance policy as a dependent or domestic partner, the challenge is to be sure you have long-term insurance protection if the relationship ends. You should be eligible for the federal version of COBRA, the law that provides extended coverage for the nonworking spouse upon divorce, as it's a federal benefit. And in some states, state law provides similar protections to some employees, so if you live in a marriage equality or marriage equivalent state, make sure to check into it. You may be able to maintain coverage if you don't terminate the relationship formally, but if cohabitation is a basis of your receiving the benefit, as is often the case with domestic partner benefits, that's going to be a problem. If there's a risk that you may become uninsurable in the future in the absence of your partnership, it may be prudent to maintain your own insurance coverage even when partnership coverage is available, so that you will have your own insurance to fall back on if things go awry.

Children

Lack of planning with regard to your children can lead to heartbreak. If you live in a state where second-parent or stepparent adoption is possible, do it—even if your state is a relationship recognition state. If you're unable to do an adoption, make sure you have signed paperwork that documents the non-biological or nonlegal parent's relationship with the child, including a will, a nomination of guardian, and an authorization to consent to medical care. Even if the courts don't literally "enforce" a private contract between parents, having one will maximize the likelihood that the two of you will honor it, and a judge might pay it some attention in the event of a custody fight. If you have children, it's important to commit to a conflict resolution process, like mediation, that minimizes the chances of harm to your children from custody or visitation disputes between parents. There's more about mediation in "How to Resolve Conflicts at Divorce."

How to Resolve Conflicts at Divorce

If despite all your best efforts you find yourself in a divorce and there are conflicts that need to be resolved, you'll have the choice of three methods for achieving resolution without litigation: negotiation, mediation, and a relatively new approach called collaborative divorce.

Before getting into the details, though, a word about compromise—the soul of conflict resolution. In 20 years of handling these sorts of conflicts, I have yet to see a single situation where there was no ambiguity, uncertainty, or legitimate disagreement. Even when there are written documents that seem self-evident, there always can be extenuating circumstances that are important to one or both parties. "Winning" is never inevitable, and fighting to the end can be extremely costly, both personally and financially. Most often a compromise leaves both parties better off.

I once asked a client why she was fighting so hard over a small sum of money and she said she didn't want to cave into her ex's unreasonable demands, which she felt would feed what she saw as self-centered narcissistic behavior. I asked her why she thought that point would get through to her girlfriend now, when it hadn't in the last two decades? If you're stuck in a desire to force your partner to change in the course of your breakup, ask yourself the same question.

However angry you may be, my advice is to remember it is always in your best interest to stay open to all options.

Negotiation

Negotiation is simply the process of talking out a dispute until it's resolved. It can involve you and your spouse sitting down together and deciding how to divide your property, or it can mean that you each hire lawyers who negotiate on your behalf and at your instruction.

Negotiating Directly With Your Partner

Many divorcing spouses feel they're too emotional to work directly with each other to decide how to divide property and deal with issues involving children. This may be true for you, but if you are able to negotiate directly you will save yourself thousands of dollars in attorneys' fees. What is needed is a clear understanding of your position and a willingness to also understand your partner's point of view (no matter how much you disagree with it), an ability to keep your eye on what is really at stake, and a persistent openness to compromise. Sometimes, it can help to set up a "cooling off" period to allow emotions to settle down a bit before trying this approach, but don't give up on it too early, especially if cost is a factor. If you can manage it, it costs less than any other way of resolving your disputes, and also has the potential to result in a resolution that really works for both of you.

Negotiating Through Attorneys

If you don't want to negotiate directly with your partner, you can ask a lawyer to negotiate on your behalf by working with your partner's lawyer to exchange possible settlement scenarios back and forth until an agreement is reached. If you are going to hire a lawyer to negotiate on your behalf, make sure you hire the right lawyer. You need someone who will follow your wishes and work toward a settlement, rather than escalating things by being aggressive or stonewalling. Once you hire a lawyer who is qualified to negotiate, make sure you clarify how you want the negotiation to proceed. Remember, it is your money that is being spent on the negotiation, not your lawyer's, and it's your life that is being debated, not some abstract legal case. Stay on top of the negotiations, and take an active role in deciding what issues are worth fighting over and when a settlement should be pursued. If you sense that your lawyer isn't able to focus on how you want the case resolved, be prepared to switch lawyers.

Mediation

Mediation is a form of negotiation that involves a neutral facilitator, called a mediator. The mediator is not a judge or an arbitrator and doesn't make decisions or issue rulings. Instead, the mediator works with both of you to resolve your disputes by helping you communicate effectively about your needs and interests until you've reached an agreement.

What mediation looks like can vary depending on the mediator and the circumstances. Sometimes the mediator meets just with you and your partner, but if you have lawyers the mediation might include them as well. Sometimes, the parties both stay in the same room for the entire meeting, and other times the mediator moves back and forth between joint and private sessions. In some situations, there are marathon meetings that last all day, and other times, a series of shorter sessions of two to three hours will work better. If you reach an agreement, the mediator will write it up, you will sign it, and it will become binding—but nothing in the process is binding until that point. (Some mediators—but not all—will also help you prepare and file any paperwork required to dissolve your relationship.)

Mediation is particularly appropriate for same-sex dissolutions. Many of us haven't organized our lives along the strict lines of marital rules, either financially or socially. Even the most traditional of same-sex couples often think about and structure their families differently from the hetero-normative model. Gender roles don't sort out in strict husband/wife roles; money is often not shared; and sexual and social obligations may be arranged in unconventional ways.

Mediation allows a couple to choose their own mediator, set the terms for the conversation, and be fully themselves in this stressful situation, without either party's running the show. It provides a private space for people to struggle through issues on their own terms and resolve them on the basis they believe is most fair, rather than automatically using marital rules. The great advantage to any mediation, straight or gay, is that the parties can settle their dispute on any basis they wish; in contrast to a court case, they are not bound by the legal rules.

Mediation also is the best approach for a couple who expects their relationship to continue into the future because they are raising children together, are continuing to co-own property, or simply want to maintain a close relationship. Mediation supports the partners in working with each other, listening to each other, and creating a resolution together, on their own terms. It can even improve their communication skills, which has a powerful long-term benefit. Litigation, by contrast, supports an adversarial approach that drives people farther apart and at the end of which at least one party is unhappy.

Mediation does require an ability to be relatively calm, to articulate your concerns, and to respond to proposals in a timely way. If your breakup has been highly emotional, it may be necessary to wait a few months before beginning mediation, to steady yourself emotionally.

Collaborative Divorce

Collaborative divorce contains some elements of lawyer-assisted negotiation and some elements of mediation. In a collaborative case, each party has an attorney, and the attorneys act as advocates for their clients—but both spouses and both lawyers agree at the outset, in writing, that they will not take the case to court and instead will work to settle it. If one person does opt for litigation, both attorneys must withdraw and each party must find a new one—who has to begin virtually from scratch.

The collaboration involves a series of meetings—attended by both clients and both attorneys—in which the spirit of cooperation prevails and the goal is to arrive at a workable solution for everyone. Often, other professionals such as accountants or child custody evaluators are involved, but typically there is no third-party neutral mediator involved.

This is a unique framework that can be very effective for complicated divorces, especially when a great deal of money or property is at stake or when parenting rights are in dispute. Collaborative divorce is not inexpensive. But as compared to a lengthy court fight, it can be an efficient and cost-effective solution.

Collaborative divorce only works when the partners and the lawyers have the awareness and discipline to act collaboratively, and when both sides are truly able to let go of any desire to have a referee or judge manage their divorce. In some states, you may find that most of the trained collaborative attorneys have so far only worked on heterosexual marital divorces and could need some additional training to handle same-sex breakups. But it should always be considered as an option.

To learn everything you need to know about mediation and collaborative divorce, see *Divorce Without Court: A Guide to Mediation & Collaborative Divorce*, by Katherine E. Stoner (Nolo).

In the end, the best way to avoid the ugly gay divorce is to accept that the relationship has ended and focus on how to go your separate ways in the lowest-cost, fairest, and most humane way possible. You'll be doing yourself and everyone around you an enormous favor if you do.

The Burden of Being Wedlocked

One of the most painful ironies of the lack of full marriage equality nationwide is the problem of being "wedlocked"—that is, not being able to get divorced even though your relationship is over. The reason for this problem is complicated, but it all harkens back to the doctrine of domicile. While you are able to get married without being a resident of the state in which the marriage takes place, residency has historically been required to get a divorce. The reasoning behind this rule was that it would be improper for one spouse seeking a divorce to flee to a state with minimal protections for the other spouse if the couple had been living in a home state that offered better spousal protections.

This doctrine makes sense when marriages are recognized in every state, but unfortunately, courts in some of the nonrecognition states have ruled that since they don't recognize same-sex marriages, they won't grant a same-sex couple a divorce. In our opinion, the couple *should* get divorced, even if they live in a nonrecognition state, in case one of them relocates again to a recognition state or if federally imposed duties are at stake. Fortunately, some of the states that issue marriage licenses to same-sex couples (California and Washington, D.C., most recently) have included provisions in their laws that allow out-of-state couples to come back to the state of marriage to get a divorce if their state of residence won't grant one.

If you find yourself in this situation, make every effort to resolve all your money and property issues in advance, as it isn't entirely clear what a judge will do if you have significant financial disputes. If you got married in a jurisdiction that doesn't offer you the nonresident divorce option, you should consult with a gay-friendly lawyer in your area to see if there's a local judge who will have compassion for your situation and grant the divorce (assuming neither party is contesting the request).

If none of these options work, you may have no alternative but to relocate to a recognition state for a few months or even a year's time, to establish residency and file for divorce there. Only one of you has to live in the state where the divorce petition is filed. We know this is no simple task, but waiting until your home state recognizes your marriage for the purpose of divorce may be more than you are willing to do. In my humble opinion, the only thing worse than not being able to get married is not being able to get divorced!

Avoiding the Ugly Gay Divorce When You're Unmarried

Much of the information and advice in this chapter so far applies whether or not you are married or legally partnered. But there are certain ways that ending your relationship when you're not legally committed is different. For one thing, you're not required to go through a court-controlled divorce proceeding. You may end up in court, but it won't necessarily be family court. For another thing, how you divide your property generally will be determined by how title is held and by any written agreements or contracts you have, not by your relationship status as a married or "married equivalent" person. And finally, if you have children, things can go very differently depending on how your relationship is defined and whether you have legalized the parent-child relationship.

Dividing Property

When my clients say "they" bought a house or "they" own a business, I ask whose name is on the title or the incorporation papers, and, often, I must correct them and say that "he" bought the house or "she" owns the business. It's sometimes painful to accept this correction, but mislabeling legal ownership when you talk about your assets may cause you to delude yourself about the legal rules that apply to you.

   As an unmarried partner, the general rule is that you are only entitled to that which is in your name and are responsible only for your own debts. If you and your partner take joint title to an asset or incur a debt with both of your names on it, the legal system will presume that your ownership shares are equal. If you separate, you'll each get what you own alone and half of what you own jointly, and most of the time, that's the end of it.

Types of Contracts

There are four types of legal contracts: implied in fact, implied in law, oral, and written.

An implied-in-fact contract is a pattern of actions that demonstrate that the parties had made an agreement even though they never really talked about it. We enter into such contracts every day when we share expenses with friends or make future plans. Offering to "meet someone" for dinner typically implies something different than saying you'll "take someone out" to dinner, even though the financial terms are rarely articulated in detail. So if one partner has paid one-third of the house expenses for years, chances are there's an implied agreement that this owner has a one-third interest in the equity. The problem with implied-in-fact contracts, however, is that they are very hard to prove, and so disputed claims based upon implied-in-fact contracts are hardly ever successful.

An implied-in-law contract is what happens when everyone agrees there was never any express agreement but a court decides that it is fair to impose a contractual structure on the parties retrospectively. If you put $50,000 in your partner's bank account because you are leaving town for a few months and don't have time to open up your own account and then your partner buys a new car with those funds, chances are the judge is either going to conclude that there was a loan that must be repaid with interest, or conclude that there was a co-ownership contract implied and you are part owner of the Lexus. Again, it's rarely so clear-cut, so it is rare for the court to find an implied-in-law contract.

An oral contract is just what it sounds like—a contract created by speaking words out loud. The problem with most oral contracts is that even if both parties admit that they talked about the situation, they rarely agree about the details. Judges tend to be conservative in nature, so they are typically suspicious of oral contract claims.

Finally, a "real" legal contract is a written contract—which doesn't mean it has to be drafted by a lawyer or even be very formal at all. A handwritten set of notes can constitute a contract, though there has to be something in writing, like signatures, that shows that both parties agreed to the terms—not just that one partner wrote down some notes reflecting one point of view.

In some states, an unmarried partner may seek a portion of an asset that is titled solely in the other partner's name or claim postseparation support (nicknamed "palimony"). Support claims are often referred to as *Marvin* claims," because the right to ask for such support was first enunciated in a court case by the girlfriend of actor Lee Marvin more than 30 years ago. The case was notorious, but it's often forgotten that while Michelle Marvin won the right to sue, she ultimately lost her case. The fact is that winning these claims is almost impossible. Some states don't allow them at all, and others only allow an unmarried partner to pursue a palimony claim if there is a written agreement.

And as hard as it has been to win such claims in the past, it's actually getting harder as the notion of marriage and legal partnership for same-sex partners takes hold. If you live in a state that allows same-sex couples to register or marry, you won't get much sympathy from a judge if you haven't done so.

For all these reasons, it should be evident that relying on the possibility that you might have a legal claim if things unravel doesn't make much sense. Instead, you should prepare written contracts as early as possible, to memorialize the agreements you and your partner have made. There are three common circumstances in which a legal agreement can be very useful for unmarried (or unregistered) same-sex partners.

A written agreement can call for one partner to provide financial support or share property with the other. Some couples have made or are considering agreements about their money or assets. For example, you might be contributing time and labor to renovating a property that's in your partner's name alone, or working in a business that's titled in your partner's name but that you both are committed to. You might have a vague agreement that involves a debt, such as where you are rolling one partner's student loan debt into a line of credit secured by a jointly owned residence with an agreement that the student owner will be paying all of this debt. You might even have an unstated assumption that one of you will provide some limited financial support to the other one in the event of a breakup. In each of these situations, you will need to have a valid written contract, not an amorphous unwritten agreement or expectation.

It will be up to you to decide how detailed your agreement needs to be and whether you need a lawyer. Having an attorney can be helpful in sorting out what you actually mean by the things you believe you are agreeing upon. For example, I frequently meet with couples where they say they agreed that the one contributing the down payment should get "credit" for the contribution, but they never figured out whether it should be a loan (and if so, with or without interest) or whether the contributor should own a greater share of the property. Or, they may have an agreement that presumes they are going to pay all bills equally, but they haven't thought about what to do if one partner fails to pay the agreed amount. A lawyer—or a tax preparer—can also identify and help you avoid tax complications.

EXAMPLE: Here's an example of a situation where a written contract really would have helped. Richard decided to buy a house that needed some work, at a time when his boyfriend, Martin, was out of work and couldn't qualify to be a legal co-owner. Martin had skills at simple construction, so they struck a deal that Richard would pay the bills and Martin would work on the house repairs for a few months, in lieu of paying any "rent." Martin ended up spending nearly two years on the renovation—though not working as efficiently as a hired contractor would have done, and not always doing the work in ways that Richard was happy about. Richard and Martin never really talked through what was going on—Richard was fine with paying all the bills and Martin was enjoying the renovation work, especially as he wasn't earning much in his part-time consulting career. Seven years later, the couple broke up, and Martin asked for half of the house's appreciation during the time they were together, arguing that his renovation work was key to the uptick in value. Richard, said "Wait a minute, we had an agreement: I paid the bills and you didn't pay rent so I owe you nothing." Martin argued back that Richard had really paid the bills simply because he was earning a lot and loved Martin, and asserted that he had ended up putting in far more labor than they ever expected.

They went through months of negotiation and mediation without reaching a resolution, and eventually their dispute ended up in a nasty six-day trial. Martin didn't do very well in court, because he couldn't prove that there was an agreement to share the equity, either oral or implied. Worsening his case, the judge viewed the value of the renovation work as being worth less than the combination of the free housing and other benefits Richard had provided to him by paying all the bills, so Martin lost on that count as well.

Richard was thrilled to be the victor, but it cost each of them more than $100,000 in legal bills to end up with a ruling on this claim—all of which could have been avoided if they'd simply written up an agreement that covered their arrangement.

A written agreement can provide for legal co-ownership of property in shares other than the 50/50 legal presumption of the title. In most states, co-owners are presumed to own property in equal shares regardless of their respective contributions to purchase price or maintenance. If this is not what you have in mind, you should have a written agreement.

The most common reason for unequal ownership is that one partner has contributed more to a down payment or renovation expenses. There are two ways to address such situations in a written agreement. One is to allocate ownership in proportion to your respective contributions and agree from the outset that you will own the property 70/30 or 80/20, or whatever the total respective contributions end up being. The other and more typical approach is to agree that the one who contributed more will get some or all of that money back off the top, with or without interest, when the property is sold, and then any other equity or proceeds of sale will be split equally between the co-owners. (That is what the marriage rule is in most states, and I believe it's a fair way to do it.)

Other reasons for unequal ownership include situations where one partner contributed labor to renovate property while the other partner paid for materials, or one partner owned property for several years before the other became a co-owner. In these cases you must calculate what portion of the equity belongs to the each owner and how you're going to divide equity if you break up.

There may be details to work out later, but what counts most is that you get the basic terms worked out and put down on paper. What you don't want to do is what a recent client of mine did.

EXAMPLE: Ellen originally owned a house with her former girlfriend, Grace, and then bought Grace out—with the help of her new lover Fran, who went on title, helped Ellen get a new loan, and then contributed renovation labor as her buy-in contribution. Over the course of the next ten years, they contributed unequally to the property expenses, did different amounts of labor on the renovation, and borrowed against the house in unequal amounts for various business and personal debts. When they broke up, it cost more than $50,000 in legal and accounting fees to resolve this dispute—first to sort out who had contributed what amounts to the expenses and the renovation labor, and then months negotiating over what was a fair allocation of the $500,000 in equity in the property—all of which could have been avoided if they'd had a rational and well-written co-ownership agreement from the outset.

A written agreement can reassure partners that neither will make a legal claim against the property or assets of the other. It's not unusual for a wealthier partner to support a lower-earning one by providing housing, paying expenses, and supporting educational or other endeavors. Especially where there's a dramatic difference in financial capacity, the wealthy partner often wants to be sure that if they break up the other won't make a claim for yet more money. In such a case, the partners may agree in writing to an amount of postseparation support to be paid to the dependent partner in exchange for a waiver of any further claims. By the way, even when such an agreement exists, there is nothing to prevent the richer partner from helping out an ex. The key is that such generosity is voluntary, not a legal obligation.

For sample contracts covering some of the common situations for which agreements are needed, see *A Legal Guide for Lesbian & Gay Couples*, by Frederick Hertz and Emily Doskow (Nolo).

Parentage Issues

In same-sex families where the parents are not married or legally partnered, there's frequently one parent whose relationship with the children is legally at risk. In a lesbian couple with a child birthed by one partner, it's the partner who isn't biologically related to the child. In a lesbian or gay couple where one partner has adopted from another state—or another country—as a single person, it's the partner who didn't adopt. In a situation where one partner has a child when the relationship begins and the second partner takes on a parenting role over time, it's the newer parent.

In all of these cases, if you're the second parent and you don't take whatever legal steps your state allows to protect your relationship with your kids, you may find yourself in the tragic situation of having little or no contact with children who are in every sense yours—except legally.

There's a wide disparity among the states as far as what's allowed for second parents who aren't married or legally partnered, and the rules change frequently. If you're a second parent and you want to establish a legal relationship with your kids, talk to a knowledgeable local lawyer or one of the national LGBT rights organizations about what's possible in your state.

If you live in a state that allows second-parent adoption, do it. It's generally not a very complicated process, and it shouldn't be extremely expensive. Whatever it costs, it's worth the security of knowing that your legal status reflects your reality—and your child's. In addition, as of 2011, there is still an adoption tax credit in place that provides a tax break for adoption expenses, unless you are married to the other parent.

Some states don't allow adoptions but do have other ways of establishing parentage, using the Uniform Parentage Act that's in place in a number of states, or procedures that have been established specifically for particular states. However you can make it happen, make it happen.

If you live in a state that doesn't allow same-sex adoptions or any equivalent procedure, there isn't a reliable legal solution. In that case, it's important that at a minimum you and your partner sign a coparenting agreement that declares in no uncertain terms that you are both parents and should be considered so legally. Not every court will defer to such a document, but it may make a difference (and did in a recent North Carolina case). And going through the agreement formation process could iron out differences in advance.

In addition to the coparenting agreement, the legal parent should sign a will that grants custody to the second parent in the event of the legal parent's death, as well as a guardianship nomination that names the second parent as guardian in the event of the legal parent's incapacity. The legal parent should also authorize the second parent to obtain medical care for the child. Finally, both of you should make sure to tell family, friends, caregivers, teachers, and your pediatrician that you consider yourselves equal parents and you want to be treated that way. Along with your written coparenting agreement and the other documents you've prepared, this could serve as evidence in a later court case.

Just like couples who are married or legally partnered, we urge you to honor the agreements you've made and the realities of your relationship, and respect parent-child relationships that exist in reality, even if not in the eyes of the law.

Whether you're married, legally partnered, or committed but not legally bound, divorce is always a possibility. The part you have control over is making choices that will help you avoid ugliness if that's where you end up. ●

Estate Planning for Same-Sex Couples

Planning for death and disability is one of the most important things couples can do to protect each other, whether or not they are married or legally partnered. There are entire books on the subject (see the resource list in Appendix B), so one brief chapter can't possibly do full justice to this important topic. We'll try to cover the high points and key issues, and then you can move on to address your own situation and create an estate plan that's right for your family. The core message is that getting married or legally partnered isn't all that is needed to protect your family. Planning for the future and signing the appropriate documents is also crucial.

We all know that estate planning means considering things that most of us don't particularly like to think about. But preparing for contingencies will bring you peace of mind and protect your family.

Planning for Disability

Planning for disability means establishing legally binding instructions about who will take care of you and your business affairs if you become incapacitated by illness or injury to the point where you can't make decisions for yourself. If that happens, you'll need someone to make medical decisions for you as well as to take care of your financial and business concerns. You use two separate documents to establish these two aspects of your plans.

Health Care Directives

A health care directive is a document that lets you give written instructions about your health care, including who should make medical decisions for you if you are unable to communicate your own wishes. All of the other terms you've heard—power of attorney for health care, medical directive, directive to physicians, and living will—are in the category of health care directives.

A living will or declaration about medical care is a document that lets you state what type of medical care you wish to receive—and not receive—if you are unable to give instructions for your own care. It's basically a set of instructions to your doctor.

A durable power of attorney for health care, also known as a medical power of attorney, allows you to name a trusted person to make medical decisions on your behalf if you can't make the decisions yourself. The person you name is usually called your agent or attorney-in-fact.

In many states, the living will and medical power of attorney are combined into one document that names a health care agent and gives instructions about your care. This form is most often called an advance health care directive. We'll assume that's what you're going to do, as it's the simplest way to get all your instructions in one place.

Preparing an advance directive forces you to address two important questions. First, you must choose who is going to be in charge of the medical decisions—you'll need to pick a primary and a backup agent. See "Practicalities and Formalities," below. Next, you must decide how you want your agent to approach decisions about your end-of-life care: Do you want your agent to instruct your physician to provide the maximum intervention, no intervention, or something in between? You can be as specific as you wish in setting out your wishes about medical care.

Some people who are married or legally partnered believe it's not necessary to prepare an advance directive. If no advance directive exists, a married spouse typically is treated as the agent. But even if you are married or legally partnered and you live in a state that recognizes your relationship, these documents are still crucial.

If you travel to or even end up living in a nonrecognition state, they could mean the difference between your partner's being kept in the waiting room or being allowed to be with you in an emergency. And, a marital or legal relationship is not the be-all and end-all of authority to make decisions for a spouse—if you don't have your wishes clearly spelled out in a valid legal document, your agent could face challenges from others. Surely we all remember Terry Schiavo, whose husband had the legal right to make decisions, but whose parents challenged those decisions because his wife hadn't written down how she wanted him to deal with her potential incapacity.

Power of Attorney for Finances and Property

A power of attorney for finances and property (sometimes called a durable financial power of attorney) empowers your agent to manage your finances if you are disabled, including property or business assets if you include them in the list of powers. The term "durable" refers to the fact that the authorization remains in effect if you are completely incapacitated, and not just temporarily unavailable.

Like a medical directive, a financial power of attorney requires that you choose an agent and make several additional decisions.

You can make your power of attorney effective immediately upon signing, to cover situations where you might need your agent's help even though you're capable of making your own decisions—for example, if you travel or are otherwise unavailable a lot of the time. Or, you can have the power of attorney become effective only if you become incapacitated.

You can leave the definition of incapacity open, or require confirmation by one or two physicians. (It usually is wiser to go with the second approach, to protect from abuse of the authority.) And you must decide how much power to give your agent. You can limit the agent's authority to paying your bills, allow your agent to do anything but sell real property or some other important asset, or allow unlimited powers to do just about anything with your property.

When you're considering what to do, think about your assets and properties and the actions that the agent might be required to take. If you have significant assets in a variety of forms (for example, real property, bank accounts, and stock accounts), it's possible that a power of attorney that gives your agent unlimited powers could run into trouble at financial institutions, and you might want to consider making separate documents. It's a good idea to check with your bank or another financial institution—especially brokerage companies—to find out whether there's a particular form they prefer. Powers of attorney for real estate, for example, typically need to be notarized, and they should make specific reference to the address of the property in question, so making a separate one can be a wise choice.

Practicalities and Formalities

It's very easy to prepare medical directives and financial powers of attorney. Many states offer forms online at no cost—check your state department of health services or the like. You can often pick up a form at a local stationery store and at most hospitals. Nolo's estate planning software, *Quicken WillMaker Plus*, contains forms that you can be confident are valid for your state. If you have an attorney preparing a will or trust for you (see "Planning for Death," below), the attorney will very likely include these planning documents as part of the package. And if you are preparing a trust, you have the option of designating a "substitute trustee" who will take over your affairs if you are incapacitated. If you do that, a power of attorney is less critical—but still a good backup, as long as you name the same person in both documents.

While most folks select their spouse or partner to serve as agent, you're not required to do so. Nor do you have to choose the same agent for your advance directive and your financial power of attorney. Just be sure your agent is someone who lives nearby, knows you and your family well, and is capable of handling emotionally difficult situations. If your partner travels a great deal or is often unavailable, or if your family mistrusts your partner, it might make sense to pick a close friend, sibling, or even a professional adviser instead.

Don't minimize the consequences of what you are doing. By signing these documents you are bestowing upon your agent enormous power over your assets and, in the case of a medical directive, your very life. It is crucial that you appoint someone you trust completely.

Once you figure out what documents you need to sign and what you are going to include in each of them, be sure that you follow the formalities for having them properly signed. Each state has its own rules, but typically you either need to have your signatures notarized or have at least two witnesses verify that you signed the document and were mentally and physically competent when you did so. In order to avoid any accusation of undue influence or pressure, neither your agent nor anyone who is an heir should act as a witness.

Planning for Death

Estate planning is the process of compiling a list of your assets and obligations (which comprise your estate), and making decisions about how you want your estate to be distributed after your death. Making these decisions is never easy for anyone, because it forces you to anticipate your own and your partner's mortality. Being legally partnered gives you a great many rights, and it also imposes duties on you as a spouse, making your estate planning somewhat more complicated than when you were living outside of any legal relationship.

Things are particularly complex for high-net-worth same-sex couples because of the differential treatment same-sex partners receive at the hands of the federal government when it comes to bequests to spouses. Even for less wealthy couples, there can be problems with interstate recognition that affect your estate planning. All of this complexity makes it especially important that you create a legally enforceable estate plan. Everyone should have a will, and many people who own property or have children should also consider preparing trusts. Here are the basics on both of those documents.

Wills

A will is a set of written instructions stating who should get your property and possessions upon your death. You can make lists of specific possessions, and you should always include a "residuary" clause that covers assets you forgot to list or that you acquire after you sign the will. Your will may also include funeral and burial instructions and recommendations as to who should serve as guardian of your minor children. Your will also names an executor—your spouse or a relative, friend, or agreed-upon professional, and a backup executor in case the person you chose isn't available at the time of your death. The executor is the person who makes sure that assets are properly distributed at your death, often in the context of a probate, discussed in "Probate Procedures," below.

The Rules of Bequests

"Bequest" is the legal term for the gifts you make under your will. You can use your will to distribute all of your personal property, your money, and any real estate you own, either with specific bequests or by leaving certain percentages of assets to a specified number of people. For the most part, you have total control over what you give to whom. However, being married or legally partnered subjects you to a set of special rules that, in most states, require that you leave at least something to your spouse in a will. (If you don't have a will, your spouse will still get some of your assets—see "Intestacy Rules," below.)

Each state has different rules about what you can and can't do with your property vis-a-vis your spouse. For example, in community property states, you and your partner jointly own everything acquired after marriage, so you can't give away your partner's half of the community property in your will or trust to someone other than your partner, even if it is titled in your name alone. On the other hand, you aren't required to give any of your own half of the shared property to your partner—you can leave it to anyone you choose, along with your own separate property.

Most other states impose what is called the "forced share" rule, which establishes a minimum share of your estate that must go to your spouse at your death. If you don't leave at least the required percentage to your spouse, some of your other gifts will be invalidated in order to provide the appropriate amount for your spouse.

EXAMPLE: This isn't just a problem for gay people. An older man's first wife died quite young, and he remarried a woman to whom he gave significant gifts of money and property during his lifetime. Believing he had cared for her in this way, he didn't leave her anything in his will, instead leaving everything to his adult son. The second wife challenged the will based on the forced share rule, and ended up with most of dad's property and money.

It is possible to leave your spouse less than the state-required minimum if you wish, but you must follow specific procedures to accomplish this, and you'll need a lawyer's help. Your spouse may have abundant assets and not need the inheritance, while you have children or other relatives who need help, or favorite charities you want to benefit. However, if your plan is to leave your spouse less than the legal minimum, most states require that you get your spouse's written approval, typically in the form of a pre- or postmarital agreement. (See Chapter 7.)

You'll usually also be required to get your spouse's approval if you wish to leave your retirement plan assets to someone other than your spouse. It's very important to make sure that your beneficiary designations and your will are consistent. If they're not, the beneficiary designation will control who gets the benefits, no matter what is in your will.

Changes in marital status—getting married or divorced—can also have an impact on your estate planning. In many states, if you divorce, any provision in your will leaving assets to your spouse will be automatically void. Thus, if you want to provide for your ex-spouse after you've divorced, you must renew your will after you complete your divorce. And getting married generally requires that you update your beneficiary statements, even if your spouse was the prior beneficiary.

If there's any question in your relationship about who owns what and in what shares, you'll need to get that resolved before making your estate plan. In some situations, you may need to meet with a family law attorney as well as an estate planning attorney, so that you can evaluate who really owns what and avoid making mistakes when it comes to drafting your estate planning documents.

Joint Tenancy Property

Many couples own property as joint tenants, meaning that the ownership share of the first person to die passes to the survivor without the necessity of a will or a probate. This arrangement generally makes sense for heterosexual married folks (though in community property states it is better to title the asset as "community property with right of survivorship"), because there's no gift or estate tax on transfers during life or at death between married partners.

Joint tenancy also works fine for unmarried partners who aren't at risk of paying estate taxes (meaning they don't have assets worth more than

$5,250,000). But if the first partner to die is very wealthy, it might not be the best way to hold title. That's because joint tenancy ownership means both partners own the entire property—that's why it goes to the second partner without a probate at the death of the first partner. But it's also why the entire value of the property is attributed to the first partner to die, unless the survivor can prove that he or she actually contributed to the property expenses or purchase. If the partners instead held the property as tenants in common with each partner's share defined as 50%, the first partner to die would only have half the value attributed to his or her estate, which could improve the estate tax situation. (See Chapter 4 for the basics of estate taxes.)

This could be a problem for all unmarried partners, both straight and gay, but now that our marriages are federally recognized, it will no longer be a problem for married same-sex couples. Joint tenancy can still create confusion if the titled property is not properly described in the will. In most states the automatic inheritance rights of a joint tenancy preempt anything written in a will or trust, so if you don't integrate the various documents and deeds carefully, you can end up leaving more to one person than you intended—the joint tenant will inherit the entire property even if your will says that a percentage of it should go to someone else.

Remaining Tax Concerns for Same-Sex Couples

Not all states have inheritance taxes. But if you're married or registered under the laws of the state where you file taxes and there is an inheritance tax in your state that exempts spouses, that exemption will cover you. If you are legally married, your spouse can take advantage of the marital exemptions from federal estate taxes. Couples who are state registered cannot take advantage of federal tax benefits.

The federal tax exemption limit for 2013 is $5,250,000—minus what you've given away in excess of the annual $14,000 per year gift tax exemption. (See Chapter 4.) Most likely, this is not going to be a problem for most of you, but if you happen to be worth anywhere near (or more than) this amount, your survivor could face expensive estate taxes when you die.

There are numerous ways to minimize or even avoid the estate tax, and if you are wealthy enough to be worrying about it, you should find an estate planner who has experience working with high-net-worth folks who are unmarried—gay or straight—to figure out appropriate strategies to avoid or limit the tax.

Probate Procedures

Probate is the process by which the court supervises the distribution of your estate. Not everyone has to go through probate. If your assets other than real estate have a total value that's under a certain amount—defined by your state—and you either don't own any real estate or your real estate is titled in joint tenancy, your executor will be able to carry out your wishes upon your death without court supervision. Also, if your property passes to your heirs through a trust, discussed below, probate rules don't apply.

Each state has its own rules about how much property you can own at the time of your death and still have your property pass outside of probate. States also have their own rules about how the probate process goes, but in pretty much every case the local probate judge reviews your will to make sure it is valid, supervises the executor's plans for carrying out your wishes, and reviews the final accounting to make sure everything went where it was supposed to go. Along the way, the judge rules on any disputes raised by heirs, friends, or relatives; issues orders to enable your executor to sell assets; and sometimes sets the fees for any professionals who assist in the probate process.

Probate can take a year or longer and can cost upwards of $10,000 or more in professional fees, which is why so many folks want to avoid it.

Trusts

One way that you can avoid probate is to use a legal instrument called a living (or revocable) trust. You wouldn't want to use an irrevocable trust in most instances, as that would prevent you from changing your plans if your relationship came to an end or other circumstances changed.

A trust is a legal entity, and it functions like a briefcase: Once it is created on paper you can place any of your assets into the trust entity. You can set up the trust so that you continue to control the assets that are in the briefcase while you are alive, and then you can designate a person to control them upon your death (or if you become disabled). At your death, the briefcase goes to your trustee, who will transfer the assets in it to whomever you name in the trust, without the requirement of probate. Because the probate court isn't involved, the terms of your trust stay private and it is more difficult for a hostile relative to challenge your plans in court.

You can change your trust instructions any time during your life, without having to start over creating a new trust. You can make specific provisions in a trust that can't be arranged in a will. You can provide, for example, that upon your death your partner can continue living in your house, but upon your partner's death the house must pass to your relatives. Likewise you can set up your trust so that upon your death some of your money is used to support your partner during his or her lifetime, but whatever is left when your partner dies goes to your favorite charity or your chosen relatives.

Typically, although your trust assets can be transferred without court supervision, you should also make a will that leaves your remaining property to the trust, to be sure that any assets you don't deposit into your trust will be distributed under the same terms.

For some people, despite the advantages, a trust may be inconvenient and overly complicated, and not have much short-term value. For example, a trust requires that you change the names on your bank accounts and the title to all of your property in order to put the assets into the trust briefcase. Some lenders won't lend to trusts, so you may be required to take the property out of your trust if you want to borrow money against your house later. And depending on which state you live in, you may have to set up multiple trusts if you share some property with your partner and own other assets on your own.

Setting up a trust can be expensive. Only a small category of people can use do-it-yourself products to create a trust—those who are putting property into trust solely to protect it from probate. Anyone who wants to make more complicated provisions, like allowing a partner to live in a house but then transferring it again at the partner's death, should consult a lawyer, as should anyone with significant assets. Fees for creating a trust generally run between $2,500 and $5,000.

In my opinion, people who have more than $1,000,000 in assets or real estate, are over 55, have complicated plans for their assets upon death—especially involving the care of children—or have been diagnosed with a life-threatening illness, probably should go ahead and spend the money to create a trust. And if you have more than $5,250,000 in assets, then you certainly should consider creating a trust and absolutely should hire a lawyer to help you.

The Relationship Between Estate Planning Documents and Other Agreements

Many same-sex couples, especially long-term couples for whom marriage hasn't been an option until recently, already have written agreements that state how their property will be divided in the event of a breakup. Some of these documents also purport to address what happens to their property at the death of one partner. In general, these documents won't meet the standards of a will or trust, which means the provisions about transferring property at death are unlikely to be honored, unless they are restated in a valid will or trust.

Thus, if you have such an agreement, be sure to bring it to the attention of your estate planning lawyer so that your estate planning documents can be created or revised appropriately. If you're doing your own will, make sure that the provisions of your will and of your property agreement are entirely consistent.

The same is true for partners who enter into a premarital agreement. It's critical that you make sure that your premarital agreement and your wills are consistent. Your premarital agreement doesn't substitute for a will, nor will it override a will if the provisions are in conflict.

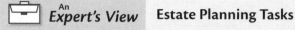

An Expert's View   Estate Planning Tasks

Because of the confusing patchwork of rights for same-sex couples, you need to have a complete estate plan in place, regardless of what legal union you enjoy. That way, no matter where you are and no matter how (or whether) your relationship is recognized, you and your beloved will be protected in the event of the Three Big D's: death, disability, or dissolution (breakup). This is the "belt and suspenders" theory, as you can't be too prepared when it comes to these important protections.

Everyone should have a will, even if you have very modest assets, and be sure your property and accounts are titled as you want them to be. A crucial document to have in place is the designation of health care surrogate, health care proxy, or health care power of attorney—whatever your state calls the document that allows you to have access to and make medical decisions for your partner.

Other documents, such as a power of attorney and a living will, also are good to have, depending on your wishes. A trust might be appropriate as well, depending on the probate scheme in your state and your asset level. Please, consult a gay or gay-friendly lawyer with specific estate planning competence for more information.

Be sure you understand the limits and possible pitfalls of entering a legal relationship. It may not give you all of the benefits you may be seeking— for example, you won't be entitled to the marital deduction for estate tax purposes if you are in a civil union or domestic partnership, or be guaranteed parental rights when your partner is the sole legal parent of a child you're helping to raise. And remember, romance is exciting but it's crucial to be deliberate when it comes to these issues.

Elizabeth F. Schwartz is an attorney in Miami, Florida, with an emphasis on addressing the unique estate planning needs of the LGBT community, as well as divorce and creative conflict resolution. Her work also includes assisting with the legal aspects of adoption, insemination, and surrogacy.

Intestacy Rules

Intestacy rules determine who gets to inherit from a person who dies without having signed a valid will or a trust. Every state has laws about where your money goes if you don't state your wishes: Generally, it's to your spouse and your close family members (parents and siblings) in various shares.

One of the most valuable benefits of getting married or legally partnered is the possibility that your state's rules about intestacy will apply to you. I say "the possibility" because it won't always be true—if you live in a nonrecognition state, you won't have the benefit of your state's laws. And even in some of the relationship recognition states, you don't get all the same protections as heterosexual married spouses (see the chart in Appendix A). But if intestacy rules do apply, they should be a factor in your decision about whether marrying is the right choice for you.

If you are not married or legally partnered, your legal "next of kin" will be your parents, siblings, nieces or nephews—not your partner. This means that if you don't have a will or trust leaving your things to your partner, your partner will inherit nothing. (See "Estate Planning When You're Not Married," below.) If you are married or legally partnered and you live in a state that recognizes your relationship, that state's intestacy rules apply, and if you die without a will, your partner will inherit the spouse's share. But in most states, this "share" isn't everything—sometimes the rules say that half of your estate goes to your spouse and half to your parents or other family members. If you want to leave your partner more than that, a will or trust is crucial.

On the other hand, if you are married or legally partnered and you live in a state that doesn't recognize your relationship, it's unlikely that your state's rules will apply—it will be the same as if you weren't married, and your legally recognized family will inherit instead of your partner. Given how much uncertainty there is about which states recognize which relationships, you'll be better off if you presume a lack of recognition and act accordingly by preparing a will or trust.

If you rely solely on intestacy rules as the basis for transferring property to your partner at your death, you are inviting a challenge. In part, that's because our legal relationships are new and not always recognized, but another reason is that the domestic partner registration process is relatively informal and often just requires signing a piece of paper and mailing it in to the designated state agency. Family members may challenge your partner's inheritance on the grounds that you didn't know what you were signing when you registered, and didn't intend to distribute your estate that way.

It's also very likely that you want to leave more to your partner than the state intestacy rules would provide. Or you may want to arrange things differently than the state would prescribe, by giving certain preferred items to your spouse and other things to other relatives. The bottom line is that it's always better to make your own decisions than to let the state make them for you.

Other Ways to Transfer Property at Death

There are some other ways to transfer property outside of probate that you should know about.

Pay on Death Accounts. You can designate your partner (or someone else, of course) on bank and brokerage accounts as "payable on death." Once the designation is made, the account will go to the designated person immediately upon your death without any court involvement—regardless of whether you've signed a will and regardless of what intestacy rules are in your state. This is an efficient way to transfer cash and other accounts that might otherwise be tied up after your death. Just ask your banker for a pay on death form. If the first person you ask at the bank isn't familiar with the procedure, go up the chain of command until you find someone who is—every bank has the forms somewhere. Be sure to keep track of what you have done, so that your other estate documents are consistent with these designations.

Beneficiary Designations. If you have retirement accounts, you have undoubtedly designated a beneficiary to receive those benefits in the event of your death. The designation means that the person you list will get the account, regardless of what your will says or what intestacy rules would mandate. In other words, if there's a conflict between your will and the beneficiary designation, the designation will be enforced. The tax consequences of transferring retirement accounts to a same-sex partner at death are complicated, and you may want to consult a financial adviser about the best way to deal with them.

Joint Tenancy. If you own an asset (such as a house or a bank account) as joint tenants with right of survivorship, your half automatically passes to your co-owner immediately upon your death. A will that says otherwise will be ignored. (See "Joint Tenancy Property," above, for reasons why some people might not want to hold property this way.) Some states also allow for a "payable on death" arrangement for real estate assets.

Community Property. If you are married or legally partnered and you hold title to property as community property with right of survivorship or, in some states, as tenants by the entireties, your share will pass to your co-owner notwithstanding any contrary provisions in your will or trust, or what the intestacy rules provide. In some states, similar rules apply to any asset that is in fact community property, even if it wasn't titled as such.

Fiduciary Duties and the Problem of "Influence"

Spouses and legal partners in every state owe each other legal duties called "fiduciary duties." This means that both partners are under an obligation to act in the financial interests of the other partner and the partnership, not just in their own self-interest. In addition, all states have laws regarding "undue influence," intended to protect people—whether married or not—from financial overreaching on the part of a family member, friend, or caregiver, especially when it comes to making decisions about bequests.

How do these rules affect you? They become relevant if your partner's relatives challenge your partner's will or trust on the basis that you exercised undue influence to force your partner to leave you money or property. The law assumes that spouses don't exercise undue influence on each other, but if you are unmarried or living in a state that doesn't recognize your marriage or legal partnership, you could be at risk of an undue influence claim if your partner's relatives are hostile to your relationship.

This problem can be avoided with the right kind of estate planning. If either you or your partner has significant assets, if you live in a state where it is unclear whether your marriage or partnership or marriage will be recognized, or if there is any chance that a relative would attack a bequest, the best way to avoid potential problems is for each of you to have your wills prepared by separate lawyers. Each of you should see your own lawyer on your own, in private—don't even bring your partner with you to sit in the waiting room. That way you can be sure that your lawyer can verify that you were fully competent to make the crucial decisions and that you made your plans of your own free will.

Special Issues for Parents

If you, your partner, or the two of you together have children, you have some special considerations as you prepare your estate plan. If you both are legal parents, it's clear in every state that if one of you dies the other retains custody of your minor children. But if only one of you is a legal parent, it's important that you make your intentions clear about who should take care of your kids if you die while they are minors. You won't have absolute assurance your partner will be selected, because you can only nominate a guardian. The local court will make the final determination, but your wishes will be respected unless someone objects and shows a good reason why your decisions aren't in your children's best interests.

If you die when your children are minors and you have a partner who's also their legal parent, you'll most likely leave your money and property to your partner on the assumption that your partner will continue to care for your children. If you're a single parent, you can leave money and property to your children in trust under the Uniform Transfers to Minors Act. You can name your partner or another adult to act as trustee and manage the funds until your children reach adulthood.

Cautionary Tales

In case you haven't been sufficiently motivated by all these positive exhortations about the need for estate planning, consider two examples that should prompt you to act now.

EXAMPLE 1: Bill and Ed were long-time partners who owned a valuable old mansion they had operated as a bed and breakfast for more than 20 years. In 1995, Bill was suffering from AIDS and was sure he was going to die, so he transferred his interest in the mansion to Ed outright instead of writing up a will or trust. Then, when the HIV drug cocktails became available and Bill's health improved, they bought standard trust documents from a local office supply store—but filled them out wrong and forgot to list the property in the right place or designate clearly who was to inherit it. Even though they registered as domestic partners later on, they only registered with the city and not under any state-mandated process, so the intestacy rules didn't apply. Ed's sister ended up as the presumptive intestacy heir, and Bill had to file a lawsuit against her to claim the property he always thought would be his. Eventually the lawsuit settled with Bill receiving the property, but he had to pay a settlement to Ed's sister and pay his lawyers as well.

EXAMPLE 2: Elaine and Terry co-owned their house for nearly a decade, but when Elaine was having financial troubles she deeded her half to Terry so they could refinance at a better interest rate. They never added Elaine back on title, but when Terry was diagnosed with ovarian cancer they state-registered as domestic partners in California. They believed that as spouse-equivalents they had protected Elaine fully, but when Terry died, her parents claimed that the registration was defective because Terry wasn't completely alert when she signed the registration form and hadn't signed a will either. Elaine had to file a lawsuit to establish the validity of the registration, and even if she wins her case she may only inherit a 50% interest in the residence, because Terry's parents also claimed that because the house wasn't a community property asset, the intestacy rules provide that half go to the parents and only half to the spouse.

Both of these tragic situations could have been avoided if the people involved had received just a minimum amount of advice and made considered decisions about how to plan their estates.

Estate Planning When You're Not Married or Legally Partnered

The freedom to marry also bestows on you the freedom to not marry—but if that is your choice, please do not put your partner at risk of being thrown out of your home, being denied access to your shared possessions, or having to wage a legal battle against your legal relatives. Put simply, if you aren't legally partnered or registered then you aren't legally related to each other, and intestacy rules don't apply. This means that your closest legal relatives are your parents and siblings, and they will have the power to make decisions about your medical care if you're incapacitated and about the disposition of your property at your death. This also will be the case if you register or marry but live in a state that doesn't recognize your partnership. (See Chapter 4.) And as unmarried/unregistered partners, neither state tax exemptions for married spouses nor any of the federal spousal exemptions apply to you.

You should plan on signing the documents described in "Planning for Disability" and "Planning for Death," above, to protect each other in the event one of you is unable to make medical or other decisions. If you do nothing else in your immediate planning, make sure you sign these simple documents. While we strongly recommend that even married or legally partnered couples create planning documents, it is absolutely crucial that unmarried and unregistered couples have wills and powers of attorney. Without these documents you may not be able to take care of each other in the event of illness, and the survivor may be left with nothing at the first partner's death.

All of the information above that explains what these documents are and how to create them applies to unmarried couples as well. ●

Legal Change in Action:
How Change Happens and What to Expect

B elieve it or not, sometimes there are no clear answers to legal questions —even important questions that cry out for answers, like whether your legal relationship is valid and recognized. And there sometimes *see*ms to be no rhyme or reason to how or when the legal questions do get answered. While we can't answer every one of your questions, we can, at least, give you an understanding of how legal changes come about and what you might expect in the near and longer terms.

How Legal Change Happens

The fundamental rules of same-sex partnering have changed dramatically in the past ten years. While the underlying impetus for these transformations has no doubt been the broad social changes we've all witnessed, the changes have been implemented, as all legal changes are, from three sources: the courts, the legislatures, and voter-passed ballot measures. Here's a bit about how each type of change has played out in relation to same-sex families.

Court Decisions

The United States has separate court systems for state and federal cases, but each one operates in the same basic way: Trial courts are the first stop for anyone with a beef, whether it's personal between two individuals, a dispute between two or more entities, or a challenge to an official act or a legal rule.

Once the trial court rules on a case, the losing party can consider bringing an appeal to a higher court, called an appellate court. Not everyone can appeal—the appellate court won't generally revisit a factual finding, or the resolution of a factual dispute. There has to be some kind of legal error or violation of a fundamental constitutional principle in order for a court to consider an appeal. When an appeal is decided, the ruling is generally binding not only on the parties in the case, but also on anyone else in the same position. In that way, appellate courts shape and refine "the law" by issuing written opinions that govern everyone in the state or at least in the district where the court presides.

The losing party in an appellate case may want to take the case even higher. At that point, there are only limited circumstances under which the highest appellate courts will consider a case. Each state high court has its own rules for what cases it will consider, and very few cases are accepted for review. For the most part appellate courts only take up cases that involve fundamental legal doctrines or constitutional issues. The U.S. Supreme Court also accepts only a tiny percentage of cases it's requested to consider—usually cases from a federal circuit court (the federal appellate court) and, occasionally, cases from a state supreme court dealing with federal constitutional issues.

Most of the cases described in "Marriage in the Courts," below, are cases from state appellate courts, either intermediate appellate courts or the state high courts. That's because for the most part marital law in this country, as we've *see*n, is state based. However, if someone wants to challenge a federal ruling or law, such as the immigration rules or the tax code, that challenge will be taken up in the federal court—and then climb up the federal court ladder if the losing party files an appeal. And in some cases, such as the Prop. 8 case in California, federal courts will render an opinion on the federal constitutionality of a state law.

Legislative Action

Each state has its own legislature, made up of elected representatives whose job is to enact laws and regulations. There are state assembly members and state senators. Each state also elects a number of congresspeople and two senators to represent the state in the United States Congress, whose job is to enact federal legislation and regulations. Otto von Bismark, a Prussian leader of the 19th century, once said that laws are like sausages, and it's better to not *see* how either one is made. But in brief, both state and federal legislatures enact laws by drafting proposed laws and sending them through various committees for consideration and amendment, eventually coming out with a final product that both houses of the legislature approve and the state's governor, or the president, will sign or veto.

Voter Initiatives

About half of the states have voter initiative systems that allow citizens and organizations to gather voter signatures in order to bring issues to a public vote, with the end result being the enactment of or amendment to a law, issuance of a bond, or even an amendment to a state constitution.

And initiatives can themselves be challenged in courts and be overturned by judges, just as legislative statutes can be thrown out by voter initiatives.

Now that we've surveyed the basics of how the law is formed, let's look at how marriage equality fares in each of these realms.

Marriage in the Courts

In general, the most positive legal developments for same-sex couples have come from the courts, which have the job of interpreting our laws (including constitutional laws). This will likely continue to be true into the future, with some exceptions.

Steps Toward Marriage Equality in the Courts

As we've *seen*, the first major court advance took place in Hawaii, in 1993, when the highest court of that state issued a ruling that required the state government to justify, in court, its ban on same-sex marriage.

Then, in 2003, the U.S. Supreme Court decided *Lawrence v. Texas*, which overturned its earlier decision upholding the validity of sodomy laws. *Lawrence* was a landmark case and *see*med to turn the tide—ever since then, the trend in the courts *see*ms to be in favor of LGBT rights—again, with some notable exceptions. Consider the following positive decisions beginning with Lawrence.

Lawrence v. Texas: Dramatically reversing its own decision issued just 18 years earlier, the United States Supreme Court tossed out all remaining laws criminalizing homosexual conduct between consenting adults. This decision represented a major transformation of how the law in this country treats homosexuals and laid the groundwork for other decisions, especially in cases where the criminalization of homosexuality formed the basis for discriminatory treatment.

Goodridge v. Dept. of Public Health: In 2003, the Massachusetts Supreme Court ruled that only full legal marriage would meet the legitimate need for dignity and respect that same-sex couples deserved and that civil union or domestic partnership options were not just "separate," but were unequal.

California Parentage Cases: In 2005, the California Supreme Court overturned decades of decisions hostile to lesbian parents and ruled that nonbiological coparents who could demonstrate an intent to coparent at the time of the child's birth could establish parentage, even where no adoption has been finalized.

In Re Marriage Cases: In May 2008, the California Supreme Court pushed the marriage envelope even further, ruling that only full legal marriage would meet constitutional standards and also that LGBT people are a protected class, entitled to the highest level of constitutional review when discriminatory laws are challenged. However, a ballot initiative in November 2008 rendered the court decision moot as the voters approved a constitutional amendment banning same-sex marriage; that amendment was upheld by the California Supreme Court in May 2009 and remained in effect until 2013.

Varnum v. Brien: In April 2009, the Iowa Supreme Court ruled in a unanimous opinion that Iowa's marriage statute, limiting marriage to a man and a woman, violated the equal protection clause of the Iowa state constitution.

Kerrigan et al. v. Commissioner of Public Health: In October 2008, the Connecticut Supreme Court concluded that marriage is a social institution of great importance, not just a "bundle of rights" that could be designated a civil union. The court held that same-sex marriage is legal in Connecticut.

Perry v. Hollingsworth: This California case began in 2009 when two same-sex couples challenged Proposition 8, the ballot initiative that became law in November 2008 and provides that only marriage between a man and a woman is recognized in California. In July 2009, federal district court Judge Vaughn Walker issued a 132-page opinion that eviscerated the arguments against same-sex marriage and ruled that Prop. 8 was unconstitutional and that same-sex couples should have the right to marry in California. The proponents of Prop. 8 filed numerous appeals and finally, in June 2013, the U.S. Supreme Court ruled that the proponents of the ban on gay marriage lacked standing to appeal the case. As a result, the Walker decision was reinstated, and the same-sex wedding bells promptly rang again in California.

Parentage cases: These cases aren't technically about marriage, but many of them test the marriage and marriage equivalent relationships in some way. For example, a New York court granted recognition to the parental rights created by a Vermont civil union, and a Virginia court recognized a North Carolina parentage decree in favor of two gay men who were registered as domestic partners in California. Other cases support the validity of adoptions across state lines and require a birth state to issue a new birth certificate to a child adopted by gay parents in another state.

New York Appellate Court Rulings: In a series of recent rulings, the generally conservative New York state courts have upheld parentage and property rights based upon Canadian and Massachusetts marriages, thus opening the door for marriage recognition in a state that has not itself authorized same-sex marriages. In sync with these rulings, Governor Paterson issued an executive order providing that all state agencies should recognize same-sex marriages legally entered into in other states.

State Recognition Decisions: In New Jersey in early 2009, a judge ruled that two lesbians married in Canada could be divorced in a New Jersey court. California courts have likewise granted divorces to same-sex couples married in Canada. But a Texas appeals court recently ruled that two gay men married in Massachusetts could not get divorced in Texas, an Oklahoma court of appeals refused to grant a divorce to a couple married in Canada, and a Pennsylvania trial court judge also denied a divorce petition by a couple married in Massachusetts. The court in that case, however, suggested that the couple ask the court to declare their marriage void under Pennsylvania law—not exactly the political statement that any same-sex couple wants to make.

Steps Toward Federal Recognition: While narrow in impact, a few federal judges recognized same-sex marriages early on. In a bankruptcy case in 2007, a same-sex couple was treated as married, and in a lesbian employee's challenge over health insurance regulations, a federal judge ruled that her California marriage required that she be given the same rights as a heterosexual married employee.

Also in early 2009, two federal court judges ruled that the Defense of Marriage Act (DOMA) unconstitutionally denied benefits to the same-sex spouses of federal employees. One ruling was issued on behalf of a Los Angeles federal public defender, and another involved claims by a federal court staff attorney. While neither ruling sets precedent that can be cited in other cases, the decisions were positive, hopeful signs that courts were beginning to recognize the serious impact that federal nonrecognition has on employees.

And in *Gill v. Office of Personnel Management*, a federal trial court in Massachusetts ruled in August 2010 that Section 3 of the Defense of Marriage Act (DOMA) is unconstitutional. Section 3 is the part of DOMA that says the federal government does not have to recognize marriages legally entered into in states that have marriage equality. In other words, the law requires all federal departments and agencies to disrespect the valid state-licensed marriages of same-sex couples.

These trends were especially relevant to the most central issue of marriage equality: the lack of federal recognition of same-sex marriages and partnerships. Finally, in June 2013, the United States Supreme Court handed down its landmark decision in the case of *United States v. Windsor*, which invalidated the section of DOMA that prevented the federal government from recognizing otherwise valid same-sex marriages. The appeal resulted from the imposition of a federal estate tax on the estate of Thea Spyer, who had married her longtime partner, Edith Windsor, in Canada several years earlier. The Court concluded that New York State would have recognized their marriage, and it was wrong for the federal tax authorities to disregard her marital status in denying her the spousal exemption. Interestingly, even though the Obama administration had elected to not appeal the adverse decision by the lower courts, the Supreme Court decided to rule on the case anyway, *see*ing the significance of issuing a decision on this important case.

The Court's decision embraced the "liberty" rights of same-sex couples to live together and raise families, concluding that it was a denial of equal protection and due process for Congress to deny same-sex married couples the same federal benefits that straight couples enjoy.

The Court limited its decision to one issue—federal recognition of a legally married same-sex couple. The justices did not reach the broader issue of whether every state must allow same-sex couples to marry or recognize same-sex marriages celebrated in other states. Many legal observers have stated that the broad policies enunciated by the Court will eventually lead to state bans on same-sex marriage recognition being tossed out, and lawsuits raising this sort of claim have been filed in many of the states that still ban same-sex marriage. This issue will likely come back to the United States Supreme Court in a few years, and hopefully the results will be as positive as what occurred in the *Windsor* case!

This list is not comprehensive; it's merely a representative survey of some of the major decisions that have impacted or involved marriage equality. Obviously, not all the court decisions in recent years have been positive. Courts in numerous states have issued decisions denying parental rights to nonbiological same-sex parents, and state courts have rejected marriage equality cases over and over again. Judges also continue to issue homophobic decisions limiting custody or visitation for LGBT parents raising children with their former opposite-sex spouses.

Organizations like the National Center for Lesbian Rights, Lambda Legal Defense and Education Fund, the ACLU, and Gay and Lesbian Advocates and Defenders, among others, are constantly working on important cases on the state and federal levels. To learn more about their work, *see* the website listings in Appendix B.

The Future of Court Decisions

The next five to ten years will undoubtedly be extremely active in the courts. First, local family law courts (the first court most people go to when they end a legal relationship) will begin to face more and more cases involving partners of the same sex. Some disputes in those cases will involve garden variety family law issues that the courts will know how to deal with, but many will be more complex. Some of the unique issues will be the date of marriage for a couple who legally married more than once, in several different jurisdictions; the characterization of property purchased before the legal relationship began; whether a couple's time together before the legal relationship should count for purposes of calculating support; and whether parentage rules of one state apply in another state, especially one that doesn't recognize the adults' legal relationship.

The trial courts will make decisions about all of these issues and more, and if one partner is dissatisfied with the ruling, feels there's a principle at stake, and has money to burn, the case will be appealed to a higher court, and decisions will be made in the appellate court that affect all of the same-sex couples in that state. We are already hearing about lawsuits filed in states that don't allow same-sex couples to marry and eventually, those cases will very likely end up at the U.S. Supreme Court.

In other words, courts are going to be making a bundle of decisions that will affect our relationships. Some will go well for the individual but badly for the community and some will be the other way around. Over time, there will be enough court rulings for you to have greater confidence in predicting your own future and making your own decisions. It's also possible that the very complexity of these cases will generate greater consciousness of the problems that arise as a result of state nonrecognition. Judges are bound to be just as frustrated with the patchwork of legal options and the chaos that results from inconsistent treatment of same-sex relationships as you are.

It is for these practical reasons as much as any others that I predict that marriage is going to emerge as the winning solution. It won't happen nationwide immediately, but ten years from now, chances are very good that it will become the new norm for all of us.

In the interim, courts will be called on to interpret the validity of marriages and to decide crucial issues. The actions the courts take will determine how long the marriage equality fight continues.

Marriage in the Legislature

LGBT family issues may have begun to find some support in the courts, but the opposite is true in the legislature.

Marriage in Congress and in the Statehouse

The United States Congress enacted the first "defense of marriage" act (DOMA) more than fifteen years ago; this also led many federal agencies to issue rules and policies that negatively affect same-sex couples. The

Respect for Marriage Act, introduced in Congress in 2010, would have recognized same-sex marriages in every state, even states where same-sex marriage isn't legal. For example, a couple living in Kansas could travel to Iowa to get married, and when they returned to Kansas, they would still be married for purposes of federal recognition. Ironically, however, nothing in the Respect for Marriage Act requires states to respect other states' laws about marriage—so that couple could find themselves married for federal purposes but not considered married in their home state. As of 2013, the federal issue has been resolved in our favor, but more than half of U.S. state legislatures have passed DOMA laws that prohibit same-sex marriage and, in some cases, prevent the state from recognizing same-sex marriages and other relationships authorized elsewhere.

On the positive side, 45 individual states have enacted hate crime statutes that include sexual orientation as a protected status, and many state laws now protect LGBT youth and prohibit discrimination in business and employment. Of course, these laws relate to LGBT rights generally, not marriage equality, which remains a hot-button issue unlike any other. According to most observers the "line in the sand" for most antigay advocates is marriage. The new approach *see*ms to be that it's fine to be gay and even to have some of the rights and duties of marriage, as long as "real" marriage is saved for heterosexual couples. Marriage is truly the new battleground for gay rights in this country.

The Future of Marriage Equality Legislation

Despite incremental positive change in areas other than marriage equality, for many years, the legislative horizon has been rather bleak. In recent years, however, that trend has begun to change, with numerous states passing legislation in favor of same-sex marriage and a number of other states with marriage equality or marriage equivalent legislation moving through state legislatures, albeit in fits and starts.

In the states that have DOMAs or other laws that discriminate against same-sex couples, it will take affirmative legislation—or a court case—to overturn the existing laws. This may be particularly challenging in states that have passed constitutional amendments, which are difficult to change once enacted.

Now that the federal DOMA is repealed but states are allowed to keep their DOMAs, there will be further uncertainties. Some federal agencies, such as the Social Security administration, recognize all marriages that are legal in the states where the couples live. Other agencies, such as the IRS, recognize any same-sex marriage as long as it was legally formalized in a state that allows it, regardless of where the couple lives.

It's also becoming clear to some politicians that watching the gay marriage bandwagon go by without jumping on could be costly for their state. When the Massachusetts legislature was debating whether to lift the ban on out-of-state citizens marrying there, the debate was briefly about justice and fairness, and then turned to the issue of revenue that would be lost to the state if out-of-staters flew to San Francisco for their lavish gay weddings instead of to Provincetown.

The New Business Approach

A telling example of how supporting gay marriage has become the business-savvy position is how the corporate mainstream supported the opposition to Proposition 8, the ballot initiative to ban same-sex marriage in California. An editorial in a mainstream business newspaper of Northern California explained that attracting the "best and the brightest" workers was key to California's economic success and argued that regions that are open to diverse workers (including gay ones) demonstrably "out-perform their less-creative peers in job creation and income." In other words, there is no justification for intolerance, either morally or economically.

So where does this analysis take us? I predict that we are likely to continue to gain some unexpected allies because of the extent to which the current system is downright cumbersome and confusing, and not just for same-sex couples. Financial institutions, title companies, credit card companies, human resources departments, companies doing business in multiple states, and many other institutions and organizations don't want to have to figure out 50 different versions of marital status when it comes to dealing with their customers and employees. In particular, given how mainstreamed many same-sex couples have become and how much more common it is for people to be open at work, American business is likely to be a strong advocate for removing barriers to marriage equality.

For all these reasons, we are confident that eventually the tide will turn, but it will take time. In the next five to ten years, there will continue to be significant ways that our relationships will not be fully recognized by some states' laws. As a result, the extent to which your relationship is legally protected will depend in large part on where you live. Perhaps instead of talking so much about blue states and red states, we need to be highlighting the lavender states!

Marriage and the Voters

As is often true in a civil rights context, the battle for the hearts and minds of the voters is the hardest to win.

Setbacks From the Initiative Process

Where the legislatures have declined to pass DOMA laws, voter initiatives have often taken up the slack and put them on the books. More than 35 states have statutes in place that define marriage as between a man and woman only, and 30 state constitutions expressly prohibit same-sex marriage. Most of these were passed by voter initiatives, and three of them—California, Arizona, and Florida—were amended in the November 2008 election, a disappointing result in an election that also saw President Obama's historic victory.

Future Voters of America

So why do I remain optimistic? Many polls indicate that the younger they are, the more likely voters are to support marriage equality—and younger voters are becoming more active and gaining more of a voice in each successive election. The visibility of same-sex couples is also on the rise. As an increasing number of couples becomes known to their straight neighbors and relatives, I am convinced that the barriers to full equality will eventually fall.

Government Agencies

Another way that incremental change happens is through the movement of government agencies. For example, even before DOMA was invalidated, federal government employees were eligible to participate in a limited form of domestic partnership that granted benefits such as long term care insurance, child care subsidies, and employee assistance to the same-sex partners of federal employees. Also, the Office of Personnel Management redefined "family member" and "immediate relative" to include same-sex partners for purposes of sick leave, funeral leave, and other time and leave-related issues—but not for purposes of the Family and Medical Leave Act, which is a federal statute. In addition, State Department employees were able to bring their same-sex partners along on postings and have travel and other expenses paid for, for the entire family. And the IRS issued a "private letter ruling" to the effect that community property income in California and Washington—the only community property states among the marriage equality and marriage equivalent states—would be treated as such by the federal tax authorities in addition to the state tax agencies.

What Does the Uncertain Future Mean to Your Present?

The newest form of discrimination against LGBT people is this: legal complexity. Opposite-sex couples don't have to worry about what their rights will be if they relocate to another state, or how laws might change in the future. Instead, they can make their decisions about marriage based upon the organic development of their relationship—at the time and place that makes most sense to them alone. Unfortunately, we don't yet have this privilege. So how do we go about making our relationship decisions in light of the uncertainty?

Look to the preceding chapters for the answers, especially Chapters 4, 5, and 6. You'll *see* that my advice is that you should factor in the probable availability of marital rights and obligations on the state and federal levels, while at the same time organizing your lives in ways that take into account the problem areas that remain and the ways they may affect you. Here's a quick summary of the important steps in making your decision:

1. Start by evaluating your own state's rules, and decide whether non-recognition problems are sufficiently serious for you to hold off marrying until they are resolved.

2. Evaluate the effects of the invalidation of the federal DOMA, and get a sense of whether any of the federal agency rules might create serious problems if you got married or legally partnered.

3. If the downsides of nonrecognition are not wildly punitive for you, make the marriage or partnership decision based upon your emotional needs and subjective desires, knowing there are some legal risks and uncertainties, and take the necessary steps to protect yourselves in the face of this nonrecognition.

4. If you decide to wait, make regular reassessments of both the legal landscape and your own personal situation, and be prepared to update your plans accordingly.

5. If you are taking any major actions that involve legal status (such as bringing a child into your home or purchasing or changing ownership of a house), establish those relationships by court action or contract, as appropriate, regardless of whether you are in a legally recognized relationship or not.

6. If you marry or legally partner and believe there is any risk of non-recognition of your relationship, ratify your decisions about dissolution and death in private documents, rather than relying solely on your legal status.

And keep your eyes on the prize. Full marriage equality is coming; the only question is when. ●

The End

I often try to think of metaphors for the legal aspects of maintaining a successful same-sex relationship in these rapidly changing times. Clinging to each other on the deck of a ship on stormy seas, perhaps, or dashing hand-in-hand across a busy road, or maybe snuggling together on a gyrating rollercoaster. However you see it, we're all trying to hold onto our partners and our dreams and have long and satisfying relationships, while the still-homophobic political culture and the outdated legal system toss us from side to side and put barriers in our way.

There are moments where one can feel and see the power of our love and our flexibility and creativity in the face of these challenges. I felt it when my partner and I celebrated our 30th anniversary with our close friends, tearfully thanking each other for so many years of love and support. I experience it every time I attend a commitment ceremony or a wedding, reflecting on how secretive such events would have been in earlier times or in other lands. It's readily apparent when my gay friends show off photos of their young children attending their first year of school. And I see it in the simplest of moments, when a young lesbian couple enthusiastically tells me about the condominium they have just purchased together.

Part of what is special about all of these events is that it hasn't been simple for any of us to get to this point. It's not just about the personal dramas that every couple faces. It's also about the decades of legal advocacy and political work that have made it possible for us to live together safely, with our partners and children, in our own homes and our chosen communities. So many activists and advocates have fought for so many years, in so many places, for us to share in the same public and private benefits that our straight friends and relatives have taken for granted for so long.

And as you know from having read these chapters, it still isn't easy for many of us. Until there is marriage equality in all 50 states, same-sex couples will be burdened by unfair inconsistent laws of property and parentage, and uncertainty as to how they will be treated when they travel.

As daunting as it has been to establish the very real legal rights that we now have, each of you also face your own questions and uncertainties about how best to exercise those new liberties. I'm confident you can master these challenges.

In my ideal world, our community is filled with happily single folks choosing to stay unattached, happily married couples enjoying all the rights and privileges of marriage, and equally happy couples electing to opt out of the marriage system and form their own kind of commitment arrangement. Whichever option you choose, I believe that you can face the questions presented in this book and organize your legal affairs in a way that supports your goals and nurtures your partnership for the long term. And should things not work out for the two of you as a couple, I hope that you have made the appropriate arrangements to allow you to move on with the resources you need and deserve, without regret or rancor.

Fundamental to the practice of law is a belief that information bestows power and freedom, by giving everyone the tools to best organize their lives, meet their personal needs, protect their families, and create a sustaining legal framework that fosters their dreams and goals. You now are in possession of the basic knowledge relevant to the formation of your legal lives together, and you have the deeper understanding that will enable you to ask, and answer, the central questions and make the necessary decisions for your lives together. Keep your balance, stay on track, resolve your disagreements, and cherish the hard-won freedoms that you are now able to enjoy.

I wish each and every one of you many happy anniversaries! ●

Relationship Recognition Chart

This chart shows the states with some form of relationship recognition for same-sex couples and answers some of the most common questions that come up about the laws of each state. If there's no answer in a box, that means the law is unclear on that issue. This chart was current as of November 2013, but things change quickly! Stay up to date by checking our blogs at www.makingitlegal.net and www.queerjustice.com, and Nolo's update pages at www.nolo.com/legal-updates, as well as the resources listed in Appendix B.

Relationship Recognition Chart

	California	California	Colorado	Connecticut	Delaware	District of Columbia
Type of relationship	Domestic Partnership	Marriage	Domestic Partnership	Marriage	Marriage	Marriage
Effective date	1/05	6/2013	2012	10/08	2013	2010
Marriage equivalent	Yes	Yes	Yes	Yes	Yes	Yes
Must be same sex	Yes (or 62)	No	No	No	No	No
Hospital visitation, medical decisions	Yes	Yes	Yes	Yes	Yes	Yes
Spousal privilege	Yes	Yes	Yes	Yes	Yes	Yes
Community property or equitable distribution	Community property	Community property	Equitable distribution	Equitable distribution	Equitable distribution	Equitable distribution
Presume parentage	Yes	Yes	Yes	Yes	Yes	
Court dissolution required	Yes	Yes	Yes	Yes	Yes	No
Intestate succession	Yes	Yes	Yes	Yes	Yes	Yes
Joint tax filing	Yes	Yes	Yes	Yes	Yes	Yes
Spousal support available	Yes	Yes	Yes	Yes	Yes	Yes
Tenancy by the entirety	No	No	Yes	No	No	Yes
Body disposition rights	Yes	Yes	Yes	Yes	Yes	Yes
Priority for appointment as deceased partner's representative/administrator	Yes	Yes	Yes	Yes	Yes	Yes
Divorce revokes will bequests and beneficiary designations	Yes	Yes	Yes	Yes	Yes	Yes
DOMA or constitutional amendment	No	No	Yes	No	No	Yes

Relationship Recognition Chart, cont'd

	Hawaii	Illinois	Iowa	Maine	Maryland	Massachu-setts
Type of relationship	Marriage	Marriage	Marriage	Marriage	Marriage	Marriage
Effective date	12/13	6/14	4/09	2012	2012	5/04
Marriage equivalent	Yes	Yes	Yes	Yes	Yes	Yes
Must be same sex	No	No	No	No	No	No
Hospital visitation, medical decisions	Yes	Yes	Yes	Yes	Yes	Yes
Spousal privilege	Yes	Yes	Yes	Yes	Yes	Yes
Community property or equitable distribution	Equitable distribution	Equitable distribution	Equitable distribution	Equitable distribution	Equitable distribution	Equitable distribution
Presume parentage	Yes	Yes	Yes	Yes	Yes	Yes
Court dissolution required	Yes	Yes	Yes	Yes	Yes	Yes
Intestate succession	Yes	Yes	Yes	Yes	Yes	Yes
Joint tax filing	Yes	Yes	Yes	Yes	Yes	Yes
Spousal support available	Yes	Yes	Yes	Yes	Yes	Yes
Tenancy by the entirety	Yes	Yes	Yes	Yes	No	Yes
Body disposition rights	Yes	Yes	Yes	Yes	Yes	Yes
Priority for appointment as deceased partner's representative/administrator	Yes	Yes	Yes	Yes	Yes	Yes
Divorce revokes will bequests and beneficiary designations	Yes	Yes	Yes	Yes	Yes	Yes
DOMA or constitutional amendment	No	No	No	No	No	No

Relationship Recognition Chart, cont'd

	Minnesota	Nevada	New Hampshire	New Jersey	New York
Type of relationship	Marriage	Domestic Partnership	Marriage	Marriage	Marriage
Effective date	2013	10/09	1/10	2013	2011
Marriage equivalent	Yes	Yes	Yes	Yes	Yes
Must be same sex	No	No	No	No	No
Hospital visitation, medical decisions	Yes	Yes	Yes	Yes	Yes
Spousal privilege	Yes	Yes	Yes	Yes	Yes
Community property or equitable distribution	Equitable distribution	Community property	Equitable distribution	Equitable distribution	Equitable distribution
Presume parentage	Yes	Yes	Yes	Yes	Yes
Court dissolution required	Yes	Yes	Yes	Yes	Yes
Intestate succession	Yes	Yes	Yes	Yes	Yes
Joint tax filing	Yes	Yes	Yes	Yes	Yes
Spousal support available	Yes	Yes	Yes	Yes	Yes
Tenancy by the entirety	No	No	No	Yes	No
Body disposition rights	Yes	Yes	Yes	Yes	Yes
Priority for appointment as deceased partner's representative/administrator	Yes	Yes	Yes	Yes	Yes
Divorce revokes will bequests and beneficiary designations	Yes	Yes	Yes	Yes	Yes
DOMA or constitutional amendment	No	No	No	No	No

Relationship Recognition Chart, cont'd

	Oregon	Rhode Island	Vermont	Washington	Wisconsin
Type of relationship	Domestic Partnership*	Marriage	Marriage	Marriage	Domestic Partnership
Effective date	2013	2013	9/09	2012	2012
Marriage equivalent	Yes	Yes	Yes	Yes	Yes
Must be same sex	Yes	No	Yes	Yes	Yes
Hospital visitation, medical decisions	Yes	Yes	Yes	Yes	Yes
Spousal privilege	Yes	Yes	Yes	Yes	Yes
Community property or equitable distribution	Equitable distribution	Equitable distribution	Equitable distribution	Community property	Equitable distribution
Presume parentage	Yes	Yes	Yes	Yes	Yes
Court dissolution required	Yes	Yes	Yes	Yes	Yes
Intestate succession	Yes	Yes	Yes	Yes	Yes
Joint tax filing	Yes	Yes	Yes	Yes	Yes
Spousal support available		Yes		Yes	Yes
Tenancy by the entirety	Yes	No	Yes		No
Body disposition rights	Yes	Yes	Yes	Yes	Yes
Priority for appointment as deceased partner's representative/administrator	Yes	Yes	Yes	Yes	Yes
Divorce revokes will bequests and beneficiary designations	Yes	Yes	Yes	Yes	Yes
DOMA or constitutional amendment	Yes	No	No	No	Yes

* Recognition of out-of-state same sex-marriage

Resources

This resource list is intended to direct you to books, organizations, and websites that we think might help you in your education and decision making about marriage. It's far from complete, so do your own research and gather whatever information you need to make the decision that's right for you.

Books

Legal

Prenuptial Agreements: How to Write a Fair & Lasting Contract, by Katherine Stoner and Shae Irving (Nolo)

Prenups for Partners: Essential Agreements for California Domestic Partners, by Katherine E. Stoner (Nolo), available as download at www.nolo.com

A Legal Guide for Lesbian & Gay Couples, by Denis Clifford, Frederick Hertz, and Emily Doskow (Nolo)

I Do, Don't I?, by Mary Kearny Stroube (Wit's End Press)

When Gay People Get Married: What Happens When Societies Legalize Same-Sex Marriage, by M.V. Lee Badgett (NYU Press)

Nolo's Essential Guide to Divorce, by Emily Doskow (Nolo)

Quicken WillMaker Plus, estate planning software (Nolo)

Make Your Own Living Trust, by Denis Clifford (Nolo)

Financial

Gay Finances in a Straight World, by Peter Berkery (MacMillan)

Four Steps to Financial Security for Lesbians & Gay Men, by Harold Lustig (Ballantine)

Personal

Get Closer: A Gay Men's Guide to Intimacy in Relationships, by Jeffrey Chernin (Alyson Books)

The Male Couple's Guide, by Eric Marcus (Harper Perennial)

When the Past Is Present, by David Richo (Shambala)

How to Be an Adult in Relationships, by David Richo (Shambala)

The Hard Questions: 100 Questions to Ask Before You Say "I Do," by Susan Piver (Tarcher/Putnam).

Websites

There are more websites addressing LGBT legal, financial, and personal issues than we can count, including general and news sites like www.advocate.com, as well as a myriad interesting blogs. We've opted to list primarily organizations working specifically on marriage equality and family and civil rights for same-sex couples and the LGBT community.

Organizations

National Center for Lesbian Rights: www.nclrights.org

Lambda Legal Defense and Education Fund: www.lambdalegal.org

Gay and Lesbian Advocates and Defenders: www.glad.org

ACLU LGBT Project: www.aclu.org/lgbt

Freedom to Marry: www.freedomtomarry.org

White Knot for Equality: www.whiteknot.org

LGBT legal information: www.gaylawnet.com

Human Rights Campaign: www.hrc.org

Transgender Law Center: www.transgenderlawcenter.org

Marriage Equality USA: www.marriageequality.org

Equality California: www.eqca.org

Iowa Marriage Equality: www.oneiowa.org

MassEquality: www.massequality.org

Washington State marriage equality: www.equalrightswashington.org

Vermont marriage equality: www.vtfreetomarry.org

Maine marriage equality: www.equalitymaine.org

New Hampshire marriage equality: www.nhftm.org

Connecticut marriage equality: www.lmfct.org

New Jersey marriage equality: www.gardenstateequality.org

Divorce Information

www.nolo.com

www.divorcenet.com

www.divorceinfo.com

www.bonusfamilies.com (information for blended families after divorce)

Author Information

Frederick Hertz: www.samesexlaw.com

Emily Doskow: www.emilydoskow.com

Blogs: http://blog.nolo.org/lgbtq/, www.makingitlegal.net

The Marriage License Test

We don't let teenagers drive without passing a drivers' license test, nor do we let adults practice law or sell real estate without passing the appropriate exams. Many other professionals must pass licensing tests before they can legally practice their trade. So why do we let people enter the most important relationship of their lives without making sure they understand its terms? In other words, shouldn't everyone have to pass a "Marriage License Test"?

Here's a multiple-choice test that is designed for same-sex couples. Give it a try. If you get more than half the answers wrong, maybe you should consider boning up on the legal consequences of marriage.

You'll find the correct answers, with explanations, at the end of the test.

The Marriage License Test

1. *Could I ever be liable for debts that my boyfriend incurred before I even met him?*

   a) No, that rule only applies to heterosexual couples.

   b) Yes, unless the debts were incurred buying things for his ex-lover.

   c) Yes, if you live in a community property state.

   d) No, unless he gives you the things he bought on credit.

2. *If I'm listed as a parent on the birth certificate of our child, does that make me a legal parent?*

   a) Yes, and that makes you legally responsible for your child.

   b) Yes, if the child has your last name.

   c) No, because a birth certificate alone isn't enough to establish legal parentage.

   d) It depends. How many diapers did you change last month?

3. *My partner and I are about to marry, and I anticipate inheriting some money next year. If I don't make a will giving it to him, will my partner have a right to any of that money if we later break up or I die?*

   a) No, because inherited money never has to be shared with a spouse.

   b) In some states yes, and in others no, depending on the law of a state.

   c) Yes. Everything that either of you receives from any source during your marriage is owned 50/50 by the two of you.

   d) No, unless your partner was the one who restored contact with your parents after you cut them out of your life when they rejected your last partner.

4. *If I own a house before my girlfriend and I get married and we share the mortgage and other expenses thereafter, but I remain the only person named on the title, does she get a share of the house if we break up five years later?*

a) Yes. Once you get married, the house will be owned 50/50 regardless of contributions or ownership history.

b) It is still your house completely because you owned it before marriage and you never added her to title.

c) You are entitled to whatever the equity was when you got married, and any subsequent appreciation is shared 50/50.

d) There is no simple answer. It depends on the law of your state and several factors, including what funds were used and whether you paid off your mortgage while together.

5. *My partner makes a lot of money. We live in Massachusetts, and I'm wondering whether getting married will prevent my son from obtaining a college scholarship based upon my much lower income?*

a) If the scholarship is federally funded, probably yes, and also if it is state-funded or mixed state and federal, probably yes, because state law will recognize your marriage and consider both incomes in determining financial need.

b) No, unless she adopts your son before he turns 21.

c) Yes, because household income is what determines eligibility for scholarships.

d) That depends on how long you have been married before he goes to college; if the marriage was longer than ten years, her income will disqualify your son's application.

6. *Even though he seems in good financial shape now, I suspect that my boyfriend went through a bankruptcy, and he won't talk about these issues at all. Does this mean I shouldn't marry him?*

a) Not at all. If he's in sound financial shape now, his past troubles really don't affect you at all.

b) Possibly so. His prior bankruptcy could affect his credit rating, which could affect both of you. It also could be an indication of a tendency to mishandle money.

c) Definitely stay away from him. Once a debtor, always a debtor.

d) It's impossible to learn anything about his financial history and he probably won't share it with you, so probably you should just ignore this issue altogether and do whatever you think is right about the marriage.

7. *I'm about to lose my full-time job with good health insurance. I'm planning to become self-employed so I'm planning to register as domestic partners with my girlfriend so she can put me on her health insurance. We are living in separate apartments. Is there anything wrong with getting registered if we don't live together?*

a) Nothing wrong with that at all, as long as you are planning to live together soon.

b) No problem, so long as you register at least six months before she adds you to her policy.

c) There's no legal problem, but is this really sufficient reason to enter into such a serious legal commitment?

d) It depends on whether your state requires you to live together in order to register. If you aren't living together then you'd be lying on the application, which could lead to a cancellation of your insurance just when you most need it.

8. *If my partner and I break up and we don't have any conflicts over our stuff or money, do we have to go to court to get a divorce?*

a) Yes, unless you qualify for a summary termination in the few states that offer it.

b) Yes, unless your partnership or marriage lasted less than a year.

c) No. If you can work out all your financial conflicts you don't have to file anything in court.

d) No, unless you have minor children.

9. *I got married in Canada and never got a divorce from that partner, and now I've registered as civil union partners with my new boyfriend in Vermont. Can I put him on my health insurance as my civil union spouse equivalent?*

a) Yes, because he's your current partner.

b) Yes, if your civil union ceremony had more people at it than your Canadian wedding.

c) No, because you are technically a bigamist and your second marriage may be legally void.

d) Yes, because the civil union ended the Canadian marriage just like a divorce would have.

10. *We live in Massachusetts and my wife-to-be is pretty casual about running up credit card debt. If she owes a bank in North Carolina money on a credit card and North Carolina doesn't recognize same-sex marriage, can the bank force me to pay her bills after we're married?*

a) No, because your marriage isn't recognized in North Carolina.

b) No, because she obtained the card and ran up the bills before you were married.

c) Yes, if the purchases were made in Massachusetts.

d) Yes, because it is the state of your residence, not the bank's location, that sets the rules.

11. *If my partner and I get married and I die before him, will he be able to receive my Social Security benefits instead of his own, since mine are likely to be much higher than his?*

a) No, because Social Security law is federal, federal law doesn't recognize your marriage at this time, and it's the law as of the date of your marriage that counts.

b) Yes, because Social Security law now defers to state law that recognizes your marriage, and that's what other married people get.

c) Not now, but if the federal law changes before you retire and the federal government starts recognizing same-sex relationships, he should be able to take advantage of this rule then.

d) It depends on whether he's still working after you marry; if so, the answer is yes.

12. *We registered as California domestic partners a few years ago and are considering getting married next month in Connecticut. If we break up and we are living in Connecticut at the time of our divorce, which date will the divorce court consider our "date of marriage?"*

a) The court will set the date as the midpoint between your two celebrations.

b) Whichever one had a religious blessing will count as the real marriage.

c) Your California registration will count, because California domestic partnership comes with all the rights and duties of marriage, and the Connecticut court will likely recognize this rule.

d) Only your Connecticut marriage, because that is where you live now and where you are getting divorced.

13. *If we marry in Connecticut and my partner dies without a will while we are still living there, will I inherit any of his assets, or will they all go to his mother?*

a) They will all go to his mother, because she has priority in the absence of a will.

b) You will share them with his mother, as provided by Connecticut's rules about intestacy (what happens when someone dies without a will).

c) Everything will go to his mother, because your marriage will not be recognized by federal law and federal law determines inheritance rules.

d) Neither you nor his mother will inherit anything, as in the absence of a will all his assets are turned over to the state government.

14. *My partner and I are planning to register as California domestic partners soon. She recently lost her house to foreclosure in Nevada, and in Nevada the lender can come after the homeowner if the debt is greater than the sale proceeds of the house. She knows the lender is going to come after her for this shortfall. If we get married and the lender pursues the claim in California, am I liable?*

a) No, because the debt was incurred before you got married.

b) No, because Nevada law doesn't recognize your domestic partner relationship.

c) Yes, because you knew about the debt before you got married.

d) Yes, because community property income can be tapped to satisfy all debts of either partner.

15. *My partner and I aren't married or registered, and she just had a baby that we planned for together. We chose the sperm donor together from a catalog of anonymous donors and I was involved in all the prenatal appointments and was there when the baby was born. If we break up, will I have any parental rights?*

a) No, your partner is the only legal parent.

b) Yes, if you put your name on the birth certificate at the hospital.

c) It depends on where you live. In some states your participation in planning and in parenting will mean you're considered a parent, but in others your partner has all the power.

d) It depends on how old the child is when you break up.

16. *My partner and I are in a New Jersey civil union and we have two kids. I'm the birth mom and my partner adopted both of them. They're really young, so if we break up now will I get more time with them because I'm the birth mom?*

a) It depends on who spends more time with them now, not who was the birth mom.

b) Not necessarily. You both have equal legal rights so the court would look at the children's best interests to decide how you should share time.

c) Yes, because courts think young children should be with the person who breast-fed them.

d) Yes, if you're willing to give up child support.

17. *We want to create a new last name for our new family identity. Can we do this without a court order?*

    a) Yes, as long as the new name has parts of each of your names in it.

    b) No, you'll have to get a court order if the name isn't one of your names.

    c) No, you're not allowed to make a new name—you must pick one name or the other.

    d) No, unlike opposite-sex couples, same-sex couples must keep their own names.

18. *My partner and I are registered domestic partners in Oregon. We hired a surrogate to have a baby for us, using my partner's sperm and a donor egg, and she's six months pregnant now. Who are the child's legal parents?*

    a) Both of you are automatically parents because you are registered domestic partners.

    b) Your partner and the surrogate are the legal parents.

    c) You'll have to take legal action to establish that both of you are legal parents.

    d) Your partner is the only parent.

19. *My girlfriend and I got married in Massachusetts last year, and we are now renting an apartment in Boston. Our landlord is insisting that we have to submit two applications and pay two deposits, and is refusing to treat us as a married couple. Can he do this legally?*

    a) Yes, because your marriage is not federally recognized and all rental laws are federal in nature.

    b) Yes, because the apartment building was built before your marriage was allowed.

    c) No, because landlords can never make such a request, even of unmarried couples.

    d) No, because as a legally married couple you are entitled to all the same rights and protections as a straight married couple.

20. *My partner and I registered as civil union partners in Vermont, and now we live in New York City. Can we list ourselves on our bank account as married spouses?*

   a) Yes, because New York officially recognizes civil union partners as equivalent to married spouses.

   b) Yes, because the banking system is controlled by federal law, which recognizes your partnership as a legal marriage.

   c) Maybe. New York State agencies are supposed to recognize out-of-state marriages and partnerships, but the rules have not been clearly established for all agencies, so you may need to request a ruling from the agency that regulates banks if your bank is not cooperative.

   d) No, because you are not married and are only civil union partners.

And just so you don't think we only care about legal issues at Nolo, here are a few "extra" questions that call upon your own sense of gay etiquette. You may not want to count these in your score!

21. *Should I invite all my ex-boyfriends to our wedding?*

   a) Yes, but leave off the invitation some critical details like the address of the ceremony, in the hope they won't show up.

   b) Mostly yes, but not any who have hooked up with your spouse to be.

   c) No, there wouldn't be enough room.

   d) Definitely not—what if your fiancé thinks one of them is cuter than you are?

22. *My partner believes that because we live in a state that allows same-sex marriage, unless we get married we aren't really committed to each other. Is my partner right?*

   a) I'm afraid so. Now that same-sex marriage is legal in some states, not getting married demonstrates a lack of commitment.

   b) No, but if you later relocate to a marriage recognition state, you will need to get married within one year of your relocation, to avoid having your relationship fall apart.

    c) That depends on your gender. If you are lesbians, probably so, but not if you are gay men.

    d) Not at all. The right to a legal marriage does not mean that it is required to demonstrate emotional commitment, any more than it has been for straight couples.

23. *My family is devoutly Catholic and my girlfriend is Jewish. Each of our parents wants us to persuade our partner to convert to our religion, but neither of us are observant and this is not that important to us. What should we do?*

    a) As always, do what your parents tell you to do.

    b) Given all the grief you've already visited upon your parents, do what they say this time.

    c) Politely decline the suggestion, as being inauthentic and not religiously appropriate.

    d) You can become Jewish and your girlfriend can convert to Catholicism, and then you can each spend holidays with your in-laws instead of your own family.

The Answers

Question 1:

c) In a community property state where same-sex couples are covered by marital rules, all income earned during your domestic partnership is considered community property, which means that either partner's creditors can grab that income to pay either partner's debts—including debts incurred before the two of you even met. In other states, you generally are on the hook only for debts incurred during marriage.

Question 2:

c) Birth certificates are not sufficient on their own to establish legal parentage. Parentage is based upon specific legal rules, which look to factors like biological connections, marital status, intent to parent, and adoption judgments. A birth certificate can be evidence of parentage, but standing alone it is not conclusive.

Question 3:

b) It depends on what state you live in at the time of your death or divorce. In most states, inheritances are not considered marital property, and if you spend some of your inheritance buying a house that you own jointly with your spouse, you can get your down payment back even if you don't have a written agreement. In other states, however (such as Massachusetts) the divorce court can take all assets into consideration and can allocate the funds "equitably" based upon a variety of factors.

Question 4:

d) Every state has its own rules about this sort of situation, and oftentimes the rules don't really match what either of you think would be fair. In California, for example, who gets what depends on whether you spent money on renovations and whether the mortgage principal was paid down during the marriage. But in most states most of the equity remains the property of the original owner, and the spouse only accrues a very small interest.

Question 5:

a) Probably yes, if it is a state-based scholarship that focuses on financial need, rather than being based on merit alone. If your partnership or registration is considered equivalent to a marriage, then you will be held to the same rules as a married couple, which means that both spouses' incomes are taken into consideration. And now that the federal government recognizes same-sex relationships, your partner's income will also affect your son's eligibility for federal aid.

Question 6:

b) As conservative as this response may seem, my advice is to try living together without marrying for a few more years, until you really understand what happened in his financial life and are sure that it isn't going to recur. One of the benefits of remaining unmarried is that you are not responsible for each other's finances, and sometimes that's a good thing.

Question 7:

d) (and c) Unlike the marriage statutes, most civil union and domestic partnership statutes require cohabitation. In some states the rules are somewhat loose. But you never want to give your insurance company an excuse to cancel your policy after you've incurred medical expenses. By the way, even if you live together, I still don't think this is a good idea—the long-term consequences of registration or marriage are just too serious to take on simply for reasons of health insurance.

Question 8:

a) In almost every instance the answer is yes, you must use a court process to end your legal relationship. Some states have provisions for an easier process under certain limited circumstances; for example, California allows domestic partners with few assets and no real estate or children to file a termination form with the Secretary of State. Everyone else has to process their dissolution through the court system. But this doesn't mean you have to argue in court! If you are able to reach agreement on all the issues, it's likely you can get your divorce based on written paperwork, without having to appear in person.

Question 9:

   c) Sorry, the answer is no, because your civil union registration is technically bigamous and therefore invalid. You will need to find a court that will grant a divorce to end your Canadian marriage, either here or in Canada. In some instances, you can have the court do this retroactively, rendering your civil union valid; in other instances you will also have to reregister with your new boyfriend, to create a valid registration.

Question 10:

   d) It's most likely that Massachusetts law will apply to your debt. It may seem unfair that a company that doesn't honor its own employees' right to marry can use your marriage to come after your income, but each set of rules is distinct, and they don't have to be consistent to be valid.

Question 11:

   b) Under current law, the answer is yes, because the federal government now recognizes same-sex marriages and Social Security is a federal program that will recognize your marriage, as long as you live in a recognition state.

Question 12:

   c) Most likely it will be the date of your California registration. Marital law in California applies as of the date of your registration, and Connecticut recognizes same-sex marriages, so chances are they will also recognize the period of your California domestic partnership as equivalent to being married. (Note that the answer wouldn't be the same if you are one of the couples who married in California between June and November 2008. In that case, your Connecticut marriage might be invalid, but the Connecticut court would undoubtedly take jurisdiction of your California marriage and grant you a divorce there.)

Question 13:

b) Under Connecticut law, you are an intestate heir and are entitled to a share of his assets, to be shared with his other close legal relatives, such as a parent or child. But if he wants to leave you the entirety of his assets, he must sign a valid will or trust document.

Question 14:

d) Because California is a community property state, your income is presumed to be community property, which means your spouse's creditors can come after your income even for this premarital debt, unless you have a premarital agreement that establishes all of your assets as separate property. (They can't come after your premarital savings, as that is your separate property.) Even though your marriage is not recognized in Nevada, a Nevada creditor can come to California and take advantage of your California marriage to come after you.

Question 15:

c) Some states will consider you a legal parent because of your involvement in planning for and procreating your child, and based on the fact that you've been acting as a parent. Others give all the legal power to the birth mother, and if she doesn't want you to be involved then you might be out of luck. If this is your situation, you definitely need a lawyer to help you figure out what to do.

Question 16:

b) Because your kids were born into your civil union partnership and you did an adoption, there's no question that you're both legal parents. Your best option is to work together with your partner to come up with a parenting schedule that's good for your kids and for both of you. The court isn't going to give you precedence because you gave birth; you're going to have to show why the kids should spend more time with you.

Question 17:

    b) Most states will let one partner change to the other partner's name after a marriage without having to get a court order. But if you want to pick an entirely new name that both of you are going to use, you'll have to get a court order allowing it. Fortunately, this is a pretty simple process.

Question 18:

    c) While your partner could put his name on the birth certificate at the child's birth if you don't take any legal action, that would also mean that the surrogate's name would be put on the birth certificate as mother—a result that neither you nor the surrogate probably want. So you'll need to first get a parentage judgment that says your partner's a legal parent and the surrogate isn't, and then proceed with an adoption to make sure that you have parental rights as well.

Question 19:

    d) Housing law is primarily state based, so state law applies here. And, under Massachusetts law, there is no separate category of "same-sex marriage"— all married partners are entitled to the same protections, regardless of their sexual orientation.

Question 20:

    c) New York State law is still a bit in flux, and banks are regulated by both state and federal agencies. The federal rules now allow such recognition, whereas state law may be unresolved. If that is the situation, your bank may have no choice but to reject your request. On the other hand, over time it is likely that the state will issue rules on this issue, so this problem may be resolved shortly.

Questions 21, 22, and 23:

    Sorry, you're going to have to figure these out for yourselves!

Index

Businesses
  and challenge of dealing with variety
    of laws, 231–232
  and income from LGBT weddings,
    231
  and prenup, 150, 154
  of unmarried couples, 193

C

California
  court for family disputes, 67
  effect of community property laws on
    taxes, 82, 83
  as marriage equivalent state, 44–45
  overview, 38–39, 238
  parentage legal cases, 225
  Proposition 8, 20–21, 39, 90, 225,
    231
  same-sex marriage legalization cycles,
    1–2, 20–21, 90, 131, 142
  summary dissolution of domestic
    partnerships, 62
  See also Community property states
California Supreme Court, 225
Canada, 30–31
Children
  adoption of a child, 70, 72, 107–108,
    187
  adoption tax credit, 199
  discussions about raising, 119–120,
    122
  and divorce, 187

  and estate planning, 199–200, 217
  invalidity of prenup clauses on,
    151–152
  See also Parentage
Citizenship and Immigration Services
  (USCIS), 79–80
Civil partnership system (PACS) in
  Europe, 18
Civil unions, 19, 21, 32, 45–46. *See
  also* Marriage equivalent registrations
COBRA continuation of health
  insurance, 150
Cohabitation
  breakups, 174–175, 193, 195–200
  and challenges to estate plans,
    216–217
  as contractual relationship, 53
  and estate planning, 218–219
  overview, 193
  parentage issues, 198–200
  will or trust vs. written agreements,
    212
Cohabitation agreements, 162,
  169–170, 194, 195, 198
Collaborative divorce, 191–192
Collaborative process for creating a
  prenup, 147
Colorado, 46, 238
Commitment to your marriage, 113,
  121–124, 180–185
Common law marriages, 35
Community considerations, 120–121

⚖ NOLO *Online Legal Forms*

Nolo offers a large library of legal solutions and forms, created by Nolo's in-house legal staff. These reliable documents can be prepared in minutes.

Create a Document

- **Incorporation.** Incorporate your business in any state.
- **LLC Formations.** Gain asset protection and pass-through tax status in any state.
- **Wills.** Nolo has helped people make over 2 million wills. Is it time to make or revise yours?
- **Living Trust (avoid probate).** Plan now to save your family the cost, delays, and hassle of probate.
- **Trademark.** Protect the name of your business or product.
- **Provisional Patent.** Preserve your rights under patent law and claim "patent pending" status.

Download a Legal Form

Nolo.com has hundreds of top quality legal forms available for download—bills of sale, promissory notes, nondisclosure agreements, LLC operating agreements, corporate minutes, commercial lease and sublease, motor vehicle bill of sale, consignment agreements and many, many more.

Review Your Documents

Many lawyers in Nolo's consumer-friendly lawyer directory will review Nolo documents for a very reasonable fee. Check their detailed profiles at **www.nolo.com/lawyers/index.html**.

On Nolo.com you'll also find:

Books & Software

Nolo publishes hundreds of great books and software programs for consumers and
business owners. Order a copy, or download an ebook version instantly, at Nolo.com.

Online Legal Documents

You can quickly and easily make a will or living trust, form an LLC or corporation, apply
for a trademark or provisional patent, or make hundreds of other forms—online.

Free Legal Information

Thousands of articles answer common questions about everyday legal issues
including wills, bankruptcy, small business formation, divorce, patents,
employment, and much more.

Plain-English Legal Dictionary

Stumped by jargon? Look it up in America's most up-to-date source for
definitions of legal terms, free at nolo.com.

Lawyer Directory

Nolo's consumer-friendly lawyer directory provides in-depth profiles of lawyers all
over America. You'll find all the information you need to choose the right lawyer.

LGM3